Me, Kniest & Understanding

FIONA PORCH

OTHER PUBLISHED LITERARY WORK BY FIONA PORCH

A collection of Poetry:
Soul Cried

Me, Kniest & Understanding

Embrace the life you gain,
When you push through the pain.

FIONA PORCH

First Published in 2018
By F.P. Publishing

Copyright © Fiona Porch, 2018

All rights reserved. No part of this book may be reproduced or transmitted in any form or by any means, graphic, electronic, or mechanical, including photocopying, recording, taping or by any information storage retrieval system, without prior written permission from the author, except in the case of brief quotations embodied in critical articles and reviews. The Australian *Copyright Act 1968* (the Act) allows a maximum of one chapter or 10 per cent of this book, whichever is the greater, to be photocopied by any educational institution for its educational purposes provided that the educational institution (or body that administers it) has given a remuneration notice to the Copyright Agency (Australia) under the Act.

Books may be ordered through leading booksellers globally or by contacting:
   Fiona Porch
   www.FionaPorch.com

The author of this book does not dispense medical advice or prescribe the use of any technique as a form of treatment for physical, emotional, or medical problems without the advice of a physician, either directly or indirectly. The intent of the author is only to offer information of a general nature to help you in your quest for emotional and spiritual well-being. In the event you use any of the information in this book for yourself, the author and publisher assume no responsibility for your actions.

This work is an autobiography. It reflects the author's recollection of her experiences over a period of years. Certain names and identifying characteristics have been changed to protect the identities of persons involved. Dialogue and events have been recreated from memory, and, in some cases, have been compressed to convey the substance of what was said or occurred.

Front Cover Image Copyright © Fiona Porch.
Interior Design by Fiona Porch.
Interior Photographic Images Copyright © Fiona Porch and Carmen Darmo.
Illustrations Copyright © Fiona Porch.
Poetry Copyright © Fiona Porch.

Cataloguing-in-Publication details are available
From the National Library of Australia
www.trove.nla.gov.au

ISBN: 978-0-6482737-0-7 (Paperback)
ISBN: 978-0-6482737-1-4 (E-book)

This book which strives to give insight and understanding of my personal life's journey and what it's like living with Kniest Dysplasia. I dedicate, to new parents of children born with Kniest, as well as all the people who've been a constant support throughout my life. My fellow Kniestians, you changed my life forever and are an extension of family to me.

I dedicate, this especially to my mum Carmen; I appreciate every sacrifice you ever made for me. Most importantly, I thank God, who has given me strength even when I felt weak. Strength to push through my pain and embrace the life I have gained!

Contents

Introduction 1
1. Hello World 3
2. Baby Steps and Bumpy Beginnings 14
3. Let's Get Educated 20
4. Where's the Queen? 29
5. Cast towards Mobility 34
6. Growth Hormone Therapy 38
7. Childhood Memories 42
8. Ilizarov Method 50
9. Flower Girl Fee 63
10. Round Two 67
11. Fusion and a New Way of Life 75
12. Breaking Barriers 85
13. Pilgrimage to Lourdes 95
14. I Still Call Australia Home 105
15. Action Packed Adventures 109
16. Reaching My Breaking Point 121
17. Driving Towards Independence 129
18. Youth and Teenage Memories 135
19. Seeing Is Believing 148
20. Enemies in Low Places 153
21. S-U-G-A-S-U-G-A 161
22. My Turn to Fly 166
23. LPA in the US of A 172
24. Into the Workforce 184
25. Taking a Chance on Romance 191

26. Broken and Alone 203
27. Pick up the Pieces and Start Again 211
28. Musical Memories and Facing Fears 222
29. Out of the Blue Injuries 236
30. Eyes Wide Open 242
31. You Are Not Alone 246
32. What Lies Ahead? 252
33. Mission Impossible 257
34. Point Of View 263
35. Spread Your Wings and Fly! 267

Acknowledgements: 271
About the Author 272

Introduction

Writing this book of mine has been a long time coming. I recall at the age of ten saying to my mum, "One day I'm going to write a book about my life." I began journaling from then on, and during the years I've kept many diaries.

Time sometimes just continued to pass me by and this dream remained on the sidelines due to surgeries and life getting in the way. Plus, I wasn't sure when it would be the right time in my life to share my story. I had to have experienced a fair amount before the actual release and publication of this type of book. Be at a stage in life where I had enough to say to serve the purpose I hope to achieve by sharing my life story with you.

I still have my notes and diary entries from my younger days collected. So it's great because a big chunk will allow me to express my thoughts and emotions, at the time when I went through those major moments in my life. It wasn't until I was approaching my 30th birthday that I took it more seriously. I have been through so much already throughout my life; I figured now is the right time to take action. So here we are a few years on but YAY, I got there.

I'm sure as you read on you will come to know the many sides of my personality. The good times and bad, the determination, my silly humour, including many of the hard times and struggles of my daily life. How having Kniest plays a huge part in every aspect of my life. As much as I'd like to say my genetic condition doesn't define me, in reality it does. But for me, admitting that truth in all honesty isn't a bad thing. It has taught me so much about myself and given me a perspective to live my life in the best possible way. A way which most people wouldn't even dare to consider, because they need not think about simple things that aren't so simple for someone like me.

I will also share the many ups and downs of my family life, friendships, relationships, and horrible bullying. The tough surgical procedures I endured and the moments of utter joy when I achieved some of my greatest dreams.

Okay, now that that's out of the way, why don't you join me on my life's journey so far! Into the wonderful life of Fee (Me), Kniest & Understanding, I'm just an open book waiting to be read...

Chapter One

Hello World

On a winter's day in 1982, the time had come where I took my first breath and joined the world. Born in the western suburbs of Sydney Australia; it was a Monday afternoon on the 12th of July. I weighed a mighty seven pounds nine ounces and measured at 19.5 inches, with not a care in the world. I was an adorable baby, if I do say so myself, just look at that cute innocent face! ☺

(My Mum and I on my Christening Day)

Both my parents came to Australia from Malta on the 1st of April in 1976. Malta is a small European Island just underneath the boot of Sicily in the Mediterranean Sea.

(And no, that wasn't an April fool's joke.)

They were none the wiser about what was in store for me and the journey I would have in life. But the doctors at the hospital had their suspicions immediately after I was born, that something may not be quite right. The medical staff constantly kept asking my mum questions about my older sister.

She is one year, two months and four days older than me.

(Maybe that was a little too specific of me.)

But my mum kept telling them;

"Her sister is fine, why?"

She was getting anxious and couldn't work out why they seemed so concerned. Why did they keep asking if everything was fine with my sister? What did they see in me to make them so concerned in the first place?

(My Sister and I)

Before leaving the hospital they advised my mum that it'd be wise to make an appointment with a pediatrician when I approach my first birthday.

My mum told me that as soon as they suggested making an appointment she was so confused, worried and wondered what could be wrong. Seeing as, to her and everyone else I looked like any other baby would, and I didn't seem to possess any obvious differing features to the untrained eye. It was difficult for her to shake the concern she now had, and she refused to wait until I was a year old to find out if anything was wrong. So mum made the earliest appointment they would allow, for when I was roughly six months old. I needed to be a certain age for them to run a few of the tests and scans. They rarely liked to probe babies too much, if it could be avoided.

The time had arrived for mum to take me to my appointment. As the years went on I questioned her about how she found out. We've talked about that day many times, as far as how she felt and what was said. Even though my memory is great and I remember things as far back as the age of four quite clearly, I was way too young to remember many things from before that time. Now, the doctor who my mum was referred to by the hospital was not only incorrect on many levels, but also very inconsiderate to say the least! He gave me a check up, ran whatever tests and scans they could back in those days, and broke the news to my mum. According to him I had Achondroplasia, which is the most common form of dwarfism. People living with Achondroplasia have shorter arms and legs with a more average proportionate torso, as well as other defining features. Generally, when a person is born with Achondroplasia it's fairly obvious at birth, due to those characteristics. Personally, I don't know where he got his medical degree. Making a statement like that, you'd expect to see those obvious characteristics, which I didn't have. But this was the eighties to be fair, and my mum hadn't even heard of dwarfism before, so it's not like she would have known any difference.

He then blurted out;

"She will be one of those people who'll work in the circus." *(Encouraging right?)* As he continued stating I wouldn't grow past a metre in height and people would make fun of me for the rest of my life. My mum began to cry, naturally overwhelmed with shock of the whole revelation.

"Will she go to a normal school?"
"Will she be able to walk?"
"Will she be able to do things like everyone else?"
He responded by saying, "Yes, but she will be laughed at and made fun of by others."

Now I'm sure you are thinking what any decent human being would think. How could a professional speak like that to my poor mum about me? About anyone really! Extremely unprofessional and cold-hearted! Okay maybe you weren't thinking about it that politely. Trust me, when I reflect back to when my mum first told me this story, I was pretty angry to say the least. It still baffles me to this day that this encounter went down the way that it did. Imagine being in my mum's position, she was so emotional and angry. Full of concern and questions as to what kind of life I would grow up to have. I can tell you now, sometimes I wish I could go see that doctor as an adult and say:

'Really! Firstly you were wrong about so many things.'
'Secondly, you need a lesson in what is an acceptable way in breaking news to a mother. A mother who just found out her daughter has a physical disability and may struggle through life.'
After which I'd most likely not be able to stop a few choice profanities from pouring out of my mouth; but could you blame me?

Mum left his office feeling completely unsure of what this would mean for me, so she sought after a second opinion elsewhere. The new doctor my mum took me to specialised in various forms of dwarfism; my mum hoped he'd be able to ease her concerns. It wasn't until we went to the second appointment with the new specialist, shortly after seeing Dr. Jerk-face that my mum was able to have many of her questions addressed as to what this could mean for my future. He answered all of her questions in such a way for her to understand what obstacles I could face throughout my life due to my condition. To my mum's surprise I was diagnosed with a much rarer form of dwarfism called Kniest Dysplasia.

(As if the title of this book wasn't a dead giveaway.)

Turns out I didn't have Achondroplasia after all, and I was completely misdiagnosed by that first unprofessional monster. Kniest is entirely different from Achondroplasia; I will explain this in more detail shortly.

The second specialist we met became my regular doctor and from then on has constantly played a massive role in my life. Especially with regards to many of my medical challenges and decisions which you will learn about as you continue reading. To simplify things I will refer to him as Profs from here on. Profs showed more compassion when he explained my condition to my mum. Plus, he had studied overseas and seen many forms of dwarfism over the years of his medical career. He was definitely more qualified and possessed greater knowledge on the subject. My mum felt slightly more at ease as he informed her of the challenges I would likely encounter. Even though she was still full of worry as to how severely it would truly impact my life, she felt an element of relief. He went on to state that my condition wouldn't affect my intellectual abilities in any way, and how the challenges I'd face throughout my life would mostly be physical. Naturally, he knew I was more than likely destined to a lifetime of struggle and hurdles. But he confidently told my mum he would do his absolute best to help make my life easier in any way he could.

During the appointment he also informed my mum of an organisation for little people. The organisation is there as a support network for people with various forms of dwarfism and their families. They organise special events and gatherings all across Australia, as well as state only events in New South Wales, which were more relevant to us. Profs thought this would be something both me and my mum would benefit from. Especially so my mum could meet other little people and see how many of them lead very fulfilling lives despite their physical challenges.

At our next appointment we had with Profs, he introduced us to two ladies, Grace and Ruth. They were both active members of the organisation. Ruth was an average height lady in a similar situation to my mum; she had a daughter with Achondroplasia. Grace on the other hand, had a comparable form of dwarfism to mine, called SED (Spondyloepiphyseal Dysplasia.) *(Try saying that word when you're drunk,*

Haha.) Since there was no-one else in Australia known to have Kniest, Grace was the closest to my condition. She was more than happy to meet with mum and I, and take us under her wing. Mum found this meeting to be such a positive impact in further reassuring her I would grow up to be okay. Ruth and Grace were a real comfort to my mum. Especially Grace, such an upbeat lovely lady who was so positive and enjoyed a good laugh; she was actually a great support through much of my childhood. This enabled my mum to see that I too could be a positive light in the world.

A Little Bit of History

I happen to find it interesting knowing the history of when Kniest was first documented. So, I'd like to share that history with you, of how the condition got named and came to be.

The disorder was first documented by a doctor who was a chief resident of the Children's Hospital at the University of Jena in Thuringia. It was during 1952 when the chief resident had a unique patient. He filed a report stating that his patient was fifty years of age, severely handicapped, and short in stature. It was noted the patient had restricted joint mobility, and blindness, but was mentally alert and leading a very active life.

The molecular analysis of the patient's DNA showed a single base (G) deletion, destroying a splice site of the collagen II (COL2A1) gene. In simple terms, this means they identified the specific gene mutation that effectively causes people to be born with Kniest. This gene is involved in producing a particular protein that forms type II collagen, and is essential for normal development of bones and connective tissue. Changes to the composition of type II collagen lead to abnormal skeletal growth causing a variety of conditions known as skeletal dysplasias, such as Kniest. The mutation affects the ability to form cartilage around the joints in the body.

Kniest is an autosomal dominant disorder, and seeing as I have Kniest, there is a 50/50 chance of any children I'd have to be born with my condition. Autosomal dominant means that one mutated copy of the gene in each cell is sufficient for a person to be affected by an autosomal disorder. In some cases the affected individual may inherit the condition from an affected parent. In many other cases, it is quite common for the condition to result from a new mutation in the gene, and occur randomly in people with no known history of the disorder in their family. With the majority of autosomal dominant conditions, if both members of a couple have the same condition then their children would have 25 percent chance to be born with the non-dwarfism gene and be of average height. There is also a 25 percent chance that their children would inherit the dwarfism gene from both, this is known as double dominance. In many cases, a child born with double dominance inevitably ends in death at birth or shortly afterwards.

Now I won't overload you with too much medical jargon that didn't even make sense to me for the longest time. But I feel like it's important I give you a brief lowdown, so that you have the basic understanding of what Kniest entails.

There are less than two hundred people worldwide known with Kniest Dysplasia. As far as my doctors were aware, I was always told that I may be the only one in Australia with Kniest. Not one person born with the condition is exactly the same as the next. There are many levels of severity, I like to think I belong somewhere in the middle. I don't have all the issues a person with Kniest can have, nor am I the best case scenario. There's very limited information about Kniest available, it isn't even listed in many medical books and the information that's available now on the internet can seem to be more puzzling than helpful. If someone doesn't live with Kniest or know about it but they read the limited information available, it can be overwhelming and frightening. The information lists every possible issue that could be present in people with the condition as a whole. It doesn't make it clear enough that each person can be affected differently. Some people are more severe than others in a range of different physical areas, and then not so much in other attributes. This is partly why I always wanted to write this book. To give insight to parents who have a child with Kniest, and to help provide people in general form a better understanding of the condition, who may simply just be curious. I feel that by sharing a point of view of someone who is living through it, rather than the mildly available medical jargon it will be more beneficial. Also, if I can be there as a support network for others with Kniest I'm sure it would mean a lot to them. I know growing up I wished I had someone to turn to, someone who really understood and could be there for me, even if it was just a listening ear to vent to from someone in a similar situation. This was something I lacked being the only one in Australia, but also something I craved.

Over the years I tried doing my own research, but if I wasn't living with the condition myself and knew nothing about it I'd freak out reading the limited resources available online or in books. Mostly because there are so many variables, and way too many medical terms that barely make sense to someone who doesn't have a medical degree. I will leave no stone unturned in hopes that it will shed some light in providing a better understanding, to the best of my ability.

Having Kniest has caused Osteoporosis-like issues and other arthritic joint problems for me since birth. My joints all appear larger than normal and are very restricted in movement. I don't have the flexibility and rotation most people are born with, this has been and still is my greatest cause of pain. Another major Kniest defining feature is my spine; I have terrible Kyphosis creating an outward curvature of the top section of the spine. And Lordosis, an inward curvature of the bottom part of the spine. My spine is quite compressed and severely curved from top to bottom. This causes my torso to appear significantly shorter than most. If you were to look at an x-ray of my spine today you would probably wonder what the heck is going on in there. Even Radiologists tend to go into 'freak out' mode when they review x-rays or MRI's of my spine. Sometimes I joke about it making me look like ET. "It's like ET phoned home and sent me to the wrong planet." The funny thing is watching people's reaction when I say this to them. Especially, if they only just met me for the first time and ask me about my spine, they aren't sure if they should laugh or feel sad. I tend to throw people off with that comment, and the look on their face is priceless. Additionally, my left pointing finger is double-jointed, so the way I can bend and move it when I'm saying my line, feels like a total ET moment. It always reminds me of the part in the movie when his finger glows. I do have a pretty good sense of humour even if it's at my own expense. I figure if I can't laugh at certain things myself and beat people to the punch it would only hurt more if someone else says it.

As I mentioned earlier Kniest is a rare form of dwarfism, therefore my whole life I have been significantly shorter than my peers. Today I stand at 128 centimetres tall which is approximately four foot two inches. *(Yes, I surpassed the horrible doctor's prediction of being only a metre tall, Lol.)* My limbs are fairly average length wise, but due to the curvature in my spine my body appears short. This is where I lose the majority of my height; I imagine if my spine was straight I'd be closer to five foot tall.

This constantly has made it difficult when buying clothes. All throughout my life I have had to accept that even if I love how something looks on a hanger in a store, it doesn't mean it will fit my body shape. No amount of alteration or wishful thinking would allow me to look good or feel comfortable in every piece of clothing. I have learnt what works for me over the years, and just make the most of what I've got to work with.

Onto the less obvious Kniest feature to the human eyes which ironically is my vision. The mutation in the collagen II gene that causes my joint issues, also affects the jelly in the eyes from forming correctly. Therefore, I am very short-sighted and have high grade Myopia. My eyes appear normal on the outside but inside they are more oval shaped. It causes my retina to be quite stretched, thin and prone to retinal detachments. This could potentially lead to blindness at any given moment throughout my life. Obviously it's not something I've ever focused on; I do my best not to think about that happening. I feel like if I worried too much I'd probably be too scared to live my life. What's the use of being so stressed that I don't go outside to do the things I love? There's no use living in fear of something happening that may never happen. Stressing about it every waking moment would mean I'd miss out on all the amazing things life has to offer. I definitely don't want to worry myself about what ifs; it's better to deal with what is and face my problems head on if and when they arise. Due to the extensive severity of my myopia I began wearing glasses at the young age of 8 months, right after I was diagnosed. Luckily since Profs knew all about Kniest and how more often than not it affects vision greatly; he sent me to an excellent female eye specialist straight away to be assessed. It's not like at that age I could tell anyone I couldn't see properly. I do find it pretty amazing that they could determine my lack of vision at such a young age. In fact, I still have my very first pair of glasses; my mum had to tie them around my head with a string. Clearly as a kid I found them annoying and always wanted to pull them off my face.

I'd have to say, in my case these are the main issues that shape me. I do have other Kniest defining features but they aren't as problematic to live with, I will expand on this later on. As you continue reading you'll see how all the surgeries I have encountered throughout my life tie in with these issues.

Other people living with Kniest are known to have a cleft palate at birth. Basically it's a hole in the roof of the mouth; it can affect your speech and even cause extensive breathing complications. Usually this requires surgical correction at a very young age. Some people also experience severe hearing loss, requiring hearing aids in most cases. I was fortunate not to have a cleft palate or any drastic hearing issues, requiring any hearing aids.

There are so many medical issues a person with Kniest can be born with, which is why I consider myself somewhere in the middle. Even though I feel fortunate to be in the middle, my life has still been a whirlwind of hurdles to jump over.

You may wonder how I can remember all the defining moments in my childhood. While I do have my mum to continuously bug with questions; surprisingly, I remember most things after the age of four. Although to help me write this book as accurately as possible, I paid the hospital to make a complete copy of my medical records when I was in my twenties. Anyone can pull out their own medical records, it just sucks you have to pay per page. As you will soon discover I've had an eventful life, leading to two fairly thick volumes which resulted in a costly adventure. Nonetheless, I feel it's worth having, not just for the purpose of writing this book but also for my own personal use.

So without further delay, let's get right into it, with baby steps and bumpy beginnings.

Chapter Two

Baby Steps and Bumpy Beginnings

On the 12th of August 1982 when I was precisely one month old, I smiled for the first time followed by laughter only a week later. You could say the 12th continued to be a significant date for me. I reached another milestone of recognising my mum's face for the first time, when I was just two months old. I feel like my first recorded milestone is a testament to who I am. It's gotten me throughout my life and represents me well. Even when times are tough my smile shines through. ☺

As a toddler, growing up with Kniest meant I took longer than most to do the basic physical things. Such as reaching the more monumental milestones like; sitting, crawling, standing etc. Mum was advised by Profs to hold me back from standing and walking for some time. It appeared when I first tried to hold on and get myself up I was favouring one leg over the other. He felt it was important for me to gain more strength in my lower limbs. His main concern was that my apparent unbalanced demeanour would lead to many injuries, he hoped I could avoid. It wasn't until I was two years and five months old that I began to walk unaided. Mind you, I got many bumps on my head from falling down because we had a split-level house. I constantly toppled down the two steps between the kitchen and the living room area. Miraculously, I never broke my glasses, even if my forehead was a bumpy bruised disaster area. Though it was recommended that I be held back, mum didn't want to restrict me from progressing.

Eventually when I decided I was ready mum couldn't stop me, even if she wanted to. In contrast, there was certainly a huge positive difference when it came to my early language developmental skills.

(Three year old Fee)

It was around this time Profs suggested I begin swimming and exercise hydrotherapy. He felt it would be beneficial for me to build up my muscle strength and work on my balance issues. Being in the water would allow me to do this without putting excessive stress on my body. Mum immediately organised for me to start swimming lessons at our local public pool. As odd as this may sound I can mentally visualise the experience of learning how to swim. The swimming lessons I went to weren't just to teach me how to swim, it was also to provide me with the skills to be drown proof. Meaning unless I am unconscious, I'd have the survival skills to stay afloat after completing the course. Many times I used to get thrown into the pool with all my clothes and shoes on. Although I knew this was good for me, I still screamed my lungs out and cried because I hated being thrown into the water. The initial point of impact and water possibly going up my nose or seeping through my goggles always seemed like an upsetting prospect to me. Once I was in the water I was happy and okay.

This one time at band camp ... *Just kidding!*
(You may not get my lame attempt at humour if you haven't seen the movie 'American Pie.')

But no really, this one time at swimming, I was sitting on the edge of the bench near the pool. I had a habit of swinging my legs anxiously as I waited for the instructor to call my name. Next thing you know I must have leaned too far forward because I ended up doing a somersault off the bench and rolled into the pool! At the time I didn't think this was funny considering I never did things like somersault due to my joint limitations. Now when I think about it, I'm sure it looked pretty hilarious. I almost wish I had it on tape because it was something that would never be repeated.

I did swimming lessons for many years. Fortunately my mum received some financial support from an organisation to help cover part of my swimming lesson fees for a while. Seeing as my mum couldn't work anymore, like she used to. Looking after me and taking me to all my medical appointments and physical therapy was a full time job; she needed all the support she could get. Thankfully, I passed and earned my certificates as I accomplished each milestone of the drown proofing course.

You May Be Far, But In My Heart You're Near

Let it be known, I love my mum and am grateful for everything she has done for me in my life, and continues to do for me. Although there have been times it wasn't always clear to me why she did certain things, now I'm older I can see them from her point of view. I know that even if I didn't agree with the way she handled some of my issues, she always had my best interest at heart; like any other mother would for their child. Yes, like any family there are the occasional arguments. I won't lie and say everything has always been peachy, that's just crazy talk. But I can honestly say now, as an adult that I couldn't have asked for a better mum, truly.

(No she didn't pay me to say that either.)
My mum did it tough, especially during my childhood but she has been my one constant support and advocate for me, my entire life.

Right after my diagnoses my mum called her family in Malta so that she could have someone to talk to about everything that was going on. Even though they were thousands of miles away, she felt comforted by their voice on the other side of the phone. Her dad; my grandfather, was a Sergeant in the police force and generally a very serious and respectable man. But when mum told him about my diagnoses and her concerns, he assured her that he would do anything he could to help. My grandfather hadn't had a chance yet to meet me or my sister. Shortly after talking with my mum about everything, he proceeded to make arrangements for the big trip across the world. I was a one-year-old, when he finally came to Australia to visit us. He was looking forward to seeing us all and wasn't too fazed by my whole diagnoses. I was his granddaughter, and he was my grandfather and that was all that mattered. It meant the world to my mum to see her dad who she hadn't seen for about seven years since moving to Australia.

A lovely close friend of his named Tom, who lived in London; had medical connections on that side of the world. During my grandfather's visit, my mum gave him recent copies of my x-rays as well as some of my medical information to take back to Malta, for him to pass them onto Tom. Mum wanted to see if there was any other help they could offer to make sure I was given the best care available. Especially, seeing as I was considered to be the only one in Australia. This still worried my mum because there was no-one else here to give her that extra comfort. The comfort of knowing what obstacles might be in store, for her to provide me with a positive future as much as possible. She wanted to do everything in her power to research every avenue.

Unfortunately, even though my mum's side of the family lived in Malta, my mum's mum Doris had already passed away. I never knew what it was like to have a loving grandmother. She had died before any of her grandchildren were born. I can't even begin to express how much it truly saddens me that I never got to meet her.

Mum always told me stories about my nanna *(nanna is grandmother in Maltese.)* Stories of how close she was with her and how she would make her clothes all the time. Mum believes if nanna would have known me she would want to make clothes for me too. I really believe that as well, because even though I never met her she sounds like the kind of grandmother any kid would love to have. As much as it would have been awesome to have had her make me clothes, I just wish I could have gotten the opportunity to know her. Everything my mum has ever said about her makes me believe she must have been the most beautiful person in the world. I feel deprived that I never get the chance to have her in my life.

Sadly, my nanna Doris died at the young age of forty-eight from pancreatic cancer. When she passed away my mum had already moved to Australia. Heartbreakingly for my mum, she wasn't able to return to Malta due to unspeakable reasons. Not when she found out her mum was sick or even to attend her own mother's funeral. It wasn't like my sister and I were even born yet. I can't even begin to understand how hard that must have been for my mum, seeing as her mother was her best friend.

In the meantime I continued on my merry way just being the kid that I was. Constantly attending multiple doctor appointments and having regular eye checkups.

Oh, my goodness! How I hated my eye appointments when I was really young. Mum and the eye specialist both had to hold my arms and legs down, just so she could get the necessary drops in my eyes to be able to check the back of my retina. I never liked anyone getting close to my eyes, and the drops used to sting so much. I imagine the poor kids in the waiting room probably felt worse. As they sat there anxiously waiting, while being subjected to hearing my loud screaming that sounded like I was being tortured. Thankfully, I handle myself a lot better at my eye appointments these days, and I manage to internalise my desire to scream.

Chapter Three

Let's Get Educated

You could say that some of the hardest times I've dealt with were during my adolescence. When I faced how horrible the cruelty of others could be. Especially with other children who tend to speak whatever comes into their mind without holding back or thinking prior. As anyone else with a disability would likely understand, these times can truly test your inner strength.

I know a few people that are short statured with forms of dwarfism who don't like to consider themselves disabled. This is totally understandable since there are mild cases that have none of the more disabling challenges; except for their height. Personally, if I was just shorter and had none of the other problems or regular pains that I have, I imagine I might feel the same way too. Me being short doesn't actually bother me at all; realistically that's the least of my worries.

I'm definitely not backwards in coming forward, if I need to ask someone at the grocery store to reach something I ask with no hesitation. My line these days is; "Can I please borrow your height and could you please pass me 'such' and 'such' item." Most people I approach don't even have to be working there. I try to gauge a person's mood, if I get a sense they aren't going to get cranky because I asked for their help then I'll approach them. I find most people are happy to oblige, usually they smile and find the humour in the way I ask for their help. Although, in saying that, this one particular memory comes to mind. I was at the grocery store and I asked a lady politely if she could please pass me something. The look she gave me was like I had just asked her to chop her own leg off and hand it to me.

Then she abruptly said;

"Do I look like I work here?"

My response was; "I wasn't sure if you worked here or not, but I didn't think it would be too much to expect another human being to pass something." I paused, then said; "Thanks anyway." She gave me the most evil look and continued to walk away.

As it happened another lady saw the whole thing, she grabbed what I wanted, handed it to me and said; "I'm so sorry you have to deal with people being rude to you like that when all you were hoping for was some common decency." I thanked the lady for her help and even though I was appreciative of the lady who helped me, I still couldn't believe the other woman's reaction.

Sorry I'll do my best not to get carried away on a Fee tangent, which is easy to do when there's so much I want to say; but let's get back to the topic at hand.

Even though I accept that I have a disability I definitely don't expect sympathy nor do I want it. I always try to live the best life possible, but the reality is; having Kniest does stop me from doing certain things. When it's something important to me I try to find alternative ways of accomplishing what I want.

I've faced many roadblocks throughout my life and I refuse to let others be the ones who limit me. All too aware of my capabilities and vice versa, sometimes it takes a little extra determination to achieve what I want. Regrettably this often means I may also suffer the consequences afterwards, by being extremely physically tired and sore. Although, I am very in-tune with my body and my limits and I'd never do something so silly to risk permanent harm to myself intentionally. If I want to do something bad enough, then I'd consider it to be worth the pain. At the end of the day we only live once and I want to live my life as much as my body allows me to. Even if that means I have to give my body a little push. It doesn't matter how long it takes or how many times I fall or fail.

The important lesson here is to never give up, to keep trying; the only true failure would be not trying at all. Someone who embodies this similar way of thinking who I admire and inspires me so much is Nick Vujicic. If you haven't heard of him I recommend looking him up. Personally, I have read every book he's ever written, I feel really connected to certain aspects of how he overcomes obstacles and his way of thinking.

It's Time I Got Educated

In 1986 I began preschool at three and a half years of age. It was recommended by Profs I attend two days at a local preschool and three days at another preschool. The other preschool was predominantly for people with disabilities. Profs thought it would be in my best interest to go there so that I could have regular physical therapy. The school had an in-house physical therapist, Margaret. By attending the second preschool Margaret would be able to assess how well I'd manage myself in a regular schooling environment. Little did I know that Margaret would end up playing an integral role during the majority of my school life.

A particular memory comes to mind, while I was at the preschool for people with disabilities. There was this lovely girl who was also attending; she had no arms. I always admired her way of managing tasks and had so much respect for her. She would eat, write, paint and do so many other things with her feet. To the average person this may have seemed odd. But to me even at that young age, I couldn't help but think how awesomely she adapted daily tasks in such a unique way. I wish I knew where she was now because I bet she has had such an interesting, and fulfilling life. I could totally see that for this girl, this was *her* normal. Just like for me and the way I adapt when doing things is *my* normal.

Realistically there is no such thing as normal, or you could say there's more than one type of normal. Everyone is different, disabled or not; short or tall. How a person chooses to live their life and how they handle life's obstacles is what's important.

Yes, it's true, many people with disabilities struggle with tasks others tend to take for granted. Trust me; even I am all too familiar with this, but I choose to focus on my abilities rather than my inabilities.

One thing I never understood for the longest time was a decision that was made by my Specialists, Physical Therapist and my mum. They thought it would be best for me to repeat preschool for an extra year. I was told due to my short stature if I repeated preschool it'd be easier to manage by the time I went to mainstream school. At first I thought this was the biggest waste of time. Regardless of how much time passed my height would always be much shorter than my peers. Aside from that, dealing with challenges was a part of my life and it would be foolish to expect that I wouldn't face obstacles. It felt like I was on pause just waiting for reality to catch up. I'm sure everyone thought it would somehow help or my mum wouldn't have agreed. The biggest challenges were yet to come, so I guess an extra year of painting and playing around was the holiday before the real school nightmare set in. Turns out that after reading my medical records it became clearer why this decision was made. In my first year of preschool, while doing regular physical therapy with Margaret she noticed a positive improvement. Physical therapy was correcting issues I had in obtaining muscle mass and strengthening my lower limbs. Even though there were noticeable improvements I still had difficulty standing confidently. Their intentions were good but I was still quite unbalanced. During the extra year of attending both schools, I continued to build up my muscles and strength further. They hoped it would aid me in managing the physical toll walking to class would take on my body.

A few minor adjustments were made at school by an Occupational Therapist during my primary years. One being an adjustable desk, it came with a slanted attachment that could be inserted. This was useful so I didn't have to constantly lean forward. At one point I even had a special chair made with a footrest so my feet wouldn't dangle. The OT had also given me these triangular rubber add-ons to put on my pencil or pen. I used them regularly in primary school as they provided a much better grip. I found they were extremely helpful since I am very restricted in my knuckle joint movement, so much so I can't make a fist. Looks like there will be no punching people if I don't want to break my hand. The inability to make a fist is actually a very common Kniest trait.

After the two years of preschool passed I went onto solid mainstream schooling. It was 1988 when I began Kindergarten regularly, five days a week. I ended up going to the same school that my sister attended, but she was two years ahead of me. During this time I remember this one boy in particular, he was my daily nightmare. Every time he saw me in the playground he thought it was fun to pick on me and call me horrible names, especially 'Midget.' For anyone out there that doesn't know, most little people (LP's) don't appreciate being called the 'M' word. It's considered hurtful and politically incorrect, and let's be real, usually meant to be an insult. Personally, I prefer to be called by my name. Fiona or Fee works just fine; most of my friends call me Fee. When it comes to referencing my height if need be, I don't mind short statured, little person or dwarf. Others may think dwarf is rude too because they think of 'Snow White and the Seven Dwarves.' But, if used politely it's actually an accurate title, as I do have a form of dwarfism after all. I do get frustrated when other short statured people seem to encourage the 'M' word in reference to themselves. It only makes matters worse for the rest of the short statured community. We all just want the respect we deserve as people, because that's really all we are. We may be shorter and appear different; but as I stated before everyone is different, not one person is the same as another.

Getting picked on almost every day at school made it really hard for me; so much so, that I dreaded going. I tried so hard not to let it get to me or show them they were hurting me. As soon as I'd get home, I'd go in my room and write in my diary. I had this little Mickey Mouse diary with a lock; it became my safe place where I wrote my feelings down. Either I'd write about what happened to me, what they said or did, and how it made me feel. I just needed to get it off my chest somehow, without involving anyone else. My mum had no idea what was going on because I never told her. If she knew she would have spoke to the school, and I didn't want that because it would have made it worse for me. Plus, if I was going to get through school life and life in general I had to learn how to deal with things in my own way. Not have my mum or anyone else fight my battles for me.

Sometimes, admittedly, I would cry myself to sleep thinking about all the hurtful things people said. It made me so self conscious about myself internally that then I'd look in the mirror and believe I was all those horrible things. It wasn't good for my self esteem, but 'The force is strong with this one' as Yoda would say. I'd pour my emotions onto the pages, and then dust myself off. I'd bury the hurt deep inside and put a smile on my face. Writing in my Mickey Mouse diary taught me a lot about myself, I found it really therapeutic. It allowed me to express everything on paper without burdening my mum or anyone else with my problems. I still like to believe and look for the good in people, no matter how many times I've been hurt.

As much as I was a target for the mean kids, I also made friends easily. While I was at school, I always tried to stay positive and be my usual bubbly smiling self. I did such a good job of hiding my hurt and pain that people never knew how much they were hurting me on the inside with all their harsh, cruel comments. I can't understand how kids or adults even, think that being a bully is okay. It baffles me how any one person could be so malicious that they seem to get enjoyment out of making someone else's life difficult. This seems to occur often especially towards people with disabilities or someone with noticeable differences. Truth be told, I've even seen this occur between people who have disabilities; where they attack each other as if one of them is better than the other.

In my case, because I can only speak for myself; as a child I always disliked confrontations or conflict. I made a conscious effort to not get in anyone's way, in hopes that I wouldn't bring further unwanted attention to myself. I was already getting enough unwanted attention due to my noticeable physical differences. Plus, I knew if anyone got physical with me I'd be the one who'd suffer and I wasn't looking to be a bully's punching bag.

Sadly, I fell victim to this situation despite all my efforts to be nice to everyone including the people who weren't so nice to me. In fact, that one particular boy who was always so rude for no reason continued to taunt me. I never said anything to him and I always consciously tried to stay out of his way. Without fail every time he saw me near the bubblers at school he'd push and shove me. Many times I asked him to please stop after initially trying hard to ignore him. He didn't seem to care; it just made him go out of his way even more. On one occasion he was so rough in the way he pushed me that I fell in the school hall. I slid on the wooden floorboards and my leg ended up somehow twisting underneath me as I hit the ground. As I mentioned earlier, my joints are quite limited in their movement. Therefore, I'm not flexible enough to even sit with my legs crossed. When I fell to the ground, my leg snapped and broke right under me. I screamed out in pain; the next thing I knew the ambulance had to come into the school hall and took me to the local hospital. This whole ordeal was quite traumatic as this incident was also when I formed a serious fear of needles. Once I got to the hospital they had given me an injection in my bottom for the pain. Next thing I knew, blood was seeping through my pants, all the way through to the hospital bed sheets. It stung like hell... For a moment I had forgotten all about the fact that my leg was broken. Now all I could think about was the pain from the needle and blood everywhere. When my mum got to the hospital she asked me what happened, how I broke my leg. Instead of telling her the truth that a horrible kid was bullying me and he pushed me, I lied. I told her that the floor was slippery and I lost my footing and fell. Maybe I should have said something, been honest with her.

What if this kid didn't just bully me, maybe other kids were also too afraid to say anything? I just knew I couldn't do it, I knew there were times when a friend of mine heard this boy taunt me. They tried telling one of the teachers and all the teacher did was told me to ignore him. The teacher said if I ignored him then I wouldn't draw attention to myself, and I shouldn't expect special treatment. So, you can see why I sunk within myself and didn't want to say anything to anyone. I never wanted special treatment; all I wanted was to be left alone instead of get taunted when I was minding my own business. Plus, I didn't want people to think I lied about things like that for attention. People don't realise I don't want the attention in the first place, especially not that kind.

Frankly, most people including those who have known me my whole life; wouldn't know I went through those hard times. I hid it well, it's always been my nature to internalise any negativity even to this day. I like to make sure the people around me are happy.

Somehow I had and continue to have the strength deep within to wear a smile on my face, never wanting a pity party. As I have gotten older, and the realisation began to sink in that people will know me all too well after reading my story; it has made me open up with certain people I feel close to.

I am ever so grateful, even with all my challenges I have faced and am yet to face to feel as blessed as I do. It's like God has provided me with an amazing, unexplainable strength and positive personality. Not to sound conceded in any way because I'm not, but, I am a firm believer, it's what's inside that counts.

There were many mornings in primary school I struggled when the time came for mum to drop me off. When I got out of the car, I tried to chase it and call mum to come back, so she wouldn't leave me. I realise how silly it must have seemed to my mum, since she didn't know why I didn't want her to leave me there. It was my occasional moment of weakness, but because she had no idea what I was dealing with she gave me the tough love treatment. She would tell me to cut it out and then left, which probably sounds harsh to some people. Sometimes I thought that too, but I knew Profs had always told my mum not to wrap me in cotton wool. He would say; "You have to be cruel to be kind, if she's going to grow up to be strong."

In her own way she was teaching me a form of independence. Added with my own will power to not complain to her about bullies and stand on my own two feet; I quickly realised I needed and wanted to make her proud of me. As soon as mum would leave I'd snap out of it, pull myself together and be a happy little vegemite. Which brings me to a funny story I think I should share; it's getting a tad pole too serious. As much as I have had a lot of hard times; I like to think that I am a funny, optimistic person. So onto my story!

Happy Little Vegemite

When I was young, the happy little vegemite commercial would come on TV and I loved to sing along with it. Those of you that aren't Australian, or old enough, may not remember or know it.
It was a black and white commercial, and the end slogan was;
'It puts a rose on every cheek.'
The only colour in the commercial was the rosy cheeks of the kids at the end. I remember begging mum to buy me vegemite, all because I wanted rosy cheeks. Mum insisted; "If I buy it, you better eat it" in her firm Maltese accent. I couldn't contain my excitement when she finally bought it for me. Instantly once I took a bite I was disgusted! I complained as I ate.
"Ewww, this is gross, I don't like it mum."
"You better eat it, you asked for it."
But I was not having it! My biggest problem wasn't just that I didn't like the taste, I was more concerned with the fact I felt cheated and sucked into their marketing ploy. Don't get me wrong, plenty of people love vegemite, but it's certainly an acquired taste.
Clearly I won't be getting a vegemite sponsorship deal...
"But mum, they lied it didn't even give me rosy cheeks."
I know I was silly for thinking it would happen, but come on, the commercial trapped innocent little impressionable Fee. Hook, line and sinker!
I guess if you haven't seen the commercial you may not get it, and you could think I've gone crazy. Maybe you had to be there... Funnily enough, I can still recite the commercial word for word, it's crazy how after all these years some things just stick. Unfortunately, copyright laws prevent me from breaking into song on these pages with all of you.

Chapter Four

Where's the Queen?

Almost two months before my fifth birthday, after much thought and planning, mum had decided to take me and my sister on our first international trip across the seas. It would be the first of many big adventures to come.

The day arrived on the 27th of May 1987 for us to start our long journey to Malta. How exciting, I would finally have the chance to meet all my aunties, uncles and cousins from my mum's side of the family. Until now I had only met our grandfather when he came to visit us in Australia. I am so blessed; I can imagine what a huge challenge it would have been for my mum to take us on such a big journey. Travelling with two kids on her own, would have been difficult enough. Then you add me into the mix and my struggles to walk for any long period. As much as I wasn't a difficult brat, I got tired easily and my joints would constantly throb with pain regularly. There were moments mum had to pick me up and carry me because I couldn't keep up. Plus, she had to carry our luggage on top of everything else. My only responsibility was to make sure that I looked after my first teddy mum bought for me. Yes, even though I was almost five years old, I loved my teddy bear. My sister had one exactly the same, except hers was white. Mine was a cute brown bear with a little bib on it that said 'My First Teddy.' I made sure he was well looked after as he was my soft cuddly friend. To this day teddy is still present in my life, he currently lives in the spare room of our house. No matter how much time continues to pass it hasn't changed my love for soft toys, I'm still a big kid at heart.

Aside from mum missing her family and returning home for the first time since moving to Australia, she also knew Tom really wanted to meet me. Once he knew we would be in Malta he came for a short holiday to meet us. From the moment we were babies even though my mum spoke fluent enough English, she also taught us how to speak Maltese. The way mum taught us was by saying the sentence in English first and then repeating it in Maltese. Even though we didn't speak much Maltese at home, we understood it well enough. It was great preparation for us not to be totally clueless on this trip. In saying that English is a second language in Malta so it's not like we would be epically lost.

While we were staying in Malta, we stayed at my grandparents' house. It was such a big house there were three stories, the first and second story were like two houses. Both floors had multiple bedrooms, a kitchen, dining and bathroom. The third level led up to the roof, the laundry room was also up there in a separate room. In Malta rooves are flat so we had some awesome family parties and barbeques.

The whole trip was three months long, seeing as it takes between twenty-four to thirty hours to get there. We definitely made it worthwhile and who knew when we would get a chance to go back again. This meant I was lucky enough to spend my fifth birthday partying with my extended family. It was such a different experience having the closeness of family around compared to what I was used to. Being that it was summer in Malta in July and the scholastic year was different to Australia, all my cousins were on summer break during most the time we were there. We enjoyed so many fun days at the beach with everyone and shared many wonderful memories. Finally, we had cousins around our age that we could play silly childhood games with.

When Tom arrived in Malta, we had a nice dinner at my Uncle Joe's house. After getting a chance to meet me, he and mum talked about how good it would be to get another medical opinion in England. Tom suggested if mum was serious and could amend our ticket we should arrange to visit him before heading back to Australia. He would set up an appointment for me to see one of the top specialists there and suggested we could stay at a mutual friends place. They lived close to the hospital where my appointment was going to be.

Mum changed our return flight and ten days before the long trip back home we flew to England. England is only a three-hour flight from Malta so it wasn't too bad. When I went to the doctor's appointment they examined my joints and ran a few tests. The conclusion they came to at the time wasn't an earth shattering revelation. They mentioned they were still undergoing a lot of research in their lab, running tests on mice. The research they were doing was to assess if they could eventually offer any treatment to help ease joint issues for people like me. My mum and I were grateful to Tom for going out of his way to get me an appointment in the first place. This at least gave my mum peace of mind and she knew she was doing everything she could.

During the rest of the time we spent in England we visited a few touristy places. The one that stuck in my memory the most was the day we visited the famous Buckingham Palace. As we wandered the grounds of the castle, I recall asking my mum where the queen was. To which we cheekily joked that she was on the throne; you know when you are referencing the bathroom throne not the royal throne. We thought this was hysterical but it simply was a time when the Queen had been away from the castle.

Funny enough, when we were in Malta I had plenty of time to get used to everyone speaking Maltese. But, because we weren't back in Australia I didn't want to stop speaking Maltese. I chose to believe Australia was the only place I had to speak English. The hilarity of my young brain not realising England is the land of the English is pretty funny, but cute right? It took some serious convincing by my mum to make me aware I should have been speaking English.

When we had arrived back in Australia, it took me days to get out of my jet lag and adjust to the time difference again. Not long after returning mum was trying to make me eat, but all I wanted to do was sleep. It was the middle of the day and I hadn't eaten yet. As she gave me food, she turned away for only a moment and I fell asleep standing up. Then, **bang, crash** next thing you know I fell on the tiled floor, head first. Mum was in a panic and rang the hospital at once to ask them if I should be taken in. She was concerned with how hard I hit my head on the floor, in case I became unconscious. The hospital advised her to keep me awake and alert for a few hours to make sure I didn't slip into unconsciousness. Thankfully aside from the big new bump and bruise on my forehead I was okay. If anything, the big bump on my head hurt so bad that I was definitely awake then. Trust me, to end such an awesome trip with a bang.

Girls Just Wanna Have Fun

Even at the age of five I discovered what I would have to say is one of my greatest passions in life. I'd record myself on my black cassette recorder singing, 'Girls Just Wanna Have Fun.' It was all the rage back then, and I loved to listen to music all the time. I'm sure the fact that mum always played cool 80's music on her vinyl turntable sparked my passion and love of music. My idol was and has always been Celine Dion. She has the most amazing, powerful voice and always sings with incredible passion. I loved listening to all genres of music, during the 80's the main artists I listened to were Whitney Houston, Mariah Carey and Michael Jackson. They were at the top of my playlist growing up, but if I had to choose one ultimate idol, it would one hundred percent be Celine.

For as long as I can remember I would say; "I want to be a singer." Many people I said that to, including my mum, always tried to discourage me and tell me how tough the music industry is. Especially that society might not be ready to accept someone as physically different as me. My mum wasn't that blunt about the last point, but she did somewhat shrug it off. She probably thought I was daydreaming, or it was just a faze I'd eventually forget about. I can see partly why my mum likely didn't want to encourage this dream of young Fee; she wanted to spare me from other people's cruelty. Although, little did she know I already knew how cruel people could be. I do understand and appreciate her wanting to protect me, but at the time I didn't care. I still think I would have preferred a more supportive approach. Of course I realise I was just a kid at the time, but I always felt so mature for my age. Constantly being put in many situations to where I had to consider things the average child didn't need to worry about. It's not that I didn't expect it to be a difficult process, because it's difficult enough for someone who doesn't have my physical obstacles, it's a tough industry, period.

Like with anything in life, you don't know unless you try, and I'd rather say I tried, instead of I just gave up. I refuse to accept the limitations others set upon me. Which is kind of ironic because there have been people in my life that have given me lectures on being independent. Yet they too were holding me back from believing in myself with something like this. Essentially, they were limiting me more than I limited myself. Still, this never really stopped me, deep inside I knew even then that singing meant the world to me. It didn't matter whether I ever became super famous or not, singing would always be a big part of who I am and what I aspired to be. Never fear, we will revisit this massive dream again as time continues on, I can assure you of that.

I never allowed anyone to crush my dreams, no matter how unrealistic some people may have viewed them as. You too should never allow someone to crush your dreams or your spirit. Nobody would get anywhere in life if they simply gave up before trying in the first place. Every actor, singer, doctor, lawyer or author even, only got to where they are by putting themselves out there. Just like I now have by finally publishing my story. Whether I leave my mark as a singer or not, is yet to be seen, but I can now say I'm a published author.

Don't lose sight of who you are just to fit into someone else's mould they set for you. It doesn't mean you have to get carried away with yourself, but it's also important not to lose yourself along the way.

Chapter Five

Cast towards Mobility

I was six years old when I had my first official surgery. See, as a kid my mobility was always not so great. My knees used to knock against each other, and my ankles were collapsed inwards. This meant my feet were never really flat on the ground. The soles of my shoes would always get so worn out because I dragged my feet a lot when walking, causing me to ruin my shoes within less than a month or two. It also made it very hard to find suitable shoes, especially ones that wouldn't dig into my ankle joint. My ankle joint is quite large compared to what's considered to be normal; as most of my joints are. If a pair of shoes comes up to the ankle bone, then it hurts and makes it more difficult to walk. This made the task of finding appropriate shoes a big ordeal.

Seeing as Margaret, my physical therapist and Profs had been monitoring my progress over the last few years; they felt it was time to take things further. They introduced me to a pediatrician, and I went through more tests, x-rays and scans while they considered the best way to help me. After numerous consultations the pediatrician suggested he would like to operate on both my ankles. The plan was to change the alignment of my ankles to make me more mobile. This was important to correct as I continuously fell a lot because I didn't lift my feet high enough or correctly when walking. The inward positioning of my feet was also interfering with my balance. Both my legs were operated on at the same time but I don't remember too much pain from that surgery. The plaster covered me all the way from the top of my thighs, down to the tips of my toes. The pediatrician had implanted a metal clip in each leg, just above my ankle joints. They almost look like an enormous staple. These clips have grown with me and are still in there to this day, occasionally setting off metal detectors.

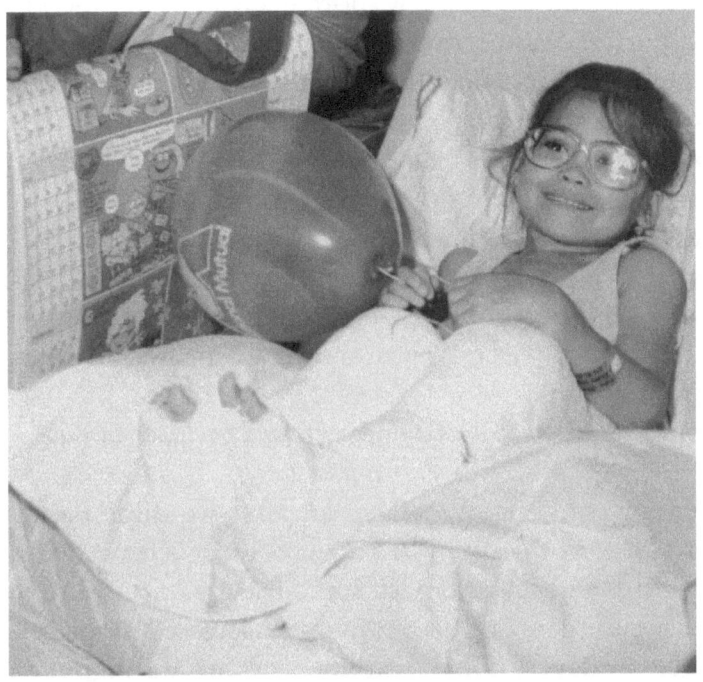

(Me at six years of age in hospital)

It was during the summer so it was fairly hot with all that plaster. My mum thought it'd be best to get me a ceiling fan for my bedroom, because she knew how itchy and hot I was feeling. The itchiness was so bad I naughtily stuck a ruler down inside my plaster; it wasn't one of my brightest ideas. Occasionally I would freak myself out when the ruler would get stuck in there and I'd be panicking to get it out before mum saw me. I couldn't walk at all due to the plaster casts; I had to rely on my mum to take me to the bathroom or anywhere for that matter. There was nothing I could do to help myself during this time, I felt very limited and it was such a challenging time feeling as though I had no independence. It was bad enough I couldn't go to the bathroom by myself but I also couldn't have full, proper, showers during that time. The casts covered the entire bottom half of me and I wasn't able to get them wet.

FIND THE POSITIVE IN EVERY STRUGGLE

Okay, so let me fill in a few more blanks I didn't mention earlier. My mum basically raised my sister and I on her own, since before I was even three years old. Mum had encountered many hardships during my younger years, raising two kids by herself. I saw many things with my own eyes that I wished I hadn't seen, the hardships and struggles we went through were horrible at times. My mum, God bless her, did so much for us to have the best life possible. Now even though no-one else in my family has any form of dwarfism, everyone is quite tall. Except for my mum, she is of average height but naturally just shorter compared to everyone else in our family.

(But let me tell you, she is a firecracker and holds her own and I'm sure I get that from her.)

When I was about five years old, after we came back from our big trip to Europe my mum had went for a much-needed night out; while my sister and I stayed with some friends of ours. My mum was at the local club dancing, as the night progressed a guy asked her if she wanted to dance. They continued talking throughout the night and he told my mum that he'd like to call her sometime. Mum was straight up with him and told him she had two kids and one of them had a disability; of course she was talking about me. He didn't seem fazed by that piece of information at all, and assured her he would call. At first mum wasn't holding her breath that he would actually call, but true to his word he did. Following from that day onwards they started to go out on a regular basis.

While I still had my plaster casts on, this was a time where we were going through many unspeakable challenges and had to move around a lot. Fortunately for us, our friend Kathy who we would visit often offered for us to stay with her until we found somewhere else to live that would be affordable for my mum.

Thank God for friends like Kathy, she kindly took us in with no hesitation until we got things sorted. Even if it wasn't the most convenient situation for my mum, as Kathy lived in an apartment up a few flights of stairs. This was a struggle for my mum to carry me with my plaster every day, up and down the stairs; but it was a small price to pay for us to have a roof over our heads.

After a few weeks of living with Kathy, we then moved into a granny flat of someone else we knew. Over the following years we moved around a lot throughout my childhood. As time went on, we then finally moved into a house of our own that we rented. A lot of those trying times we went through as kids would be an intense story for my mum to tell; if she ever wrote a book of her own about *her* life. As much as during these moments we encountered many struggles, we were also very fortunate. Thankfully with the support of good friends and my mum's new boyfriend we managed to get through every obstacle that came our way.

Mum as you read this, I realise I may not say it often enough, but I will say it for the world to know because I truly mean it. I love you so much, and I thank you from the bottom of my heart. For everything you have done for us and continue to do, and for being the strongest woman I know. You always put us first all of the time, even at your own expense.

You really did teach me a lot about life. One of the biggest things you taught me is how to be strong no matter what life threw at me. We may have been through a lot but I am grateful that I get to call you my mum. *xoxo*

Chapter Six

Growth Hormone Therapy

At the age of seven I went in for a routine check up with one of my specialists. They discussed the possibility of me being started on growth hormones, with the primary aim of increasing my bone density. The doctors had convinced my mum that the aim wouldn't be to make me taller. They were doing a clinical trial with a few rare patients to focus more on increasing bone strength. At the time of that appointment I was only 97.3 centimetres tall and weighed 16.2 kilograms. I recall when my specialist had brought up the topic with my mum and I, he questioned whether she'd be willing to consider that type of treatment for me. They also discussed a lot of the process with me. I was very inquisitive and asked many questions about what would be involved. I expressed my concerns and told my specialist that the thought of regular needles were stressing me out. My biggest fear was that I would have to learn how to inject myself when I disliked needles so much. I was not interested in the thought of having to do that on a daily basis. It scared me a lot and I wondered if the whole process would even be worth it for me. As a kid when someone mentioned growth hormones I thought they were only used to make people tall, and I didn't really care so much about whether I was tall or not. But I continued to ask my questions, and just sat there listening intently to see where it was all going to end up.

If my specialists were to put me on this program, they would have to get permission from our state capital. They'd need to plead my case to the government and inform them why this was something I had to have. Every few months over the next couple of years I proceeded with regular x-rays as well as height and weight measurements. They continued to assess how much progress I was making on my own, before the government could decide whether this treatment was something they should do.

With Kniest it's common not to grow at the average rate a regular child would without a genetic mutation. Therefore, a lot of things had to be taken into account, as to whether the hormones would negatively affect my body. Another major concern was how rapid my joint deformity could worsen, or drastically impact the severity of my spinal curvature. There are notes in my medical file that state if they went ahead with the treatment then they would have to consider bracing my spine. If they braced my spine during treatment, then hopefully the curvature wouldn't get out of control. The thing that gets me though, even though this note was in my medical file neither my mum nor me remembers them ever discussing the idea. We weren't aware that bracing my spine was an option. Whether I had growth hormones or not, my mum had previously asked if they could do something to help with my spine. But it was really just left alone because they were too worried about the unknown. I feel like me being the only one my doctors knew of in Australia really worked against me in these instances. Even though every person's severity is different with each individual that has Kniest; it still would have helped to have someone to compare possibilities and options with.

My mum allowed them to run blood tests and regular monitoring to assist them in making the most informed decision. Whether this would be a good choice for me or if it would simply just make my life worse.

As I was reading my medical records from during those moments, I found it extremely interesting. The doctors mention how curious I was about the procedure. To them they noted my curiosity into having a desire to be taller. Which at seven-eight years of age it really doesn't sound all that crazy. As much as I have always been a tough kid and accepted who I am. I was bullied a lot in school so you could attribute that curiosity to them thinking I was trying to spare myself from many more years of bullies. But then again, they weren't even aware of my bully situations so I'm not sure what they were thinking. I don't deny that I was curious about it all as I had previously mentioned. Sometimes it does make me wonder, if the doctors misinterpreted my curiosity or desire for knowledge as a sign of me wanting to be taller.

Realistically, I've always been the type of person who asks a lot of questions. I always want to understand things about myself from a more medical standpoint. Because from a physical standpoint I have always been in-tune with what my body can and can't handle. If they thought I was curious back then well, I'm sure they might love me less now. I am always challenging doctors by asking the difficult questions at appointments. Most people probably don't even want to consider knowing all the details to the extent that I do.

Back then I had asked if the doctor could show me what type of needle they would use to inject the growth hormones. For me needles were always a big deal, you could say I've always hated them and been pretty scared each time I had to get one. It was like I was trying to let my brain process, 'Do I really want to put myself through something I hated.' If it was just about height and for me to fit in, then it would be something I wouldn't consider because that sounds a little drastic to me.

Yes, when times got tough as a child I wanted to fit in. Although, fitting in didn't mean I wanted to change myself, I just wanted to be accepted for who I am by others. It's always been more about how other people perceived me that made me hard on myself. When I was eight-years-old I went in for another review. I was standing at 102.8 centimetres tall; this meant I had a 5.5 centimetre growth increase. Following that review, shortly after my ninth birthday I went back to the growth clinic for another round of tests. Even though I was still considerably shorter than other kids my age without Kniest, I actually was continuing to grow. The rate just wasn't at an average pace; I then stood at 106.2 centimetres tall and weighed 21 kilograms. It meant I was still well below the third percentile. It can be quite saddening to read notes from the doctor during that time where he wrote that the rest of the examination remained unremarkable. It's like they were expecting me to defy gravity or something. When in reality I am within the normal height range for someone with Kniest.

After many appointments over the last three or so years a decision was made at my last review. I had considerable growth velocity within the last six months of monitoring. Therefore, it meant I didn't qualify to take growth hormones anyway; which was fine by me. The doctor then suggested it'd be best to delay discussing this any further until I saw my pediatrician again. There were discussions being had that he was likely planning my next major leg surgery. Until a decision was made with whether surgery was on the cards again or not, everything else was to be left on hold. There was also still much hesitation as to the negative impact it could have had. Too much uncertainty if my body would have even responded well to the growth hormones. It could have rapidly increased issues with no way of knowing the extent of the damage that could have been caused. So that was that, after years of tests, monitoring and lots of discussion, it was all for nothing. After feeling like a lab rat being poked and prodded, I never ended up taking growth hormone therapy.

In all honesty, I'm glad they never went ahead with it. My mum didn't care either, she only allowed them to consider it because of the possible benefit it may have had in increasing my bone density. Therefore, whatever height my body decided it would be, was all there was to it.

Chapter Seven

Childhood Memories

In this chapter I thought I would cover a few random childhood memories before things get back into the more serious side of life. These memories are in no particular order but are from the first ten years of my life. More specifically memories that weren't previously covered in the major events I've already shared with you.

DEEPER WATERS

Growing up, I never considered myself to be much of a girly girl. I was never into playing with barbies and dolls but I always had a soft spot for plush toys. I used to cut little pieces of material to write the names of my toys on with colourful markers. Somehow then I'd find ways to attach them to the bows or other parts of the toys. Additionally, when I wasn't listening to music or singing along I enjoyed pulling apart watches and trying to fix them. Only problem was, when I first did this it was a bad sign if I had little springs or tiny screws left over. Speaking of watches, during these years of my childhood I had an insane fascination with owning watches that were waterproof. They were watches that could be used underwater at depths of thirty, fifty or all the way up to one hundred metres. The silly thing about this fascination was, even though I loved being in the water and I knew how to swim I never used my watches to their capacity. Whenever I was wearing a waterproof watch, instead of trying to swim as deep as I could go I barely swam at all. I had the habit of standing in an area of the pool or beach where I could reach; putting my head underwater for a split second and then coming back up to look at my watch to see if it was still working. My family used to love giving me so much grief about it; to them it looked so silly. I admit, sometimes back then it really used to upset me and I was fairly sensitive to them joking about it. As I've gotten older I realise how absolutely silly this was, because I knew how to swim. If I truly wanted to test my watch, you'd think I would have tried to get into deeper waters. When I got my one hundred metre watch, and I was testing it for the first time I was so hesitant. I wasn't sure how I would get into the water because the beach we were at had a lot of rocks. It was difficult for me; I always hated swimming at rocky beaches. Somehow I always smashed my legs into a rock and hurt myself, so this added to my nervousness. Finally, I jumped into a deep section of the ocean. Literally the moment my arm hit the water the watch blanked out, and that was the end of that!... A hundred metres was an epic fail. Afterwards I was too disappointed that my fascination with waterproof watches ended just as quickly as that watch had blanked out.

Confetti Filled Tears

In June 1991 my mum, sister and I travelled back to Malta again. It was the same time of year as the first time we went, and I was lucky enough to spend my ninth birthday with our family. During that holiday mum decided my sister and I would both do our Confirmation in Malta so we could have our family around us. Which meant my sister and I were able to choose one of our aunts to be our godparents. I loved that the two times we went to Malta were during our winter in Australia. As it was always summer in Malta during my birthday, this made it even more awesome especially as a kid. Although, I feel I need to be completely candid in admitting it wasn't always fun and games. Somehow I always managed to get upset on my birthdays and this kind of left a terrible imprint in my memories. I know kids will be kids and because all my cousins were all around the same age group, everyone wanted to be in charge. The thing that upset me the most was when it was one of my cousin's birthdays I'd be reminded of how different I was. As kids we had a tradition where the rest of the cousins had a small bag of rice or confetti to throw on the birthday person. Sadly, for me this really wasn't any fun being that naturally I was always much shorter than everyone else. Even though we were all around the same age, it was hard for me to get in there to throw the rice or confetti on them. Therefore, every time I would get upset because one of my other cousins would snatch my confetti off of me so they could throw it on them instead. This actually made me completely dislike the idea of confetti, something that should have been fun I ended up dreading. I dreaded it even more when they would throw it on me when it was my birthday. They all towered over me and it felt like I was drowning in a massive pile that would get between my face and my glasses. Instead of wanting to continue to cut my cake I would just run off in tears. I love my cousins with all my heart and I know that we were all just kids navigating through life, and I'm sure they didn't realise how much this actually upset me. Unfortunately though, those memories stuck with me because for me it was like adding insult to injury. Especially when I go back and watch old family videos, I feel so embarrassed that there's actual footage of the whole ordeal. It stung as a kid realising I couldn't even achieve the simple task of joining in the fun and throwing confetti in the way everyone else did.

Cycling through Fears

When I was a toddler I had this awesome black and red three-wheeler bike that I absolutely loved. It was the bike I had learnt how to ride on in the first place. It served as a form of exercise for me, which I needed for building strength in my legs. Eventually when I grew out of being able to ride that bike anymore I was pretty shattered. This meant I had to learn how to ride a two-wheeler bike and I knew this would be hard with my bad balance issues. The fear of falling off my bike really scared me. Mum got me a new white and pink bike with a little basket on the front.

For the longest time I had training wheels on until I built up my confidence. Even then I was always so scared to get on, to just go for it and ride because it wobbled a lot. I soon developed my own fun solution in our driveway. There was lots of sand behind where my mum parked her car, so I'd purposely bog my bike into the sandy area. This made it seem like I had an exercise bike, so I felt more confident and steady; I rode it nonstop without fear of falling over. Granted, I wasn't riding anywhere since I was stuck in the sand, but this was fun for me. Most people thought I was silly for not being confident enough within myself to just ride the way you're supposed to. In my heart I knew how injured I could have gotten if I ever solidly fell off my bike. I had already broken a few bones in the past from falling. So I knew if I was on a bike going at an actual speed I'd be in for disaster. But I never vocalised my concerns to anyone when they gave me a hard time, out of fear that they would think I was being silly. I always knew my limits and I couldn't stand the thought of having to deal with any more plaster or broken bones and hospital visits.

Sunday Fun Days

The first time I ever sang in front of lots of people or in public was also the first time I sang karaoke. I was nine years old, when my mum used to take us to Sunday family karaoke at a local club. We would go there quite often with some Maltese friends of ours. All of a sudden we were up on stage getting ready to sing. It was me, my sister and our childhood friend, the three of us had decided to sing 'Pretty Woman' by Roy Orbison. I'm not really sure why out of all the songs that existed back in the 80's we chose that one. At the time it was the song all three of us had agreed on. The coolest part was that it was a competition and the three of us actually won!

I was probably more excited than my sister and our friend because they weren't into singing in the same way that I was. Our prize was a package full of chocolates and lollies. Of course it had to be an age appropriate prize, we were kids after all and winning candy was the best prize three kids could receive.

BATTING BLUNDERS

I always did my best to participate in all school activities including sports as much as possible. The teachers actually never made any special allowances for me either. There was this one time in primary school during sports class when we were playing T-ball. It was my turn to bat, and I was focusing all my energy on making sure I hit the ball. By some miracle I managed to hit it. It wasn't a massive hit to brag about, but it still meant I had to try to run to the bases. Usually if you hit the ball you are supposed to leave the bat at the hitting post and just run to first base. Me being me; I was so focussed I ran with the bat and all, while everyone was yelling at me.

"Drop the bat!"

"Drop the bat!"

Eventually as I kept running, instead of just dropping the bat, I threw it, further than the actual ball went. It was so funny; thank goodness I didn't hit anyone or hurt anyone in the process. Don't ask me how, but I even managed to make it back to home base, even though I had no idea what I was doing.

Childhood Memories

SISTERS UNITE

When I think back to the days my sister and I were in our younger years and we were going through some pretty tough times, they were times we had each other's back. Occasionally we would listen to music, and create these funny little dance routines to the song 'Under the Boardwalk.' Some of our moves we did were so much fun. We would even let ourselves go backwards while the other would stand behind ready to catch the other one; almost like those trust exercises people do.

In the backyard of one of the houses we rented, we used to have this really big mulberry tree. My sister and I used to have these little chairs that we would take outside, so that we could sit and hide under the tree. We spent many summer days hiding in our mulberry tree making an absolute mess of our dresses. Mulberries stain everything; this meant we could never really be secretive about what we were getting up to in the backyard as our stained clothes gave us away.

We would play teacher and student games together and even invent our own silly games. We may not have had a lot of expensive things growing up but we had each other, and I'll always be grateful for that.

UNFORGETTABLE NIGHTMARE

There was a time during my childhood when our lives seemed so chaotic that I had terrible nightmares. In fact I always had this one particular nightmare that I couldn't shake for the longest time. In my dream I would be running up the stairs of a big building, while someone would be chasing me. I'd finally get to the roof, when the person chasing me would pull out a gun and pull the trigger. It was almost like I was standing on the Empire State Building, the rooftop was flat and it was pitch black outside. Right as the bullet shot out I'd be falling through the sky heading towards the street. I never knew if the bullet actually hit me or not, nor did I ever hit the ground; I always woke up as I was falling. This was so traumatising, I was so scared and didn't want to fall back asleep. To make matters worse, each time when I woke up from this nightmare it would be pitch black in the middle of the night. Just outside our bedroom window where we slept there was a big tree; the branches used to freak me out because they always looked like a skeleton was standing right outside. My sister and I were sharing a room back when I had these terrible nightmares. We were sleeping on bunk beds and my sister always slept on the top bunk because I didn't feel safe climbing ladders. Sometimes when I woke up from my nightmare I'd cry because it would seem so realistic. I couldn't understand how I kept having the exact same dream every time, it felt like a bad sign.

THE SHOCKING TRUTH OF PUSHING MYSELF TOO FAR...

On one occasion I went fishing with a few people; I don't remember the name of the actual place where we went fishing but I do remember what it looked like. I didn't want to be there because this wasn't really an outing I was interested in. As we were walking to the rocky area where they were planning to fish I struggled to keep up and I was so tired. It felt like a really long walk from the car, walking any distance is a struggle for me. As a kid my joints would throb so badly I couldn't even explain how severe the pain felt. I kept stopping every few steps I took, but as I continued to push myself tears began to run down my face.

Eventually after a decent period of time, I was picked up by one of the people who went fishing with us. They wanted to put me on their shoulders, but I didn't want them to. This felt just as bad as having to walk because I had an insane fear of heights. Also I didn't feel comfortable with other people being responsible for me and the possibility of falling gave me serious anxiety. Keep in mind I was really little, and they were extremely tall. In my eyes, they were like a giant, well realistically most people were giants compared to me. I begged and pleaded for them to put me down because I couldn't deal with the situation. When they put me back onto the ground, without even realising their own strength they had set me down on my feet too hard. It was concrete too, and that caused me to feel even more pain in my legs.

The entire day felt like an eternity. Finally, when we were back home I was in so much pain. I had pushed myself too far trying to keep up with everyone else. My joints were destroyed that day; it was so bad I was in utter agony. I couldn't walk or go to school for an entire week afterwards.

My mum told one of my doctors and they sent me to hospital for a check-up. I ended up having to go in for a few appointments while they hooked my legs up to a machine and literally performed electro shock therapy. They did this to help awaken my muscles in hopes it would calm them back down so I could walk again. This was such a crappy experience and was so painful. It took time for my legs to be relieved from the pain that one day of complete strain had caused to my body.

Chapter Eight

Ilizarov Method

As time continued on, I had doctor appointments several times a year. There were a few other minor surgeries in-between, but I decided unless they were life changing events they aren't worth mentioning here. When I was at one of my appointments with my major specialists things took a sudden turn. The next thing I knew they were having a serious talk with me. Instantly, I worked out where the conversation was headed, it meant more surgery. I sat there listening to what the process would be and asking questions here and there. Suddenly, I had an overwhelming flood of emotions. I knew no matter what I said the doctors had already convinced my mum it was the right thing for me to do. Mum began her usual routine; she had this look on her face I was all too familiar with. As she tried to convince me that everything would be worth it in the end. I was no longer able to hold my feelings in anymore. The reality of what was about to happen had sunk in, I cried my eyes out, desperately I pleaded with my mum. I didn't want to go through with it, even though I knew I had to.

Only weeks before my tenth birthday and the time had arrived for me to undergo possibly the most painful surgery. It was one of the hardest experiences I had to go through as a kid or even ever in my life thus far. The procedure I had was called Ilizarov Method. If you are not familiar with it, it's where the doctors break the leg bones in certain sections; drill and then place pins throughout the entire leg to hold the bones in place. Then the position of the leg is manipulated during the healing process. It went from my ankle up to the very top of my hip joint. It was such a heavy and big contraption designed to change the alignment of my legs. Other people who may have heard of this surgery before generally know it to be used for limb lengthening. In my case this wasn't the aim or the need for doing such an invasive surgery. After all, my arms and legs aren't that different in length. It's more my spine compression that makes me stand much shorter than I would if my back was straight. I was amongst the first handful of people in Australia they did this surgery on. Especially, where the intent focused on changing the alignment of my bones, rather than lengthen them. If I was offered this surgery just to make me taller I wouldn't have allowed it to happen, neither would my mum. My reasons were different, and even though I had the ankle surgery when I was six years old my legs still rolled inwards. The clips were still in there, but unfortunately my ankles collapsed again as I kept growing. My hips were so bad I leaned forward a lot when I walked and I could barely look straight ahead.

Prior to having this surgery, I had met one guy who came from a country of great poverty. Although I can't remember the exact place he was from, he was flown to Australia to do this surgery on one of his legs that was severely twisted in the wrong direction. They were realigning his leg to make it straight without lengthening it. It was so twisted originally he couldn't even place that foot on the ground to walk. His leg was successfully going in the right direction; I could only hope mine would too.

On the 16th of June 1992 I was in theatre for five hours whilst the doctors placed the fixture from my ankle to my knee on my left leg. They had initially planned to do the entire leg at once, but they didn't want to risk me losing too much blood.

I know this might sound silly, but at one of my appointments I went to just before the surgery took place I had a serious discussion with my doctors. Even though I was so young, it goes to show what state the world was in back then. Especially for a nine-year-old to even bring up such a subject; but it was important they knew how I felt. I had advised my doctor and my mum that I didn't give her permission to sign any documents on my behalf as my parent, if I was losing too much blood. I didn't want to allow them to give me any blood transfusions should the surgery take too long. If such a situation arose where I was losing too much blood, then they should stop the surgery immediately. I wanted nobody else's blood and I didn't care who it was. I was very serious about my feelings on this topic when I had the talk with them. Back then all I remember was people talking about how you could get sick or contract AIDS from blood transfusions. I felt like I had enough problems, so I didn't want to risk any additional medical issues.

I stayed ten days in hospital which was the time it took for me to get up and walk with a frame. It was a long process to stop myself from being sick after the anaesthetic, and the time it took to sit up in bed was agonising. My leg felt so heavy, my skin and muscles were tugging in all the places where the pins were located, and I kept having dizzy spells. Less than two weeks later I returned to hospital on the 7th of July 1992. They needed to continue the rest of my left leg from the knee to my hip. This surgery took three hours in theatre because there were fewer pins on the upper part of my leg compared to below the knee. Making my leg even heavier than it already was, I spent over a week in hospital again before I could go home. Repeating the same experience of sickness and waiting for my body to co-operate until I could sit up and walk again using the walking frame. It was such an awkward contraption the screws had to be turned multiple times a day. When the screws were turned, it would cause my leg to bleed constantly leaving me in agony.

Unluckily, this meant I spent my tenth birthday in hospital. My mum had bought me an ice-cream cake, party hats, lollies and balloons to try and cheer me up. Though I wasn't my usual cheery self, and this was a birthday I really struggled to see the bright side of things. There were quite a few kids in my ward that I became friends with. The hospital had an old Nintendo system with a television we could share. I reserved the TV as often as I could, either playing it by myself or with one of the other kids. My favourite game they had which I played most of the time was Super Mario Bros. Mum had also brought me a few things to play with for when I got bored. Seeing as she couldn't always be there with me because she had to look after my sister and take her to and from school. Plus, the hospital that I had all these childhood surgeries in was about an hour's drive each way from where we lived, provided there was no traffic. Mum always did her best by coming to see me every day, sometimes even twice a day.

One of the items she got me was this magic set because I had told her I really wanted one. It had special playing cards, a trick thumb as well as a few other novelties with a booklet on how to act out the magic tricks. She also got me a deck of UNO cards, Dominos and a fun joke book so I could entertain myself and tell jokes to the other kids and nurses. Sometimes she would bring me some of my favourite snacks to cheer me up. I absolutely loved these honey baked ham Kettle chips and Darrell Lee chocolate bullets. If you haven't had chocolate bullets before, they're black liquorice covered in milk chocolate shaped like bullets; I was completely addicted to them. Occasionally, mum would call the hospital before coming to see me, and she'd ask if I wanted her to bring me anything. I would beg her to buy me McDonald's when she was close to the hospital because I hated the hospital food. McDonald's was my favourite thing to eat, or hot chips (fries); I wasn't overly interested in much other food.

The hospital even had their own radio station, called 'Radio Lollipop.' Shortly after my surgery, my class from school made the trip to come and see me in hospital. It was nice to see some of my friends from class. They bought me a jumper from the hospital radio station. It was white with the big red radio lollipop logo on the back and smaller logo on the front. Back then it was too big for me, but it fits me perfectly now and I've worn it for so many years. The radio station was pretty cool because I used to call them up to request songs all the time. Aside from the radio station there was a special room called the 'Starlight Room.' If kids couldn't leave their beds to play games or do activities in the Starlight Room, people would come down and ask you if there were any activities they could bring. They had things like cross stitch, board games or colouring books, etc. I did a few cross stitch patterns while I was there, the one I remember the most was one I did of Donald Duck.

So, who wants to hear a joke or two that's still stuck in my mind, from the joke book of ten-year-old Fee?... Let's flip the page...

"Knock, Knock"
"Who's there?"
"Lettuce"
"Lettuce who?"
"Lettuce in it's cold out here!"

"Knock, Knock"
"Who's there?"
"Banana"
"Banana who?"
"Knock, Knock"
"Who's there?"
"Banana"
"Banana who?"
"Knock, Knock"
"Who's there??"
"Orange"
"Orange who?"
"Orange you glad I didn't say banana?"...

"So I was on TV last night"
"Wow really, you were?"
"Yeah, but mum told me to get off before I break it!"

I know; so cheesy right! It was a kid's joke book after all, and I definitely enjoyed annoying people with the banana joke.

It was a really difficult time for me being in and out of hospital a lot. As soon as I would go home, I always went back to school just days after getting out of hospital. I had to use the walking frame the entire time I had the Ilizarov fixture on my leg; not only because it was quite heavy, but also because it was hard for me to put weight on that particular leg with all the pins. My foot was always so swollen, sore and tender. When mum would put my socks on, it felt so weird and painful because I had pins that were right on my ankle joint. It was so annoying, that occasionally my sock would get stuck to one of my open wounds.

School was so full on, walking through the playground during recess and lunch breaks, because kids would play with basketballs, etc. I felt like a magnet as they managed to hit my leg almost every time. This was incredibly painful, but the teachers refused to let me stay in the classroom during lunch breaks. I wanted to stay in to avoid any injuries, and so I didn't have to go up and down the classroom stairs multiple times a day. Unfortunately, I had no other option, so I hid in the library. The library was the safest place, as no-one could run or be silly in there. I had a teacher's aide that came to the school during this time because I couldn't go to the bathroom without someone's help. Whenever I needed to sit down my leg couldn't bend much at the knee, it only had very little movement. The aide would have to hold my leg up and bear the weight for me. During class when I sat down the school chairs were quite awkward so I had to sit on the very edge of my chair. My aide also had to walk behind me and support me when climbing up and down the stairs to my classroom, in case I lost my balance.

The super annoying thing was the surgery was during the winter months, and because it was such a massive contraption I couldn't wear pants to cover it. My mum had to cut all my underwear on the left side at first; it was so uncomfortable and I was so unprepared to deal with that. In the beginning I had to tie the ends of my cut underwear back together, until mum had time to sew some Velcro on them. She even cut a few of my wider sweat pants up to the hip area so I could put them on. This way I could at least cover my right leg to avoid some of the cold. I couldn't cut all my clothes though, and mum used to buy me a lot of dresses when I was young. So even though it was winter my options were limited and I still had to wear dresses most of the time. I tried to put a blanket over my legs when I was sitting down though. This wasn't always easy, even when I was in bed I couldn't stand the weight of blankets putting pressure on the pins that were sticking out.

Finally, we had settled into a rental property that was ours a few months before this major surgery happened. We moved around a fair bit before that. Obviously we did it tough for quite some time financially because mum wasn't working. But what I haven't elaborated on yet is the guy my mum dated before I had my first surgery was still dating my mum all this time. He became such an amazing support to us all. I will elaborate more on this as we go on because there is so much that still has to be said. I just don't want to get off topic.

As you can imagine my mum had to buy us a lot of things from scratch, with all the moving around we had to do over the years. For a while there my sister and I only had these small fold away beds to sleep on, which weren't comfortable. It was even less comfortable when I had all the metal attached to my leg. It was already limiting me in how I had to sleep, without being able to move much at all. Thankfully, shortly after my surgery mum bought me my own new single bed. I was pretty lucky because mum had asked the place she bought my bed from to put extra padding in the mattress for me. This way it would handle the weight of all that metal, without making me feel like I was sinking. I loved this bed so much, it was the comfiest bed I ever owned or slept on.

The other major issue was during this time I couldn't even sit on the lounge. Firstly, it wasn't comfortable for me because I couldn't bend my leg. Secondly, it would have been more than likely the pins would have pierced a hole in the lounge, and yea, that wouldn't have been good. But mums boyfriend had got us some really cool thick army leather material from his work. Mum thought it might be a good idea if she made me a big bean bag using the strong army material. She hoped it would be comfortable for me to sit on. It had to be filled with lots of beans because of the weight from all the metal. Also so it could be as high as possible for me to get on it. Someone always had to help me sit and get up; they held my leg and me so I wouldn't fall on the floor and hurt myself.

It was such a crazy time that posed many challenges. I was constantly coming up with solutions to managing basic everyday tasks. With my family's help, we got through it together. The worst part of it all was mum had to learn how to clean my wounds. The nurses had to teach her when I was in hospital before I could go home. This was surely the most excruciating part of the whole process. It was important that my open wounds where the pins came out of on my leg wouldn't get infected. Mum had to clean them regularly; with peroxide of all things. Oh, the screams and tears I let out especially the first few times. It hurt and stung so bad, you would have thought I was being murdered. Mum had guts too, because even though I took out a lot of the frustration on her and pleaded with her to stop she knew it would have been so bad for me to get an infection. No matter how much I screamed the house down she continued to do what had to be done. I know that can't have been easy for her either, feeling like she was hurting me, and seeing me in that much pain.

I went back into hospital on the 23rd of September 1992 to have the Ilizarov fixture removed from my leg and have my leg put into plaster. I can't believe I had that thing on for a little over three months which was basically the entirety of winter. Thankfully, taking the contraption off was a much quicker process. It was done in approximately two hours compared to the total of eight hours it took to put it on initially.

This time I was only in hospital for two days before I got to go home. All I had to do was be able to get up using crutches and if I could do that it would be the ticket to going home. Dizziness seemed to be part and parcel with this entire process. I tried getting up the first few times but had to take a moment. The physical therapist said if I wasn't ready she would come back another day. I was determined to push through so I wouldn't have to spend much time in hospital; I insisted that if she gave me a moment I wanted to keep trying. As you can imagine at this point constantly having to learn how to walk over and over again; constantly getting dizzy while having to adjust every time and being in and out of hospital was getting pretty old. It just made me more and more determined to do better each time and to push myself that little bit extra.

I had the plaster on for about a month, until all my bones healed down my entire leg. Of course it was now spring time, and the weather was getting pretty hot. You'd think the doctors could have timed this better for me. First, I was freezing and then I was boiling and the plaster added with the heat was making my leg super itchy.

The time had finally arrived for them to remove the plaster cast. I was so scared of the electric saw they used to cut the plaster open and it was so loud. Plus, I was freaking out because my leg was hurting and feeling the heat from the machine which made me worry they were going to hit my actual leg. But something worse happened to add to the terrible experience of what should have been a simple plaster removal. When they tried to cut the plaster off at the top of my thigh section I quickly discovered that one of the scars from the pins must have gotten stuck to the cast, and was slightly infected. I began to cry and begged them to stop. I couldn't believe my flesh was literally stuck so badly that it was like the cast had become one with my leg. After much screaming on my part, and a swimming pool of tears, the nurse had to get the peroxide out again for them to be able to remove my flesh from the plaster. When I was eventually free, they proceeded to disinfect my wound and bandaged the area to protect it from further infection. I had to take a course of antibiotics as well to assist with ensuring the infection didn't spread. It took quite some time for my leg to heal from the whole ordeal and the plaster had caused my skin to be so fragile. My skin was peeling off down my entire leg, it was tender and painful; I had to constantly put vitamin E cream on my leg to assist with the healing process. It was also difficult not to pick at my skin when it began to dry out and fall off because it was so itchy. The stitches I had on my ankle were probably the worst section because they were so close to the stitches I had previously from my first ankle surgery. Parts of my new scars overlapped on top of the old scars. It wasn't long before I went straight back to school again. I still needed the crutches for a while until I gained my strength back in my leg because it was so weak. I felt like I was a lamb learning how to walk after they're born.

Although, unfortunately the painful memories of this ordeal didn't end there. Right away when I went back to school the teasing and picking on me continued from a few kids. Some kids made fun of how my leg looked with all the scars everywhere. Now that it was summer, the summer school uniform I had to wear was a dress; so I couldn't hide my newly scarred leg.

Other kids would take it even further with their insults. The worst was this one girl, she was much taller than me and a little bit chubby. *(I only mention this so you can understand how much smaller I was in comparison to her.)* As tempting as it might be to name and shame her, I will leave her name out from these pages, because it isn't a very common name. But it's a name that is still engraved in my mind, like the scars that now appear on my body. I will never forget her for as long as I live, she truly took teasing me to a whole new level. She used to think it was fun to try and chase me and literally poke her fingers right on the holes of my scars from where each pin was. I begged her to stop and leave me alone, but it only made it worse and it hurt so much because I wasn't even healed properly yet. For weeks she continued to torment me and for weeks I used to be scared to be out in the playground.

So I started to hide in the library again because I knew she never went in there. This in a sense gave me a deeper love of reading. I figured if I'm going to be at the library during lunch then I may as well find books I liked. I felt like I was in a movie on the run from a villain every time the bell went. More so when I had to leave the library because I wanted to make sure she never saw where I was going during lunch. I never told my mum this was happening either; because I didn't want that girl to think I was a big baby having my mum get involved. Instead I started to internally feel ashamed of how my legs looked and I was embarrassed to wear dresses, skirts or shorts anymore. But, because I kept these feelings to myself if I had to wear my school uniform dress I then began wearing stockings. I got some thick white or black stockings that you couldn't see through. Even if it wasn't cold out I pretended I just wanted to protect myself from accidently knocking my leg. This was the most believable excuse because my skin was so fragile, which was a valid reason anyway. Thankfully, it wasn't going to be much longer until Christmas and I would be on school holidays for a few weeks.

Thinking back on these moments now, it's kind of sad how this particular bully made me become so self conscious about myself; about my scars and things I had absolutely no control over relating to my appearance. Even though as a kid I never voiced these feelings to anyone, I just dealt with the internal struggle while everyone only ever saw me smile.

Never allow someone's hurtful remarks or bullying make you feel insecure about yourself. Even though I would pick myself up and dust myself off each time as far as everyone else knew, I'd be lying if I said some hurtful observations about my physical appearance didn't stick to the back of my mind. This incident from when I was only ten years old shattered a piece of my confidence in a bad way. I ended up going through such a tom boy faze after this, and buying baggy boys clothes to hide behind. Wearing tighter girly clothes would have shown all my physical differences. I completely stopped wearing dresses; it felt like I was seeing myself through the bully's eyes. The only time I ever wore shorts in summer was when I was at home with my family. My family already knew how I looked, but they never once made me feel like I should be ashamed. It took me until I finished high school to gain some of my confidence back. That's when I stopped wearing baggy boyish clothes, although I still didn't buy any dresses. By then I was so used to wearing pants, I was more comfortable in them. I took the longest time to realise I was just an easy target for people.

I'm different, it's noticeable, but that's okay. I feel like I was born this way for a reason, and I would never want to be anyone but me. Even after many people tried to break me, break my spirit, and leave a scar in my heart. I'm a better person for it, because after all the struggles I've faced my heart remains pure and genuine, and I still believe, and look for the good in people.

If you have people in your life who have made you feel less than good about yourself, ignore them; take my word for it. It bothers people more when they don't get a reaction out of you.

Love yourself, because when you do, it will radiate. Accept that everyone is different and everyone has their own struggles to deal with. Most importantly, you are not alone; everyone at some point struggles with feelings of self doubt, don't allow bullies to alter your belief in yourself. Know that you have the power and strength within yourself to rise above!

Ilizarov Method

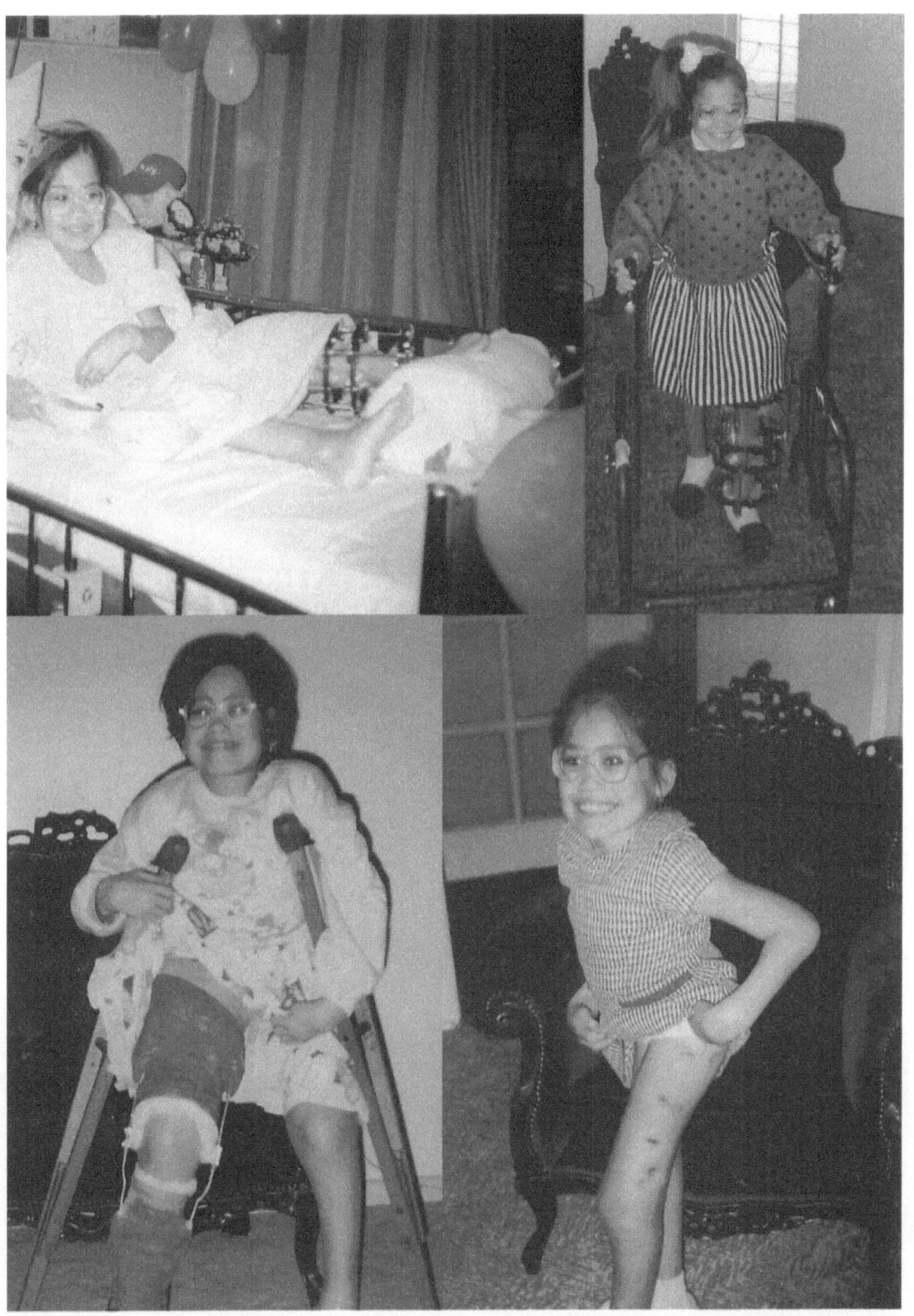

(Me with the Ilizarov fixture on my leg)

Chapter Nine

Flower Girl Fee

I like to think that I'm generally not a girly girl, as I mentioned earlier, and mostly this is true. Growing up with an average height sister who was close to my age was sometimes tough. She was always chosen to be the flower girl in family and friends weddings. I felt like I was missing out on something, it really upset me that I was never asked. It made me feel like I wasn't good enough. You know how when you feel excluded from something, then you actually want it more. I just wanted to be included like everyone else does.

Until one day I got my wish 'Flower Girl.'
I was asked by a lovely couple that knew how much I wanted to be a flower girl. I recall them saying; "If we ever get married, we would love you to be our flower girl Fiona."

Remember Grace, the lady my mum and I were introduced to after I was diagnosed. Her daughter Lynda would be getting married to another little person. Lynda had SED dwarfism like her mum Grace, but Lynda's husband-to-be David had Achondroplasia the most common form of dwarfism.

Let's rewind back a little; to two days before their wedding, back to the day my plaster was removed. It was the 15th of October 1992 and even though I still needed to walk using crutches I was thrilled my plaster came off before their wedding.

Lynda lived in a country town north-west from Sydney; which was a couple hours away from where we lived by car. We made our way there shortly after the plaster ordeal had been dealt with.

The wedding day had arrived, and I was wearing a long peach coloured dress that was specially made for me. Lynda had also arranged for the florist to decorate my crutches with nice flowers. While we were all at the house getting ready for the wedding Lynda gave me a special gift to say thank you for being in her bridal party. It was this lovely gold necklace that had an oval shaped little locket with a blue stone on the outside; I appreciated the sentiment and loved the locket so much. Little did she know that I felt more like I needed to thank her for wanting me in her wedding party. For making me feel welcome, and for giving me a chance to be a part of their special day. I still have my locket, and I've worn it for many years. I am so grateful that they believed in me enough with everything I was going through; and that they had confidence in me that I wouldn't let them down and I'd be able to walk down the aisle alongside them. Yes, I had my trusty crutches to help me, but I am so glad I had the determination to push through all the pain and walk as best as possible to fulfil my duty as 'flower girl.'

It was a lovely day aside from some of the sprinkles of rain that drizzled. Instead of hiring cars to take us to the church I got to ride with Lynda on a beautiful horse and carriage; this was another new experience for me. Granted, it was a challenge getting into the carriage, but I had my mum and her boyfriend there to help me get in and out. The ceremony was gorgeous and the reception was fun, even though I was so exhausted. It was a big day for me trying to make sure I got through it without hurting myself. Crutches and all, I even fulfilled my duty of dancing with the page boy. I remember Lynda and David gave me such a hard time saying how cute we were together. I felt a bit embarrassed, but I can also admit that he was a cute kid nonetheless. *Wink, Wink* ☺

After the wedding had passed, Grace asked me if it was okay for her to write a story about me. She wrote a story and submitted it into the little people's journal. The journal got sent out to all the active members of the organisation. I have a copy of that journal, along with my other memory keepsakes. In fact, I have so many folders I've kept mementoes in from throughout my life.

In the story Grace wrote, she told everyone a bit about me and how my sister was chosen eight times to be flower girl. As well as how now I finally got my wish and was chosen by her daughter to be their flower girl.

She also spoke of my leg surgeries I had just undergone and added a few pictures of me. There were pictures from my surgery, including some of me as 'Flower Girl Fee.'

(Flower Girl Fee)

Me, Kniest & Understanding

I can't help but think how coincidental it is that my Chapter numbers almost line up with my age at the time. Just a random Fee observation...

Chapter Ten

Round Two

It was November 1992 when we finally bought and moved into a house we could truly call our own, no more moving from one rental property to another. Our new house was approximately thirty minutes away from my primary school and where we used to live.

My sister was currently finishing the last few weeks of primary. She was in grade six, while I on the other hand was almost at the end of grade four. I knew this meant the next year I would be fending for myself one hundred percent. Not having my sister even at the same school, I was eager to change schools to the one close to our new home. I didn't even have to express to my mum that I wanted this move more than anything because I wanted to escape those particular bullies. That I was tired of all the physical and emotional attacks making my time at school hell. Besides my mum had no idea all that was even going on. I also was looking forward to teachers not wanting to approach my sister because she wouldn't be there. It would give me the opportunity to prove I could independently stand on my own two feet.

Approximately one year after I had my left leg corrected it was time to have the same thing done to my right leg. At least this time I wasn't going to be staying in hospital for my actual birthday, so I guess that was a bit of a relief. Before we get into round two of surgeries on the 12th of June 1993; exactly a month before my birthday was round two of another special event.

I was going to be a flower girl again. It was equally special if not more on a different level because I was lucky enough to be a flower girl for my mum this time around. After being with her boyfriend for approximately six years they were finally getting married. I know for my mum it took her awhile to realise this guy wasn't going anywhere. That he was more than willing to take on the big role of being a father to me and my sister, especially me with all my problems. My mum even attempted pushing him away before she finally realised he wasn't going to leave. She almost didn't want us to be burdens in his life. Not to get too in depth with all that because that's more my mum's story. Clearly he was in this for the long haul and he reassured her of that. He did so much for us during those six years and showed us so much love. He treated us as his own, even before they got married and as kids we already loved him. So much so that when we knew they were getting married, we asked him if it was okay with him if we called him Dad. No-one ever had to suggest it to us it was something we really wanted to do. It was important to me because it began to not feel right to call him by his name. In reality, he was the father figure in my life, in every way possible.

If I mention my dad from now on, it's technically my step-dad I'm talking about. I feel it's important to give you a heads up not to confuse the situation as you continue to read my story. I don't like calling him my step-dad because to me he is my dad. He has been there almost all my life and I genuinely feel like he deserves the respect of being called my dad.

Let me tell you, in my eyes it should come easily for a parent to be there for their kids that they bring into the world. It takes an amazing person to play the role of a father to kids that aren't biologically his. Especially, when they have to have such a big heart to make someone with all my challenges feel so loved. It bothers me a lot when people say that technically he is my step-dad. Most people who meet me later in life would never know any different because I always introduce him as my dad. You'd never guess we aren't actually related because he has impacted my life in such a positive upbringing, about as much as my mum has.

Back to the 12th of June 1993, they both looked lovely on their wedding day and my sister actually gave my mum away. Which I thought was fitting because it was like a symbol of us girls accepting him into our family too.

Can you believe it, after going from never being chosen to be a flower girl, to being chosen for the first time in my life, and then having the opportunity to be one twice in less than a year!

(One of my favourite pictures of Dad, Mum and I)

ROUND TWO CONTINUED...

It was earlier than the year before, on the 21st of June 1993 I had my right leg Ilizarov surgery. During the surgery they also took a biopsy of my iliac crest for testing, which is the upper part of the pelvis as per the image below.

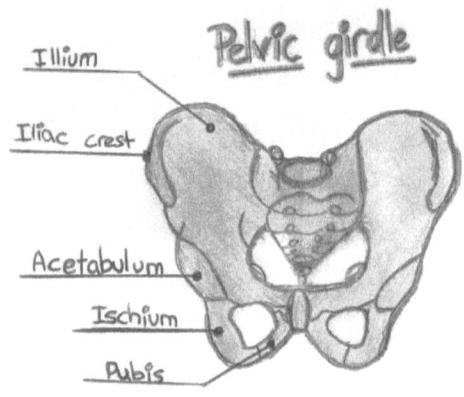

*(How do you like my artistic drawing of a Pelvis?
Sexy looking pelvis isn't it! Hehe)*

One thing I had always wondered was whatever happened to the iliac crest sample they took for testing? After reading what felt like a mountain of pages of my medical records, I finally got some answers. There was information stating that as soon as they took the sample they couldn't process any tests on it, because the bone sample just crumbled into nothing. Making the additional scar and time seem pointless. I wish they would have gone into more detail and discussed what they hoped to discover about my bones from taking the sample. Although, if this attempt says anything, it confirms how fragile my bones were to not withstand tests that it just crumbled to pieces. I should also count myself very lucky this wasn't the same outcome when they broke my leg bones to correct them. It seems almost miraculous that I didn't turn into a pile of 'Fee-crumble Pie'...

Round Two

So even though I wasn't an in-patient on my birthday, I still ended up having to go back into hospital for my eleventh birthday. This time it was just for a review at the limb clinic to see how my right leg was progressing. I still couldn't believe the doctors when booking my appointments wouldn't at least realise and give me an occasional break. Couldn't they at least make my appointment the day before, or after my birthday rather than on? You will realise further on, this topic comes into play a few times in my life where my birthday just seems like a day for medical mayhem.

My right leg seemed to do better than my left, you could say maybe I was used to the experience but that is highly doubtful. See, my left leg has always been worse than my right. I'm sure that had a lot to do with it, because even though I knew the routine with the whole experience it was such a painfully traumatic ordeal. It would be impossible to say anyone could get used to such intensity. There were still horrible moments when I would cry during the times my wounds were being cleaned. I struggled with constantly learning how to walk again and again. The second time around I could push myself harder to overcome the dizziness enough to use crutches straight away. This was better than using the bulky walking frame. Granted, that walking frame was amazing, as it completely supported my arm up to my elbow. It made it easier for me to use my whole upper body strength to support myself without straining my wrists. Considering I don't have the same flexibility in my wrists like everyone else, it was easier the first time round until I adapted. I became so confident on my crutches after all that time; I used to take big jumps instead of slowly walking, although it totally killed my underarms. I'm just glad I never injured myself or sent myself flying in all my fearless crutch jumps. During these two years of surgeries, endless pain and being in and out of hospital, with multiple months of intense physical therapy, it taught me to be tough. If I could get through something this massive twice and still have a smile on my face in front of people, then I can get through anything.

These big surgeries were full on, not just for me but for my whole family, especially for my mum. I know my mum was always trying to do her best to be there for us all. Sometimes it made me wonder if my sister resented me occupying my mum's attention so much with all my medical issues and surgeries. Obviously for me I never wanted this kind of attention and as I mentioned earlier, yes my mum was there for me especially when it mattered. But by no means did she ever baby me with too much attention. I still spent a lot of time outside of visiting hours being alone, sad and bored, wondering if this was how my life would always be. Wanting more for myself it was during these times in hospital I felt I had to grow up fast. I knew then I wanted to share my story with the world. It was during those lonely times I began writing my story. You could say this was the real birth of the story you are reading now. For complete authenticity and perspective I have a couple pages I wrote that I will share with you. These pages are of actual sections, word for word quoted from young ten-year-old Fee's point of view. You may feel like most of this is a repeat of part of the story I have already shared. But, I still feel like it's interesting, even for me reading back on how I saw things and how I viewed myself at that age. So here goes nothing, possible spelling mistakes, bad grammar and all:

(My Life)

My name is Fiona, I was born on July the 12th in 1982. I was born with a bone disorder (disability) which is called Kniest Dysplasia; it affects all the joints in the body. It is a very rare bone disorder as a matter of fact I am the only one in Australia that my doctors know about.

I also suffer from short eyesight; I have been wearing glasses since I was eight months old. It was actually around that time that the doctors found out of my disorder because when I was first born they thought I was a normal baby but I wasn't I was disabled from birth. I was healthy of course but I have to spend my whole life facing problems and suffering with pain.

Little did I know that at the age of ten
how true this statement would be.

When I was 6 years of age, I had an operation done to fix my ankles by putting like a metal clip in my ankle which would try to hold it straight and which would have to stay in my ankle for the rest of my life and never be taken out.

My bones are softer than others and the cartilage is soft too, inside it is soft like jelly, although when you touch it from the outside it feels a lot stronger than jelly. But due to the softness my bones are very easily broken when I have a simple fall and even with a simple push.

I have a sister who is of average height. My sister has been a flower girl for eight times when she was little. But due to my problems I was never asked, so Lynda (who I have known for a very long time) had said to me if ever she got married she would ask me to be her flower girl.

Year later, Lynda and David (Lynda's husband to be) got engaged and set their wedding date, for the 17th of October 1992. I would be ten years of age at that time I was very happy and excited. I was finally going to get my wish:

FLOWER GIRL!...

However, before the wedding, I was told I would need some leg operations. I went into hospital so that my doctor could straighten my left leg from hip to ankle using the ILIZAROV METHOD, *which was named after a Russian doctor who had invented the operation.*

MORE OPERATIONS! Boo!

This operation was to straighten my leg and each day I would have to use a spanner to turn a bolt which turned my leg and caused it to bleed. I was in constant pain and my mum had to carry me everywhere but this never stopped me from going to school.

Obviously she didn't carry me everywhere, but she had to carry me up stairs now and then. Until I got used to adapting to the contraption, and how I would manage stairs with how restricted I was.

On June 16th I was five hours in theatre whilst the doctors straightened my leg from knee to ankle. I stayed 10 days in hospital then I went home for two weeks and returned to hospital on July the 7th for the doctors to straighten from hip to knee. This took three hours in theatre and again I had to stay in hospital for one week, which meant I had to stay in hospital for my 10th Birthday, how boring.

THE WORST BIRTHDAY EVER!...

Yes I did actually capitalise those words back then for emphasis, I hope you enjoyed the additional insight.

Chapter Eleven

Fusion and a New Way of Life

It was 1995, and I was now twelve years old. My family had made a united decision; we all wanted to move from Australia to Malta to live permanently. This meant we would finally get to be surrounded by our extended family, like all my aunties, uncles, cousins and my grandfather. Before we could leave Australia, my mum thought it would be best to advise my specialist about our decision, to see if this would be okay for me medically. Profs suggested that he wanted to run all kinds of tests, x-rays and MRI's first to ensure I was in a stable enough condition before he could advise if I was good to go. Sitting in his office after the test results were back in was so nerve-wracking. I was incredibly worried and anxious, hoping they didn't find anything wrong with me that could ruin our plans to move to Malta.

Suddenly, everything felt like a blur, as if I was in some horrible dream I was trying to wake myself up from. As I heard my specialist tell me and my mum that the MRI showed too much space in my neck vertebrae's. He believed I needed to have a C1-C2 fusion to correct it before I could go anywhere. This can be a common issue for many people with various forms of dwarfism. Immediately, I started balling my eyes out like crazy. Deep down I knew it would not be as simple as him telling us everything was perfect with me and to go on my merry way. Tears now streaming down my face, I cried out; "Please don't make me do it mum, I don't want another surgery, I'm scared, tired and I don't want any more operations."

Mum continued to ask Profs what needed to be done and why this was important to do now. He explained I was extremely lucky nothing serious had happened prior to this. He seemed surprised I wasn't feeling any neurological symptoms. This was a shock to Profs as much as it was to us, he went on to tell us how they would likely go about correcting this issue. They would need to take a bone graft from one of my rib bones and fuse it into my neck. It was important to stabilise and remove the excess space in order to strengthen my neck joint.

The excess space between the neck vertebrae's is referred to as 'hypomobility.' Hypomobility can be the cause of collagen being weaker than it should be; which mine is as I have a collagen related condition. The tissues in the body become fragile, leading to ligaments and joints being loose and stretchy. In my case my neck joint moved ten millimetres beyond the normal stable range, causing instability to be a concern. I know ten millimetres sounds like nothing right? Unfortunately, when it has to do with the spinal cord, it is actually considered to be a lot of space. He reiterated how I was very lucky they ran the tests because not attending to this issue was not an option. If I would have been involved in a car accident or fell over badly, then my neck could have been disjointed to the point of complete dislocation. Which would either cause me to be paralysed or even death was a huge possibility.

This issue had the potential to cause me serious muscle fatigue. My neck muscles would have had to work that much harder to compensate for my weakened neck joints. This was enough reason for my mum to say; "Fiona, I know you don't want to do this but it's for the best." There she goes again with that look on her face, the look I couldn't escape when I knew my mum was being dead serious. Deep down I knew she was right; as scared as I was hearing all of this information, it scared me more thinking of what might happen if I did nothing. Internally I knew I couldn't ignore the issue and bury my head in the sand because mum wouldn't have let me either way. But, I was only twelve years old and so over surgeries after experiencing the intense leg surgeries I had in the last couple of years. I felt like it would never be over. Profs provided us with as much detail as possible and had advised mum and I of all the risks that would be involved. He then stated that once my neck begins to heal after the surgery and was strong enough, we would be okay to move forward with our plans and make the big move to Malta.

Following this, Mum and I were introduced to one of the best spinal and neck professors around. He would be in charge of doing my surgery and making sure I was treated delicately. Sometimes being known to be the only one in Australia with Kniest had its benefits. Profs always made sure I had the top surgeons on my case. A discussion was had where they thought it would be best if I met a few patients who had a similar surgery. That way I could find out more and actually see what was in store for me.

All I can say is; "Oh my goodness!" There was this one child I was introduced to who had so many complications, they had to repeat the surgery five times. As the bone they were attempting to join to support their neck kept slipping out of place and had a hard time fusing together. You can imagine how this made me feel, I was even more worried now. I truly can't imagine how that child would have been feeling after everything they went through.

> What if I was going to have the same problem?
> What if my bones don't fuse?

Doctors always told me that Kniest bones tend to be more fragile, and my bone density has always been way below average. Some medical information suggests a distinctive Kniest feature is hundreds of small holes in the bone cartilage. Making it appear like Swiss cheese on an x-ray. The holes weaken the cartilage, which serves as a connective tissue throughout the body, and causes joint stiffness and swelling. Which sounds completely weird and maybe this explains why I don't like eating cheese. *Jokes...* Well, not about the not liking cheese part. I actually really don't like it unless it's melted nicely on pizza or on lasagne. I'm a bit of an odd Fee when it comes to this.

All I could do at that point was pray and continue to have faith in my specialists. They had always looked after me, everything normally went to the plan they'd set out. I had to believe this time would be no different.

Preparation for my surgery began; I went into hospital for a few hours to get a plaster mould made of my neck. After the surgery I would wake up to a hard plastic body cast to keep my neck in place until it heals. It would be my new regular body armour. Seriously, this was an awkward experience, I felt like I was a mummy being wrapped up in mushy plaster gauze. They had placed something in-between my face and the plaster, which left me a tiny hole just big enough to breathe. I was covered from the top of my head to the base of my back, just up above my hip joints. This made me feel so claustrophobic, I felt like I was going to suffocate. Finally, the body mould was dry and solid enough to cut down the middle so I could be set free again. Thank goodness too, talk about almost having a panic attack!

Now that that was taken care of, a date was set and I was booked in for a pre-op admission on the 17th of January 1995. I had completed an extensive lung function test, spinal x-rays and a long thorough consultation with the anaesthesiologist. After two days of solid tests for the big surgery I was then discharged and advised to return for admission on the 22nd of January. They needed me to arrive the day before, being that this would be a high risk surgery. Therefore it was extremely important to monitor me for twenty-four hours prior to the big operation.

The day had arrived, and I was being taken into the operating room, tears flowing down my face. I was filled with so much fear because I knew doing the surgery was risky too. I made myself so sick with nerves I threw up just before they gave me anaesthetic. As the black anaesthetic mask was placed over my face, the anaesthetist would constantly trick me into talking so I would swallow the anaesthetic and fall into sedation. I was hip to their game at the time and mentally I knew I wanted to keep my mouth shut because I hated the taste; but it was unavoidable.

Not long after I was sedated the doctor went out and spoke to my mum. He went asking for permission to take a bone from my lower back instead of using one of my ribs. In all honesty I actually have no idea which bone they took a graft from, all I know is where the massive scar from it is located. He explained that after proper consideration he could see that this bone would probably work more effectively rather than taking a piece of my rib cage. My mum left it in their hands because they knew what was best. As long as they felt they were making the right decision then who was she to question it.

My bone graft from my lower back area was packed into the space between the posterior arch of my C1 and the laminar of the C2 vertebrae. They also wrapped some kind of wire around the vertebrae's to hold the bone graft in place until it heals and fuses together. The wire will remain in my neck forever though even after the bones have fused. After hours went by, I woke up all queasy and disoriented in a room feeling sore and stiff. I was lying extremely flat on a bed with a tube going through my nose straight to my stomach. It was there just in case I was sick, so I wouldn't choke on my own vomit. And of course what happens next was one of the worst feelings as I began to panic and tell the nurse, "I'm going to be sick." She tried to calm me down and said "It's okay that's what the tube is for." Now I don't want to gross you out too much so I am sure you can work out what happened next! Yuck...!

Aside from my nose tube, annoyingly, I also woke up to realise I had a catheter in. I would not be able to get up from the bed for the first few days. Nor was I going to be able to lift my body up every time I needed to go to the bathroom. They gave me no choice in the matter obviously it was better than swimming in my own pee. I realise this isn't the most pleasant topic but it was my reality. Every time I felt sick I wanted to sit up because it didn't feel natural. It felt like my body weighed a tonne, as if some magnetic force was trapping me. My head was in a daze and I was told it would take days before I'd even be able to sit up.

Waking up in recovery was always so confusing. It's as if you have no concept of time when you are under anaesthesia, and everything is just blank. While in reality hours are actually passing by as the doctors are actively playing a game of operation with your body. I'd always felt so lost, like I didn't know where I was and I'd hear all the machines going off around me. As the nurses are circling and trying to get me to drink some sprite or something, so they could remove me from recovery to the ward. Back in those days they didn't even let my mum see me until I was moved out of the recovery room.

As time and days went on, I began physical therapy in hospital to try to get me to sit up. But each time I tried I felt so dizzy because the body cast made me weigh more and it felt so awkward. I soon realized that they shaved the bottom half of my long beautiful hair during the surgery because my scar went halfway up the back of my skull. I was pretty sad; I've always loved my nice long hair. The body cast was so restricting I was covered all the way down to the end of my back, right above the hip joints. All you could see were holes just big enough for my ears and one hole big enough to see my eyes, nose and mouth. It ended exactly below my bottom lip, completely holding my chin solidly in place so I couldn't move my neck at all. Luckily, my arms were free as the cast had holes at my shoulder blades just under my arm pits. I also had one hole showing the top of my head allowing what little hair I had left to stick out.

I had a fairly uneventful recovery except for some mild transient 'paresthesia' *(pins and needle sensations)* of both my upper limbs, which settled spontaneously within a week from the surgery.

Finally, after some hit and miss physical therapy sessions, I was able to slowly sit up. For days the physical therapist had given me a breathing exercise tube called a three ball spirometer. I had to use it multiple times in the day to strengthen my lung capacity. They wouldn't let me move forward with trying to stand up until I was able to blow the balls high enough up the breathing tube.

Oh, let me tell you the day they removed my nasal tube and my catheter bag was such an awful experience. I hoped to never repeat in this lifetime. I won't go into too much depth because not only was it painful but it was also sickening and awkwardly uncomfortable. Once a bit of time had passed and I managed to calm down I was so relieved they were no longer attached to me. I continued to push forward after that to sitting up more regularly, to standing and finally feeling okay enough to walk with crutches. This mostly took a few days because it was a huge challenge dealing with how dizzy and nauseous I would get each time I wanted to stand up. Eventually, because I really wanted to get out of hospital, I would sing my favourite song lyrics in my head to distract myself from feeling so out of sorts. I never actually mentioned that I did that to anyone until now, but it became the best way for me to motivate myself into moving forward with my recovery.

Realistically, it wasn't long or even over a week after such a massive surgery. I was discharged on the 28th January 1995, even though it felt much longer at the time. A week or two later I had to go in for them to remove my stitches from my neck and my lower back area. I recall laying there on my stomach while they opened my brace and told me not to move as they cut away the stitches. My neck was so sensitive that some of it partially tickled or was itchy. I remember one or two of the stitches were stuck to part of my healing wound, those really hurt coming out. Luckily, even twelve-year-old Fiona was good at keeping still, not wanting to risk causing any damage to myself. As much as deep inside me I wanted to jump off that bed and be like, "okay that's enough!" Although the lower back stitch didn't hurt when it was removed, it was the weirdest feeling. Almost like a long string being slid out of my skin, it tickled more than anything. It also made me wonder how it was even possibly holding anything together because it felt like one straight piece of string being removed.

At the last review I had in the clinic on the 10th of February 1995, I was doing well with no neurological problems. My wounds were already healing pretty well and the x-rays revealed my cervical spine was fusing in a good position. I had to ensure that I kept my brace on twenty-four seven for the next ten weeks. To allow time for the bones to fuse together and effectively be able to support my head. But, as long as I did that I could now travel to Malta for the big move with my family. We finally left six weeks later, arriving in Malta on the 24th of March 1995. I was told by my specialist in Australia that after ten weeks I would need to be reviewed by a specialist in Malta and have follow up x-rays taken.

The specialist I saw in Malta was actually from England and after he reviewed my x-rays, he forwarded them onto my doctors back in Australia. At this point I was instructed to continue wearing the brace at all times until further notice. On the 23rd of June 1995 my neck specialist had written to the hospital in Malta. He requested copies of new x-rays so he could determine when it would be a good time for me to remove the brace. He also mentioned that I may need to wear a soft collar for a week or so until the muscles in my neck could support my head on their own. Due to the fact that they would be extremely weak and I would need to be able to adjust to regaining any movement.

One of the most annoying things about this whole brace situation was when I had showers; obviously the brace had to stay on in the shower too. My mum had to help me shower during this time because it was such a project and I was so restricted. I couldn't even try to wash my hair through the tiny hole I had available. It was so frustrating though because the feeling of the water running through the brace felt so weird. For me to dry off mum had to place towels on the bed and I had to lie down, while she would open the brace from the Velcro on the sides. During this time I had to remain very still. It used to hurt and be so tender when my mum even gently tried to dry the water off my body. That's not even the most ridiculous part, because after she would dry my back mum would have to close the brace back up. I would then have to turn over on my stomach so she could dry off the other side. In the process of me turning over all the water that was building up in the front would drip down into the back part of the brace. It was so difficult to ever completely dry off properly that I couldn't wait for the day I didn't need it anymore.

Because my hair was already shaved halfway up my skull during the surgery mum thought it would be best to cut my hair real short. Showers were already difficult enough. OMG seriously though, I hated my haircut during that time. It was almost like the hair dresser put a bowl on my head and gave me the worst bowl cut ever.

As the weeks were passing by, I was still waiting on instruction from my specialist in Australia. I wanted to know when I could remove the brace because it was becoming difficult to deal with. It was now summer in Malta and the heat was getting to me. I felt trapped in the brace and dehydrated all the time.

One night I couldn't sleep it was so hot, I threw up. I woke my mum up, crying, I wanted to take off my brace because I couldn't breathe. I promised her I would stay as still as possible until she could speak to my doctors but I couldn't take it any longer.

It was nearly six months after the surgery. Surely I should have been all healed up enough to safely take it off and not cause any damage. Mum ended up letting me because I was gasping for air; it was like I was hyperventilating. So I just laid there on the couch as still as possible for the rest of the night. I had a bowl next to me in case I was sick again, and some sprite to settle my stomach.

Thankfully, after that night I never had to put the brace on again. I felt like it was probably so gross on the inside at that point, so I told mum to throw my brace out. Part of me does wish I would have kept it as some kind of weird memorabilia to be put on display in the non-existent Fee museum. *LOL*

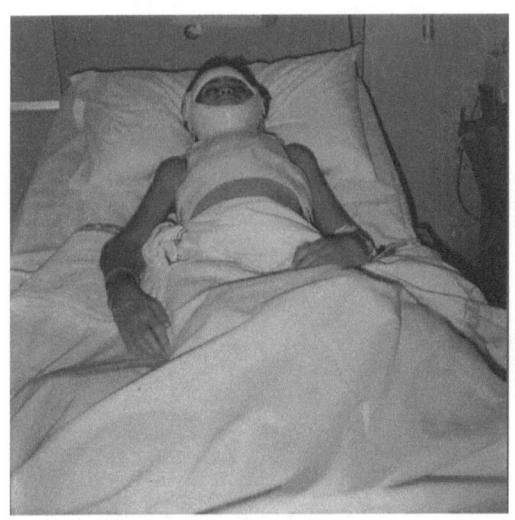

(Me during my C1-C2 Fusion)

There was a lot of hydrotherapy and physical therapy that followed to help me get my upper body strength back. When I had hydrotherapy in Malta it was so cool, they would let me use the heated pool at a major four-star hotel.

As you can imagine after all that time I was incredibly weak and skinny. Oddly, even though I couldn't wait for the day my brace came off and I could have normal showers again, I felt so weird without my body armour. At that point it felt like it was an extension of my body. For a few days I felt dizzy all over again because now my body was insanely light and naked feeling. I wore baggy clothes during the time I was wearing the brace. My clothes had to be wide enough to go over my head and above the brace. No longer having that closely tight fitted armour was truly strange. As much as I hated it and couldn't wait to take it off, it almost made me feel secure.

It just wasn't cool enough looking if I was hoping to join Thor on his next marvellous adventure. Which by the way, I am a huge Marvel fan of course. If I ever had the opportunity to join them on an adventure, I wouldn't have cared what my armour looked like.

Chapter Twelve

Breaking Barriers

If we can take a step back, to around the time I had my neck surgery earlier in the year. This was also the beginning of high school for me when I started seventh grade. My physical therapist Margaret, who I saw multiple times a week after school, suggested I go to a specific high school. She wanted me to continue our physical therapy sessions during my lunch breaks; this would avoid me having to go elsewhere after school. Since this was the logical option that's exactly what I did. It was a regular mainstream high school, but it also had a support unit for people with disabilities, which was why Margaret could complete my therapy sessions there. I was enrolled in regular mainstream classes but knew a lot of the other kids with disabilities. I got to know them because I used to be picked up by government organised door-to-door transportation, which took me to and from school. But because we left for Malta early in the year, I wasn't in high school very long in Australia.

As soon as we arrived in Malta mum was looking to enrol me and my sister into a new school straight away. The town we lived in only had two choices for public high schools that accepted students from that area. My sister chose to go to one, and I knew I wanted to go to the other. Even though these schools were literally next door to each other and only divided by a massive stone wall. I was so used to my independence and I didn't want my sister to feel like she was responsible for me. If teachers knew my sister was right there they would instinctively go to her if anything arose. Plus, being able to fend for myself was character building. I always felt like I had to prove myself even from a young age. It's easy for people to assume that because I have obstacles to deal with on a daily basis that I might not manage. But, I was already coming into my own and finding my voice.

A perfect example was when my mum and I went to the high school I was hoping to attend. We went for an interview with the principal of the school. At first it felt like attending mainstream schooling would not be an option in Malta, I was getting very frustrated during the meeting. It was like the principal was trying to get rid of us because she was insistent that people with disabilities should attend the specific school for the disabled. No-one with a disability had ever attended that school before. I mean no disrespect to others with intellectual disabilities, but the other option was not going to be the place for me. There was no way I would be pushed aside and sent to a school where I wouldn't feel mentally challenged just because of my physical disability. I continued to explain to the principal that I had never attended special classes up to then and I wasn't going to start. I pleaded with her to give me a chance to prove I could keep up in class on an intellectual level. That the only allowance I needed would be a bit of understanding with physical education such as sports class. As the meeting went on, the principal could see I wasn't giving up on the idea of attending regular mainstream school.

Fortunately, my efforts to convince her were not lost, as she decided to accept me as a student in her school. She advised if I felt like I was struggling to keep up then she would need to revisit her decision. I was pretty pleased with myself because I felt like I was also paving the way for others with physical disabilities to be taken more seriously on an intellectual level. This was a win for me and definitely a step in the right direction.

Throughout my life this is something I've noticed people seem to have a hard time separating. It's undermining when people lump everyone with a disability as incapable. Each disability physical and intellectual, whether you have one and not the other, or even both, should never be lumped into a heap of incapability. This is what the average Joe misunderstands, because everyone whether they live with a disability or not has their strengths and their weaknesses. Find me one person on this earth, who is good at every single thing in life, I challenge you to look within yourself even.

From the time we arrived in Malta at the end of March, 1995 until the end of the scholastic year there, I only had three months of seventh grade left. This meant I had three months to prove I could fit into mainstream school in Malta, after only completing three months in Australia before we left. Thankfully seventh grade was an easy year for me, the fact I pretty much skipped fifty percent of the school year hadn't set me back from progressing. I got through it with flying colours and more importantly, impressed the principal. I was even excelling in Maltese class which she wasn't expecting me to. See, as I mentioned earlier my mum had taught us how to speak Maltese as kids. Speaking and understanding was pretty natural to me at that point. The reading and writing on the other hand was a different story as we hadn't been taught that growing up. As soon as mum knew we were planning to move to Malta, she enrolled my sister and I in a Maltese crash course evening class. The class went for twelve weeks and taught us the basic grammar rules to aid us grasping the language on a reading and writing capacity, not just verbally. I was so glad we had successfully passed the crash course prior to stepping into the deep end at school in Malta.

The principal was pleased to see how well I was doing. She no longer questioned whether being at her school was where I belonged. During those first three months I got to know her pretty well, and we formed a great bond. If I was struggling physically, I would go to her and raise my concerns. This was great because after some time it prompted her to make changes within the school and evolve it into a more accessible place. Down the track she also arranged for me to have a laptop in specific classes, where there was a lot of writing. Using a laptop helped ease the strain writing tends to put on my wrist and knuckles; aside from that typing was much quicker for me.

Shortly after I started school in Malta, the principal organised for everyone in my grade to get the vaccine for Tuberculosis. It was a government standard in schools there at the time. I was not looking forward to this day when I knew I had to go to the room with the other students, I pretended to forget. Of course my name happened to be on the top of the list. The principal came looking for me because I was meant to be first. I was such a baby when it came to needles. All the tough surgeries I had been through you'd think a needle would be a piece of cake for me. I was still traumatised from that incident when I broke my leg in primary school when the injection caused me to bleed. I was arguing with the principal, telling her I didn't need or want it. She insisted that I must have it because it was required from all the students my age, otherwise I couldn't attend school. If I shut my eyes, I can visualise the hallway as she grabbed my hand while I kicked and screamed and caused the worst scene. Eventually she got me into the room; the first process involved this stamp looking injection that had about six needles in it. They'd stamp your arm and after a few days if it formed a scab you didn't need the main vaccine. But, if the area had no reaction then a week later you'd need to get the official vaccination. The principal and a nurse literally had to hold me down because I was seriously losing it. God, I loved my principal, I was so glad she never gave me a hard time afterwards, even though I was being a difficult child. All the other kids that were waiting in line outside the door were probably getting more anxious thanks to me; sorry guys!

Unfortunately for me I did not scab and actually had to get the main vaccine the week after. There was no scene in the hallway this time but I still lost it in the nurse's office. I could feel the vaccine going through my body; it had a horrible stinging sensation. Boy was I glad when that ordeal was over and super embarrassed at my behaviour. I was grateful none of the other kids made fun of me in this instance either. Usually I was very good at not appearing to be weak in front of others; not that time though.

Going to school in Malta was such a different experience than I had previously in Australia. One major difference was the public schools there are not integrated. I was at a school only for girls, not one boy in sight. *(Unless it was a teacher of course.)* Maybe this was the key because no girls were competing for a guy's attention and vice versa, so there was no drama.

During lunch breaks at school I would always carry around a diary and write lyrics of popular songs I liked to sing. The songs were from artists I idolised and admired; Celine Dion, Michael Jackson and Mariah Carey to name a few of my ultimate favourites.

In my first year of school there, they had a school disco. Yea I know; how the times have changed, but it was the Mid 90's to be fair, and they still called it a disco. All my friends knew I loved singing and music so much. Partly because they always saw me with my diary and Walkman during lunch breaks. A couple of my friends asked the DJ if he would let me sing a song. I never expected my friends to push me to the front line considering I hadn't performed in such an exposed situation like that at school before. I wasn't even sure how it even came about, nor was I prepared to sing at that moment. There were a few hundred students in the school hall, talk about being thrown in the deep end. I was nervous but excited when the DJ called me to get up on the stage; my friends didn't even warn me first. He asked me what I wanted to sing and the first song that came to mind was 'You are not alone' by Michael Jackson. The song was only just released and at the top of the charts that year. I felt like I knew it well enough to sing in front of everyone. He handed me a microphone and cued the music.

Oh, what a feeling! Everyone cheered, I pulled it off. The DJ seemed impressed, and he told me to sing another song. This time I thought maybe it would be best to get everyone in a dancing mood; we were at a disco after all. Randomly I decided to sing 'The Macarena' by Los del Rio. This was another popular song that year and surprisingly even though half of the song lyrics were in Spanish, I knew it well. I had no idea how to speak Spanish but it's different when it comes to singing song lyrics. What a thrilling experience, the DJ then gave me one of his mix tapes to keep before I got off the stage. Mix tapes were such a big thing back then. *(Wow I feel old.)* Getting up on stage and singing in front of hundreds of other kids that day made me realise more and more that my desire to be a singer was something I couldn't ignore. It was like I became a whole other person the moment the music started. My confidence felt like it was on another level. Even though I was outgoing as far as talking to people and making friends, internally I was still pretty insecure.

Being on stage like that made me forget I was Fiona for a minute; it made me forget I was different. Especially hearing the reaction from everyone at school, it was overall such a positive thing.

Christmas in Camelot

My stage days didn't end there, on the 21st of December 1995 our school was having a special Christmas performance evening. It would be something where kids from multiple grades would attend with their parents. This time though I would be on stage for a different reason, which had little to do with singing. As soon as I heard they were holding auditions for a play, for the students in my grade, I wanted to join in too.

The play was called 'Christmas in Camelot.'
The King and Queen were getting ready to throw a huge party, but the queen vocalised that the one person she refused to invite was Abigail the black witch. Everyone warned the Queen that by not inviting Abigail it would mean trouble. Naturally their prediction came true, as Abigail placed a spell on everyone in town, giving them all influenza. *(Influenza in case you didn't know is just another word for the flu.)* Guess whose part I ended up playing. Well, we were in a school with only girls, therefore some of us actually were going to have to draw moustaches on our faces and man up. I auditioned to be Merlin the Magician, which I was lucky enough to get. I was super excited because this meant I'd have the opportunity to play the character that saves the day. I practiced my lines everyday to make sure I knew them by heart. Even though it wasn't a huge speaking part, I still felt it was an important one. My hair was still fairly short then, because it hadn't grown much since my neck surgery earlier in the year. But, it worked out well since I was playing a male role.

The night of the big performance evening had arrived; I was wearing black clothes with a big cape. A teacher had given me a wand with a star on the tip of it. I had pinned my hair back and one of the teachers provided me with a magician's hat to wear, they also drew a black moustache on my face. I was ready for show time. As I was waiting on the sidelines backstage for my cue, I made a split second decision. I was going to step out on stage without my glasses. Technically, I am pretty blind without my glasses due to my extreme short-sightedness. But I knew I should be okay enough to see in front of me and not fall off the stage. I thought since everything else would be blurry I wouldn't notice the hundreds of people in the audience, then it would prevent me from getting nervous or forgetting my lines. It's funny because I never practiced without my glasses and in reality it could have made things worse. Thankfully it didn't, you'd never know how blind I truly was at the time or even if you were to watch the video because it didn't look obvious.

The moment arrived where the King and Queen, along with everyone else were infected with influenza, sneezing nonstop. As they sang: "Achoo, Achoo, Achoo, we don't know what to do." The doctors came in and advised them that there was something sinister at work, and they couldn't help. The King then asked Lancelot to call on Merlin for help. Everyone continued to sneeze as I made my way onto the stage.

<u>Merlin:</u> "I have heard my name mentioned," *I paused.*
"Oh, dear me; you do need me indeed!"
"Have you got influenza?"

The King and Queen advised me that they were checked out by the doctors and it wasn't influenza, but they could not stop sneezing.

<u>Merlin:</u> "Ah, Ah, I have got it, yes!" *Everyone continued to sneeze.*
"It's a spell." *The King and Queen pleaded with me to do something about it.*

"Very simple, simple as I say, right on the top of your noses." *Everyone seemed confused.*

<u>Everyone:</u> "Right on the top of our noses?"

<u>Merlin:</u> "Yes, simply put your finger on your nose and say, we shall invite Abigail the black witch."

Queen: "Oh no, I will not do it!"

Merlin: "Very well then, you can stay like this for the next hundred years."

Everyone: "Hundred years." *(Achoo)*

Merlin: "And More." *Sneezing continues as one of the knights pleaded with the Queen to take pity on her people. Finally the Queen agreed for the sake of all her people to allow Merlin to help them remove the witch's spell.*

Merlin: "Yes, now put your second finger on your nose and count to ten with me."

Everyone: *Everyone placed their finger on their nose and counted.* "One, Two, Three, Four, Five, Six, Seven, Eight, Nine, Ten."

Merlin: "Now, keeping your second finger on your nose repeat after me."
"We shall invite."

Everyone: "We shall invite."

Merlin: "Abigail the black witch."

Everyone: "Abigail the black witch."

Merlin: "To all our parties."

Everyone: "To all our parties."

Then the choir continued to sing a song praising Merlin for coming to their rescue. Everyone rejoiced, at last the spell was over. When suddenly a beautiful white fairy appeared, it was Abigail. Now that Merlin had reversed the spell it turned her into a good fairy. Everyone on stage then broke into song.

Singing: "When things turn well all we can do is clap. Can do is clap, can do is clap. When things turn well all we can do is clap. Can do is clap with joy. Clap, clap your hands and clap, clap your hands and clap, clap your hands with joy. Clap, clap your hands and clap, clap your hands and clap, clap your hands with joy."

It was repeated a couple times, I must admit it was the cheesiest song ever. But, I was only thirteen and although I can't sit through watching myself on the old VHS recording of this play without laughing, it was fun at the time to step out on stage as 'Merlin the Magician.' I am glad to have taken part and have the memories, no matter how cheesy they might be.

(Me on stage as Merlin the Magician)

The time I spent at school in Malta was where I started to feel my confidence grow even stronger. I began opening up more and letting people see more of who I was inside, instead of just hiding behind my diaries. I continued to strive at school so much so that my grades were something to be proud of. During the final year exams against my whole grade, I was coming first in English and Social Studies, second in Home Economics and third in Maltese. It was nice to know I could keep up with the best of them, considering I felt like I had something to prove. I finally had started following my passions with my music, acting and other creative outlets. Things were looking up!

Chapter Thirteen

Pilgrimage to Lourdes

At thirteen years of age almost every Saturday I went to a sports centre in Malta. I would be there from midday until seven or nine o'clock at night. It was a place predominately for people with disabilities. The sole purpose of this centre was to provide somewhere they could go to take part in sporting activities; maybe even make new friends. I loved going there because aside from school there wasn't much else going on that I could participate in. It was a nice escape from just going to school all week, or staying home. It felt harder for me at that age to connect with my cousins on the same level my sister did, even though we were all around the same age. My youngest cousin and I spent the most time together. Either I would take him to get ice-cream around the corner from where we lived, or we would go to the gardens, which was also around the corner.

Going to the sports centre was such a positive thing for me to do on my own. I made many new friends. Some people that attended were not necessarily disabled. They allowed siblings or family members of other people with disabilities to attend if they wanted to as well. Although for me my family never came along to the centre, I was happy that my mum allowed me to independently go almost every weekend. It was a respite type place that was organised by a Maltese government organisation. They would come and pick me up with an accessible bus from home and drop me back home afterwards.

During the time I went to the sports centre, it opened up so many possibilities for me and helped me to discover a passion for sports. See when I was younger playing sports with 'average height' kids at school was always challenging for me to keep up with. I would do my best to participate but I also suffered with many basketballs to the face. Teachers seemed to have a hard time understanding that physically I wasn't always capable of keeping up with the masses. True to my nature I would push myself and tried before ever telling the teachers it wasn't for me. I didn't complain usually even when I was struggling, I never wanted to seem like I expected special treatment. At the sports centre I played table tennis, boccia and wheelchair basketball. One time they held a table tennis tournament, which I ended up winning and got a trophy for.

I had many friends I interacted with there, but I formed two very close friendships in particular. Throughout my entire life and even at a young age I never limited myself or stuck to only forming friendships with people that were only in my age group. Maybe it was because I found it easy to relate to people of all ages. My two best friends at the sports centre varied greatly in age, Antonella was in her twenties while Anna was only eleven. The three of us would hang out all the time. Antonella was mostly wheelchair bound whereas Anna was an 'average height' girl that didn't have a disability. We would occasionally walk together to a nearby shop in the afternoon to get pastries or snacks.

The sports centre also provided the opportunity to work if you wanted to. There was a room set up where people put together toy animals for a major toy company. I of course jumped at the opportunity as I was always eager to try my hand at new things. We had to file away any excess plastic the machines may not have separated properly off of the toys. I did this for quite a long time and I must admit it was a fun experience. I put together horses, cows, dogs, etc. Then we had to separate them into bags to go back to the toy factory. In fact I asked if I could keep at least one horse I had put together as a memento which I still have.

During the night at the centre before we were taken home they would also hold a mass we could attend or participate in by reading verses from the Maltese Bible. Malta itself is a very religious Island.

All Maltese people are strong Catholics so mass is a big part of their lives and thus has been a great part of my life too.

One day mum told me that a lady from the sports centre had nominated me for the opportunity to be chosen to go on a pilgrimage to Lourdes in France. The Maltese Government had an organisation that took a select few people with disabilities from time to time on a very spiritual pilgrimage. All mum had to do was contribute one hundred Maltese pounds if I was selected. At the time that was approximately $400 Australian dollars. Plus, mum needed to decide if she would allow me to go for 10 days to Rome and France combined without her. At this point I was only thirteen years old and my condition was really kicking my butt regarding insane joint pains. I struggled more and more when it came to walking. My ankle joints would get so jammed sometimes I'd stop dead in my tracks. I felt as though I was having a panic attack and would tell mum I couldn't walk any more. Whenever I was at school or around other people, I would internalise my pain. I hated when people, especially older people would say, 'Oh, poor thing' in reference to me. When I was only around my mum, I found it hard to internalise. I felt like she should be the one person I didn't have to always wear my mask of bravery around.

Turned out I was fortunate enough to be chosen to go to Lourdes. Mum didn't want me to miss out on such an amazing opportunity, so she said I could go. She thought it would be a good experience for me, which I may never get again. Mum couldn't come with me but there would be nurses both male and female that would be with us the entire time. This made my mum feel more at ease with her decision to let me go on this journey of a lifetime. I was a little nervous knowing my mum wouldn't be going with me; I had never travelled without her before. But, I was also super excited to get to go to Rome, France and see Our Lady of Lourdes.

I was off, on an adventure of a lifetime that few thirteen-year-olds get to experience. I love that my mum trusted me enough that she allowed me to take advantage of a rare opportunity at such a young age.

In fact I wrote diary entries during the majority of the trip which later got published by an official magazine in Malta once we returned. Initially I only wrote it for myself to remember the experience, but occasionally the nurses would write my entries with me. Eventually the word got out that I kept a journal and the organisation asked me if I would mind if they published it. Naturally I thought that was awesome, so of course I said they could. To this day I still have the pages from my diary entries I wrote, and the two page clipping from the magazine I was in. I wish I had started journaling from the moment we left Malta for Rome. But, I didn't begin my diary entries until we were a couple days into our trip.

CIAO MALTA

(Ciao is like Aloha – it can be Hello or Goodbye)

First we flew from Malta to Rome; it was only an hour and fifteen minute flight. Once we arrived in Rome, we checked into a really nice hotel where we stayed for a couple days. We did some fun sightseeing in those first few days. It included a trip to the Vatican, which was absolutely magical. They told us so much history about the Roman Catholics and the Popes. I also got to visit the beautiful Spanish Steps. There were so many nice flowers all along the stairs. I even went to the famous Trevi Fountain, threw some coins in and made a wish. During our time in Rome we ate at some amazing restaurants. One of my favourite things was the Italian bread they would give us at the beginning of our meal. We used to dip it in salt, pepper and olive oil; I couldn't get enough of their amazing fresh bread.

I'm going to allow thirteen-year-old Fee to take it from here, and include my original published entries for continued realism. Even though I remember this time quite well, I may as well provide you with the experience as I went through it, not just how I remember it. Please keep in mind I was thirteen at the time and it was a very overwhelming, humbling experience at that age.

Magazine Diary Entries:

Thursday 2nd May 1996.

We went on the train on our way to Lourdes it was a twenty-two hour journey. At 1:00 pm they came with lunch which was delicious, and then we were all talking and telling jokes. Someone had given Gerald and Ella *(two of the people who were looking after us)* an enamel Maltese cross. Gerald gave me his and Ella gave hers to Janice. *(Janice was another girl with a disability who was also chosen.)* They then came and gave us lots of sweets.

At 9:30 pm we prepared our beds when a bottle of water came rolling down and fell on my head. I couldn't stop laughing at my own personal injury. I was lucky enough to wake up in the middle of the night, which was just in time as we were crossing the border into France. So I was the first one to see France. ☺

Friday 3rd May 1996.

We got up very early to get dressed. We arrived in Lourdes, took our baggage and they put us on a bus to take us to the place where we would be staying during our time in Lourdes. As soon as we got there we went upstairs straight away and unpacked some of our things.

We all were talking a lot before going to Mass. We got given medals from the Grand Master. After Mass we went to the Grotto where the shrine of Our Lady of Lourdes is located and we touched the rocks underneath where Bernadette saw her. We bought some candles to light and took a few photos.

At 6:30 pm we had some dinner which was yum, while Joan and I told some very funny jokes! *(Joan was a lovely older lady who was also selected to join the pilgrimage.)* We then went back to our rooms, but I went to bed later than everyone else. The best part was taking funny pictures of Janice in her pyjamas!

Saturday 4th May 1996.

We woke up at 6:00 am and we had breakfast which was eggs. We had to quickly go downstairs as we had to go to Mass. After Mass we headed to the baths. We went into a sort of little room where there were benches; it was such a strange experience and I felt a bit awkward as we had to take off all our clothes. We were only allowed to wrap a white wet towel around us. I walked into a small cubicle where there was a bath filled with Holy water. I started getting in, step by step and it was absolutely freezing. Generally when getting into cold water you would want to scream out loud with how cold it was. But, this time it was like I couldn't even open my mouth, even if I wanted to. It made me feel good inside because it was like Our Lady was with me and I was really taking in the whole experience. I continued to walk from the stairs to the end of the bath where there was a statue of Our Lady of Lourdes. The nurses told me to kiss her feet and then I was told to sit down in the bath. During this time my feet almost felt numb and funny especially around my ankle joints. When I sat down the water almost came up to my shoulders. While I sat there for a few moments I prayed and ended by saying, "Our Lady of Lourdes pray for us." Then I got up, walked back up the stairs to get out and I started wearing my clothes straight away without drying myself. It was like a miracle because I didn't even feel wet like you usually do when coming out of a bath.

(The nurses had told us that we wouldn't need to dry ourselves, plus there were no dry towels even if we wanted to.)

Then Edward, Marion, Janice, Joanna, and a man called Robert all went for a walk in the gardens. Robert put me on his shoulders and I must admit I was getting scared being up that high as he was very tall. We all went to lunch, and later in the afternoon we went to a procession in the streets and then headed back to our rooms in the evening.

In case you aren't familiar with the history of Lourdes it is actually the site that is near the Pyrenees Mountains in France. People go to see the site because it is where a famous vision was experienced by a young girl called Bernadette Soubirous, and to be healed by its supposedly miraculous waters.

Sunday 5th May 1996.

We went to a Pontifical High Mass, in an underground church and it was very nice. After Mass we took a group photo of the entire Maltese group. Then we went to lunch, after lunch they took us shopping so we could buy some souvenirs. I took my shopping list I had written with me and bought presents for my family. It felt like I was buying the whole shop.

After dinner we were asked to join a candle holding ceremony, called a Flambo, it was very beautiful. While we were walking down the streets, we were saying the Rosary. We even took a lovely photo of the beautiful scene all the candles made.

It was now 9:00 pm; we were up in our rooms. Joanna and I were talking when all of a sudden I went running over to Joan's bed because I thought she was going to fall out of her bed. From then on Joan would call me her life saver.

Monday 6th May 1996.

Yet another early morning of waking up at 6:00 am. I went to a Maltese Mass in the Chapel of St. Joseph. We had another Mass later in the day at the Grotto too, it was lovely. We went back to the piscine *(baths)* as I already mentioned before it was a wonderful experience. We then went shopping again and had an ice-cream with mint and chocolate topping, it was delicious. Then we went to a party where we were given gifts.

Once we were up in our room, we took a photo from our window of the procession outside. Packed our belongings to be ready for the next day and went to sleep.

Tuesday 7th May 1996.

    We finished packing, had our breakfast and then went to Mass at St. Bernadette Church. Filled our bottles with Holy water and returned to the hospital for lunch. Once we were ready, we went outside to write in my diary. At 2:30 pm the bus came for us and took us to the train station. On the train we were all reminiscing about our trip, telling jokes and looking at all the presents we got.

    6:00 pm we had pasta for dinner. After dinner we continued talking and singing songs. As we were getting ready for bed and I was getting my clothes to get changed, we discovered Coke had spilled all over my luggage. JUST FABULOUS!!! The nurses helped me clean it up, luckily we realised the Coke didn't get to the inside part of my luggage. What a RELIEF. I wasn't tired yet, so I continued to write in my diary. What a BAD DAY. Goodnight sleep tight. I love everyone.

(Hahaha... I can't help but laugh at how the Coke on my luggage turned my emotions into thinking it was such a bad day... Ahhh childhood Fee, how silly I could be.)

Wednesday 8th May 1996.

    Today is my sister's birthday. At 6:00 am Saveno came to our train compartment, put his alarm on which made a rooster sound and it said, "Buon Giorno" which is good morning in Italian.

    We brushed our teeth, got our luggage ready and ate breakfast. At 11:45 am we arrived at the station in Rome, said goodbye to all the Italian nurses especially Fiorbellina who was a really nice lady. Went on a bus to the hotel, when we got to our room I took something out of my suitcase and it fell on my leg. I ended up with a big bruise there later on in the day. After lunch I rang my sister in Malta to wish her a

HAPPY BIRTHDAY!

Then we went to the Spanish Steps, and I had a nice chocolate ice-cream with strawberries on top. We stayed downstairs at the hotel having a soft drink after dinner and chatting. The Barrellieri came over to us and gave us a doll that was dressed in the same way they dressed. Then I had a bath and went to bed. Good night.

Thursday 9th May 1996.

Got ready to go back to Malta, we took our luggage downstairs with us. Took some more photos, and I used up all the film I had left in my camera. We went on the bus to the airport, arriving in Malta at 3:00 pm. collected our luggage and went outside where there was my mum and grandfather waiting for me. I said bye to everyone and went home again. Back to my old self again! The End!

I imagine as you are reading this, you might be wondering why all it seemed like we did was went to church, and ate for the most part. Which realistically going to Mass every day, sometimes even twice a day, was a big part of the whole pilgrimage experience. At thirteen, after all I had already been through, and the place I was at in my life, from struggling to learn how to manage my physical joint pains. I truly embraced the whole spiritual experience and felt like it happened at a time in my life when I really needed it. In all honesty I was even a bit sceptical myself when people told me about the miraculous holy water of Lourdes. If I didn't go through it personally, I'm not sure I could have even believed how it could positively impact someone so much in reality. But, the truth of the matter is, I felt different after I returned from the pilgrimage. It gave me strength that I didn't feel like I had before, strength to know that no matter what I would deal with on a daily basis someone was watching over me. My faith has always provided me with peace in my heart that everything would be okay, no matter how challenging my life can feel sometimes.

(Memories from my time in Lourdes)

Chapter Fourteen

I Still Call Australia Home

Almost two years after moving to Malta my family and I had to return to Australia. Profs had contacted my mum to advise us that he wanted me to return so I could begin a medical trial. There was a new medication he believed would help with my joints, which would possibly increase my bone density. My mum weighed up all our options and because it would likely be a good thing for the whole family, the wheels were in motion. Even my dad would have better work opportunities back in Australia. I was almost three quarters through grade nine at school so mum hoped by the time I would arrive back in Australia I could slot back into year nine there. I hoped that I wouldn't have to repeat because the scholastic year had only just begun in Australia. Meaning the months I skipped in grade seven I would now end up doing in grade nine.

My sister on the other hand had important exams coming up. So she was to stay with my grandfather for an extra month or two in Malta until she completed them.

I should also mention we would now leave Malta with a new addition to our family. Almost a year into us living in Malta around 9:00 o'clock on a cool Maltese autumn night, we were waiting with anticipation as my new baby brother came into the world. Naturally, before we packed up our entire lives again and shipped them off to sea, we waited until my brother was a few weeks past his first birthday before we left.

It was the 12th of April 1997 when we left all my extended family in Malta and returned to my birth place. On our return home we had to change planes in London, but for some reason there was an airline strike preventing flights from departing. We had to wait a few hours before they would board any flights. Fortunately for us the airline gave us two adjoining hotel rooms within the airport hotel to stay in for a few hours so we could either shower or sleep in the meantime. This was awesome for me because it meant I had my own room as my brother clearly had to stay with my parents since he was just a baby, while I wasn't even fifteen yet. By the time we were able to continue our trip home it was the 14th of April 1997 when we finally landed in Australia.

Luckily, mum had kept our place in Australia, almost in anticipation that we would have to return like this. Obviously we had to wait for our container with all our furniture and important stuff to arrive. Until such time came about, we were blessed with good neighbours that we had become fairly close with. The main lady that lived next door to our property was also Maltese. Her and her husband were kind enough to allow us to stay with them until our things arrived. Otherwise we would have had empty rooms with no beds to sleep on.

Now that I was back in Australia I had to re-enrol at school, so my mum contacted the same high school I briefly attended before we left for Malta. I was accepted there almost immediately, but it felt like I was starting at a new school all over again because I didn't really know anyone. There was one friend I remembered connecting briefly with in the short time I attended year seven. It was great to see her again, but other than that I knew no-one else.

It was time to meet with my old specialists again, Profs organised multiple tests before I took the new treatment. Months rolled by as I underwent multiple blood tests, x-rays, ultrasounds to check all my organs were functioning well and bone density scans. For me to even be considered to trial this new medication my doctor had to pull a lot of strings and get permission from our parliament. Profs had to raise my case and provide the government with details why he believed I was a good candidate for this new treatment. See when this medication first became available it was solely given to people of old age to help patients that suffered from Osteoporosis. Seeing as my condition comprises of constant joint pains and osteo-arthritic issues since birth, my doctor believed the government should make an exception for me.

I was almost sixteen years of age when I got official clearance from parliament to begin treatment. It was called Alendronate Fosamax, and I was one of the first young people given this treatment trial. I had to take an oral pill once a day, seven days a week every morning. As soon as I would wake up in the morning, I had to swallow the pill with a full glass of water, and only water. I wasn't allowed to eat or drink anything else until half an hour had passed once I took the pill. I could however continue drinking as much water as I wanted during this time. For those people that know me, they would also know I dislike water with a passion. Finishing a whole full glass of water with my pill each morning was like torture for me, so the fact I drank a full glass every day was miracle enough. The other annoying thing was, during the half hour after taking the pill I wasn't allowed to lay back down. It was stipulated that I needed to either be standing or sitting upright while I waited for the time to pass. This was challenging at first because I always struggled to swallow pills, due to my neck issues and my pipes being so narrow. As time went on it got easier, after a long period of being on the daily Fosamax a new option became available to take a higher dose only once a week. Profs switched me to the weekly medication, which was so much better than having to take it every day. Every few months I had to go in for the routine blood tests, bone density scans and ultrasounds of my organs. These full days I spent getting tests regularly at the hospital were so exhausting, and the fact I still hated needles really didn't help.

I recall at one of my check-ups my little brother was with me and my mum, he would have only been close to four years of age. Pathetically I still used to cry and wasn't great at handling the blood test process. On that particular day I was almost seventeen years old, and when I began to cry my brother held my hand and told me not to cry and that I would be okay. He then asked the nurse to cover my booboo with a 'Bananas in Pyjamas' bandaid; so cute right!

Little did he know, from that day forward he actually gave me the strength to snap out of my patheticness. I was his older sister so I should have been his example, especially when I had been through so much worse than stupid needles from a blood test. From that day onwards, yes I continued to hate needles, but I had forced myself to look away. I began internalising my awkwardness so I wouldn't look like such a baby. Plus, I can always picture my innocent little brother being the one who comforted me, and that sweet gesture has stuck with me. I love you bro, thank you for giving me strength.

(My Brother and I)

Chapter Fifteen

Action Packed Adventures

The fact that I went to the specific high school that I did, opened up some different opportunities I may not have been involved in if I went elsewhere. When I first went back to high school in Australia I was managing well, as far as mainstream classes went, except when it came to sports. Now that I was a teenager alongside all my average height class mates, I knew I could no longer continue to take part in sports class. Everyone was much taller than me now, and the possibility of seriously injuring myself was all too real. Trying to keep up wasn't easy anymore, the pushing and shoving during sports class would stress me out. At first it was difficult approaching the teachers to express my concerns. I wanted them to understand that it wasn't about me wanting to be lazy or to get out of playing sports. In reality I so badly wanted to play sports just like everyone else, but physically I couldn't keep up or manage. I had a talk with my mum about it because the teacher wouldn't listen when I tried explaining my situation. It got to where my specialist wrote me a doctor's note so the teacher would no longer force the issue. This was boring for me too though, it meant I was stuck on the sidelines just sitting on a bench watching everyone else do what I knew I couldn't, but desperately wanted to. After spending a few times on the bench during sports class I decided I would approach the principal of the school. I asked him if it would be possible to allow me to play wheelchair sports during the time I had my sports class. Although, I wasn't sure if the support unit could work around my time table, seeing as I attended mainstream classes for my subjects. All I knew was that I didn't want my other classes to be affected. The only mainstream class I wasn't keeping up with was sports. I didn't want to waste time just sitting on a bench every time sports class came around. The principal spoke to my teachers, and they made this a reality for me, which was awesome. At that stage I didn't even know if wheelchair sport would be up my alley either. But I figured it had to be more feasible than regular sports. The funny thing was I didn't even have my own wheelchair to use for playing sport.

When I was younger, I had a wheelchair that my specialist had organised which I used while I was going through my leg surgeries. Surprisingly, I was too tall for that chair once I was in high school. Yep, even little ole' Fee eventually grew out of some things. I've always been stubborn though and would rather struggle to walk as much as I could. My joints regularly throbbed with pain, but I still objected to using a wheelchair in my everyday life. Occasionally when we went on family outings my mum would suggest we take the wheelchair. She wanted to make it easier for me to keep up, and even though I knew it would have been I hated anyone pushing me. My old wheelchair wasn't the type of chair I could push myself in and having someone else push me made me feel so uneasy. I didn't enjoy feeling like I wasn't in control of myself, I constantly felt anxious when others pushed me. Uneven ground made me more fearful that I'd hit a pothole or something and fall out. This fear wasn't so farfetched because it happened a few times; one time in particular was in the middle of a busy street at night.

When I went to my first sports class with the other disabled kids at my school, it was a relief to discover the school had spare wheelchairs available. They were really cool ones too, similar to what Paralympian athletes' use, with the angled wheels.

Wheelchair sports are fairly physically demanding too, I hadn't realised how hard it would be until I dove right in. Although it was tough and sometimes very rough, I enjoyed challenging myself and being able to participate in sporting events again. I played wheelchair soccer, football, hockey and basketball to name a few. The rules varied from regular soccer, football, hockey and basketball of course, but it was amazing. In the beginning I ended up with so many blisters on my hands. My skin would get burnt off my fingers from the wheels when I would get all riled up in the games. It's silly how the mind works sometimes, because as much as I could have seriously been hurt if I continued to attempt playing sports with the 'average height' kids at school; playing wheelchair sports was equally just as dangerous. At the time it was easier to be fearless in a wheelchair and not realise the truth while I was doing it. I think I fooled my brain into thinking having the wheelchair was like having protective armour.

This brings me to a wheel-a-thon I participated in at school. If you've never heard of a wheel-a-thon, it's exactly like a walk-a-thon. Usually done to raise money for a cause but instead of walking a certain distance or laps, naturally you'd complete them in a wheelchair.

I was going so well, pushing myself up hills and flying down them as we did laps around the concrete part of the school yard. Suddenly, a friend of mine who was also competing in the wheel-a-thon hit the back of my chair. He hit my chair just as I was turning the corner after an incline. Next thing you know, it's like my life flashed before my eyes as I was airborne, chair and all. My wheelchair spun so fast, I went flying and fell hard onto the concrete with a thud directly landing on my back. My friend panicked and called the teacher over while I just laid there. Not crying, not screaming, I felt numb to the world. It was like I didn't know how to react to what had just happened. When the teacher came over, someone was about to help me up. My instant reaction was;

"NO! DON'T!"

A fall like this, I feared I probably broke something, because historically this would be the case. I had never fallen on my back before so I was pretty worried. The teacher called an ambulance to come pick me up at school and take me to hospital. They also called my mum to let her know, so she could meet me there.

It had been years since I had any kind of injury like this at school. Every time I injured myself I would always think mum was going to kill me before I even reacted to the pain. Obviously she wasn't going to kill me, but I knew she would be worried about me and I hated feeling like I was causing all this grief to my mum. It turned out I had fractured my tailbone that time. My doctor was actually pleased that that was all I injured. Being on Fosamax was strengthening my bone density. If I hadn't been on that medication for some time before this incident happened my injuries could have been much worse.

This truly was a pain in the butt though; it made it extremely difficult to sit comfortably for long periods for quite some time. You would think that incident would have made me worried about continuing to take part in wheelchair sporting events. It didn't, I shrugged it off and shortly afterwards was back in the thick of it. Seeing as my school had its own support unit, they were also closely linked up with an organisation for people with disabilities.

The Organisation held multiple sports carnivals during the year. Many schools around Sydney that had support units would all travel to a location to compete against each other. I made several wonderful new friends at these sporting events, even if we were rivals on the courts. During the breaks we got to know each other well. It was so interesting how competitive I became when I was in the midst of a game. Like, I was both a cheerleader and a team member on the courts at the same time. They also had a regular athletics carnival which I participated in too; doing events like sprint races and shot put. Don't ask me how I even managed to run back then, I'm fairly certain that the Fosamax medication played a huge part in letting me push my joints further than I usually would. It was always odd being placed in specific categories to race against others with similar disabilities because for me there was no-one in Australia with my condition. Let alone, anyone similar enough to truly be placed on an equal playing field. There weren't even any other little people from other schools that attended these sporting events.

Except for this one boy who was around my age, he had a different form of dwarfism. I'm not even sure what type of dwarfism he had, but we seemed similar in many ways. He was definitely someone I felt most competitive against. It felt like every time we raced against each other we brought out one another's competitive side. I wish we would have gotten to know each other outside of competing, but he kept to himself for the most part. It does make me wonder where his life has led him, I probably wouldn't even recognise him if we ever crossed paths again.

I tell you what these sports carnivals were so competitive and intense. Don't let the fact that everyone had a disability fool you. They were fierce and tough competition to beat. At one of the swimming carnivals I was racing against many other kids. We were competing in a freestyle race across the entire distance of the pool. I was in my zone when one of the guys that also went to my school decided to cut me off by coming into my lane and totally whacked me in the head with his legs. Luckily he didn't hurt me too badly or knock me unconscious. At that point I decided it was safer to let him pass me and I just took myself out of the race. I'm pretty sure he didn't do it intentionally, he had Cerebral Palsy, and he wasn't always able to control his muscle movement and coordination. That was definitely one way to knock the competition out. Just kidding; he and I were pretty good friends, he was a sweet and intelligent guy. He used to have a mini portable electronic device to communicate, and we had many great conversations about computer nerdy stuff.

Secretly I was a massive computer nerd from the moment I had my first PC in my early teens. Actually, when I got my first computer we were living in Malta and the government there covered half the expense and my mum paid the other half. As much as having all my issues isn't a walk in the park, I have been blessed with some amazing support and opportunities in my life because of who I am too. I'd rather be grateful for those positive things, instead of focus on the struggles. But, for me to truly tell you my story, I have to mention both sides of the coin.

LET THE ADVENTURES CONTINUE...

Those organisations didn't just run sports carnivals for schools, they also organised the occasional week long camping trip, during the school holiday period. A few of my friends from school that I played sports with were planning to go on one of those trips, and suggested I go with them. They had about three or four carers that would take a wheelchair accessible bus with eight to ten teenagers with various disabilities to these camps. I knew a few of the carers already because I would chat to them at different events. Seeing as though they knew I was friends with most the kids going on that particular camp they were more than happy for me to join them.

We drove roughly two hours south of Sydney to a sport and recreation centre. The centre was located on one hundred and fifty-three acres of land and surrounded by a massive creek. Thankfully, they had brick cabins we stayed in and I didn't have to rough it out in a tent with the creepy spiders and insects. It was a tremendously accessible centre even back then; they had specific cabins for people with disabilities.

Speaking of creepy spiders and insects, I was and still am an absolute wuss when it comes to any type of bug. One morning I was sitting in our cabin chatting to a friend of mine who was in the process of putting on her socks and shoes, so that we could start our day. She stuck her hand in her sock to turn it from being inside out. To our surprise there was a massive spider in her sock. She dropped the sock on the floor, and we both started screaming. I never saw her transfer herself from the bed to her wheelchair so fast. We left the room in a hurry to find one of the carers so they could get rid of the spider for us. Luckily my friend moved her hand fast enough and wasn't actually bitten by the spider.

During my time at camp I conquered so many challenging tasks I never thought would be possible. With determination and the help of the people running the camp site and the carers, I surprised myself with how I adapted to the adventures we had.

Some of the amazing things I experienced were abseiling down a wall, archery, fencing, kayaking, canoeing and going on a flying fox. Archery was one of the hardest things for me to complete because I don't possess a lot of upper body strength to pull back the bow. They had some lighter bows that worked better for me, but this was still quite a challenge. I managed to hit the target though, so I was pretty happy with that accomplishment. Canoeing on the other hand, now that truly was an adventure. My friend from school who had previously taken me out of the swimming carnival race earlier, wanted to join my canoe. He sat in the front of the canoe, I was in the middle and we had two others behind me. I was so nervous mostly because I was afraid of capsizing. Even though I knew how to swim, I was more scared of what fishy friends I might find in the creek. Occasionally my friend's oar would slip and he would totally saturate me with water, I was screaming but laughing at the same time, it was actually pretty funny. The only problem was I needed windscreen wipers for my glasses because I couldn't see with all the water, but fortunately we never capsized.

Going up on the flying fox took some serious convincing, mostly because of my fear of heights and balance issues. I rarely felt comfortable putting myself in situations where I don't have full control of my balance. I never would climb up or stand on chairs even as a kid because I didn't feel safe. As scared as I was of going on the flying fox, I also wanted to step out of my comfort zone and not regret missing out. I asked a carer if they would climb the ladder directly behind me; I didn't feel confident enough that I wouldn't fall back. It was a fairly big wooden ladder, and quite a few metres high off the ground. As I slowly climbed I tried hard not to look down, but it was so wobbly. Finally, I got to the top of a small wooden platform that was moving slightly with every step I took. I was trying so hard to keep my anxiety at bay while they clipped my harness to the cables. For added safety I had a helmet on and they actually strapped our group onto a secure attachment that meant I would be flying through the sky flat on my stomach. As soon as I was hooked, a second later they pushed me off from the edge and I was on my way. What an intense feeling, I was screaming my face off. I stretched my arms out as I flew across the trees and paddocks. Even though I was screaming, once I was soaring through the sky I was enjoying the experience immensely. It was quite a long flying fox, when I was almost at the end I gathered my focus. The instructor had told me that I needed to be sure to catch the rope at the end. Otherwise I could bounce back and have a hard time being pulled in. I am not even sure how I caught that rope, since I can't make a fist due to my joint limitations; but I did. This was one of my highlights of camp surprisingly, even though it took some convincing to do in the first place.

Over the years I actually went on another two camps with the same organisation. One was at a completely different location, which for the life of me I can't remember the name; and the other was back at the same place I went to on my very first camping adventure. Each camp had a new set of adventures and sporting activities where I enjoyed pushing my boundaries every time.

Action Packed Adventures

(Adventure Fee at Camp)

Time to share one of my embarrassing Shenanigans before things get Serious...

FEE-LIN' EMBARRASSED

This brings me to embarrassing story time with Fee. At one of the camps I had gone to, I had met this average height boy. Let's call him Ben, he was there camping with his family and in the spirit of full disclosure I thought he was super cute! We became friends pretty instantly, and sometimes he would join our group for activities. One night a member of my group had fallen in the shower and injured herself. The ambulance had to come and take her to hospital. With all the commotion and water everywhere on the bathroom floor of our cabin, we were all advised not to use it until further notice.

This became a problem for me as I needed to go to the bathroom. I walked over to the ladies toilet block but for some unknown reason the gate of the ladies block was completely locked, just my luck! Unsure of what to do, or how long it would take for me to regain access to our cabin bathroom, Ben had a bright idea.

"Fee, why don't you just go in the men's toilet block? It's open." I wasn't too sure about that idea because what if someone came in and wondered why a girl was in the boys toilets? It got to the point that I couldn't keep waiting so I said;

"Ben, can you go check inside to make sure there is no-one in there first." There was no-one inside, so I made Ben promise me he would stay outside the bathroom door to advise any guys should they come in, that I was there. After not even a minute or two I was getting ready to open my bathroom cubical door. To my surprise I saw an older man standing at the urinal going to the bathroom. OMG... I wanted to kill Ben.

What happened to him?
Where did he go?
What should I do?

Do I shut the door and wait for the guy to leave, or just run out? It was too late, I was sure he had seen me already. I worried if I continued waiting more men would come in. So I made a split decision to bolt, and out the door I went running back to our cabin.

(Fee, running, if that's what you can call it, LOL)

Ben was there waiting for me, I told him what had happened and asked him why he didn't stay there like he said he was going to. He laughed so hard, he thought no-one would come in there within that short space of time, so he left.

The rest of the week I was so paranoid, anytime I saw the guy around the campsite I felt like he was giving me weird looks. Afterwards Ben and I kept in touch for a couple years over the phone and occasionally by writing snail mail letters to each other. Whenever we reminisced about camp, we would think back to that awkward bathroom episode and just laugh hysterically.

Chapter Sixteen

Reaching My Breaking Point

There comes a time when a person truly reaches their breaking point and for me this was definitely my day. Some people would think I should be used to being bullied by now. Honestly though, anyone who has ever been bullied can probably tell you, no matter how strong a person is or even how much they try to ignore mean comments, sometimes you just can't take it anymore. Sometimes someone says something that just tips you over the edge. Like a boiling pot that gets too hot from being on the heat too long, naturally it eventually overflows. Come on now, why should anyone be expected to be used to people being cruel to them or bullying period; in any way shape or form. I think people that stoop to lengths to hurt other people are secretly unhappy with their own life. It's as if the only way they feel important is by hurting others, which is completely sad.

In my last few years of high school there was this one girl who was almost a senior, and practically every day that she saw me she would verbally abuse me. I'd be minding my own business, not even looking in her direction and I'd hear her yell out insults across the school yard. She'd call out my name and call me a slut, bitch, anything she thought of, in hopes to insult me and get my attention. Just to let you in on some home truths we haven't even covered yet. The fact of the matter was, up to that point in my life I hadn't even had a real boyfriend or even kissed a guy yet; so I was far from slutty. I feel like she must have just felt threatened by me for some stupid reason because I hung out with more guys than girls. Sure I had friends that were girls but I felt like I got along better with the guys at school. I feel like this was a prime reason because guys were less bitchy and she was a classic example of why I stayed clear from most girls. She was one of those girls who felt the need to create drama at school. She seemed so competitive when I wasn't even looking to compete with anyone. Let me say that I mean no disrespect to any females out there reading this, because come on, I am one myself; but this is just how it is sometimes. This girl turned out to be a snake in the grass, not just a bully. She had something against me apparently; she made it a point to hang out where I would hang out during lunch time. Soon enough she caused issues with a couple of my guy friends. If anything it also taught me that they really weren't great friends of mine to begin with. If they were, they wouldn't have believed the nonsense that came out of her mouth. Not to leave anything unsaid I had a tiny crush on one guy that I hung out with. Even though I made friends with almost anyone, I was never outspoken if I liked someone as more than a friend. I knew nothing would come of it and it truly didn't bother me. I always valued friendships above all. But it hurt once she told him stupid things like; I only liked him and talked to him because I wanted to sleep with him.

Let's put on the brakes, at this point I didn't care who the guy was, I wasn't at all in the mindset of even considering something like that. There are many reasons that I will be sure to cover more thoroughly along the way. It really hurt, even though I knew it wasn't true, and that I wasn't the kind of person to sleep around. As she continued to spread these rumours I didn't feel comfortable in my own group of friends anymore, especially when she was around. You know all I ever did was be polite to everyone because that's my nature. So for me it didn't cross my mind that it was weird having so many guy friends. As far as I was concerned I really thought nothing of it. As time went on, I just kept trying to co-exist because I didn't want to let her impact me in such a way that would cause me to lose friendships I cared about. It did however impact things, and I lost trust in some of my so called guy friends. I knew they were getting involved in her nonsense, and the guy I kind of had a crush on actually started going out with her. It was obvious she only went out with him to hurt me. I had heard her talking to someone else admitting she didn't even like him. It's not like he was the popular guy in school or especially good looking either. He was just an ordinary guy, but I had a crush on him because I thought he had a better personality; clearly I was wrong about that. What hurt the most was that I didn't even feel like we had a friendship anymore and that mattered more than anything else ever happening between us did.

Now the point had came to where you could say I really lost my shit... Never in my life did I think I would ever do what I did next. It was just another school day, and I had only just arrived in the morning and got off the bus. I began walking through my regular hang out spot. She was there and of course the name calling started up again. I was really getting tired of all of her crap and I had already tried being civilized and telling her calmly to leave me alone. That didn't work; clearly she enjoyed being a bully too much.

I wasn't in the mood to keep dealing with her anymore; suddenly it was like I was on autopilot. She was sitting on the pavement which meant she was at my eye level. Let me try to paint you a better picture, if you will. This girl was fairly tall and me being my height of course she towered over me. Not to be mean but she was also a bit on the heavy side. *(So, why would someone like me even want to consider messing with her, you tell me?)*

Before I knew it, I walked right up to her not even thinking about the consequences. She was still running her mouth calling me the 'M' word even, and you all know by now how I feel about that. She tipped me over the edge so I yelled at her and said something along the lines of...

"Who you calling a slut, look at yourself. Thinking you're all that and clinging to all the guys with your skirt rolled up for everyone to see your arse. I've had enough of you, I tried ignoring you, and I tried asking you nicely. Now I'm done being nice to you, don't talk to me or about me anymore. I'm not afraid of you and I'm done putting up with your constant bullying."

Next thing I knew it's like I had no control of myself or my body, because my hand just slapped her in the face. I was running on adrenaline, I stunned her so much she didn't say a word or even get up from the pavement. All I knew was at that point I lost it bad, I was still yelling stuff at her for all the times she yelled at me and I had ignored it. Only problem was we weren't far from a window where the teachers' aides were. I recall one of them sticking their head out of the window and asking me if I was okay. But because I was still in the moment and super angry I ended up just saying;

"No, do I look okay to you?"

Shortly afterwards one of the teachers that I didn't have any classes with, but who knew me pretty well, came over and said;

"Fiona you seem a bit pissed off are you okay?"

"Do you want to talk about it?"

"Yes I am pissed off, and no I don't want to talk about it, thank you." Granted, at that point it had only just sunk in what had happened. To my surprise the whole time I ranted and raved that bully just sat there stunned, and not one of my friends or hers even said a word. I walked off and headed towards where my first class would be; I was in no mood to talk to anyone. Annoyingly word got around to a few teachers and during the day one of them came up to me and said he expected to see me in a specific room for lunch detention.

Okay, so I know I probably shouldn't have slapped her, I get that, and it wasn't like I was in the habit of hitting people. But there was no way I would apologise for finally standing up to this girl who was making me truly dislike school. When lunch time came about, I went to the room to find the bully sitting in there too. The teacher spoke to us both and said we needed to apologise to each other and put it behind us. He stated that he would put us on detention all week if he had to, until we could be friends.

Are you kidding me?

What a joke, how could he expect me to want to be friends with her? You can't force people to be friends after something like that happens. Did he actually think I wanted her as my friend after the way she made me feel? Of course me hitting her in the face was a little unexpected even for me, I wasn't planning it at all. But if she hadn't continued to push my limits with her verbal abuse, and back me into a corner for me to have to stand up for myself; then none of

Reaching My Breaking Point

this would have even happened. She attempted to talk to me during detention and I simply informed her calmly that she could talk all she wanted but we would never be friends. After detention the teacher advised me that I better be back tomorrow since we didn't resolve the issue. I explained to him how I felt about it, and that no amount of detentions would result in us becoming friends. He didn't seem interested in the fact that for months this bully was pestering me and that was why things blew out of proportion.

When I went home, I decided there was no way I would keep being put on detention to force a friendship I didn't want. So for the first time in my life I told my mum exactly what happened; my mum lost it. Never had I ever gotten my mum involved in any issues in the past, but I never had detention in my life before this. This girl made me act so out of character and now I would be stuck on detention. I asked my mum to come down to the school the next day and speak to the teacher. Considering he hadn't even seen what happened, everything was just hearsay to him, I thought it was all a bit unfair. The stupid thing was all the teachers knew this girl was a trouble maker. The one teacher who spoke to me asking if I was pissed off, later told me that it was about time I stood up to her. I really didn't want to look like an idiot having my mum fight my battle for me. But I tried reasoning with the teacher and I wasn't going to spend lunch breaks locked in a room with a bully.

Mum arrived at school just before lunch, so I walked with her to the room. She totally went off at the teacher for forcing me to be in a room with someone who had been causing trouble for me. After that the teacher told me to just go to lunch, and he hoped there would be no further issues.

I told him how I thought it was pretty sad that I had to involve my mum. If the bully left me alone then I wasn't intending to even look at the trouble maker again.

The funny thing was, after this ugly ordeal, the girl who started all this mess kept trying to talk to me as if nothing ever happened. She then broke up with her boyfriend and to my surprise she left me alone. Not that I am condoning what I did at all, but I can't believe it took me flipping out and standing up for myself in the worst way for her to develop some kind of respect for me.

Talk about reaching my breaking point, see no matter how nice you are sometimes you become a target because people might think you are a push over. When it came to people bullying me when I was younger because I hated confrontations, and still do, people saw my silence as a sign of weakness. From that moment on I swore I'd never let it get to that point, I would speak up sooner and be more firm in standing up for myself.

Don't Let Them Break You

Speaking of standing up for myself, around the same timeframe in my life, I was out shopping with my mum. Mum was in a store, and because I was feeling sore I told her I would wait outside and sit on a bench. As I was walking over to the bench, two teenagers were pointing and laughing at me. They made some comment about the way I walked. At first I chalked it down to ignorance and tried to ignore them. Not even a moment later their mother walks over to them, and asked them what was so funny; so they pointed at me. To my absolute disgust their mum laughed too. I thought to myself;

'Oh, Hell No!'

So I walked over to them as they continued laughing. Back then in the shopping centres passport photo booths were fairly common, coincidently there was one within eye shot.

As soon as I stood in front of them I said;

"Look, clearly your kids are uneducated because they have you as their example. There's a photo booth over there, if you'd like we can go take my picture and then you can laugh for the rest of your life."

The mother looked at me stunned, as if she had just came to the realisation that I have a brain. Classic example of people thinking someone who is different or with a disability mustn't be able to form smart responses. According to people like that we are all supposedly stupid or something. Just then my mum walked out of the shop having seen the tail end of the situation. She asked me if everything was okay. I asked my mum if we were ready to go, and simply told her that I was dealing with ignorant people. After telling her not to worry about it I began to walk away from them. I was proud of myself for not letting them upset me, and for coming up with such a quick witted response. Kids being ignorant I could sometimes handle, but when adults act that disrespectful towards another human being I just can't tolerate behaviour like that.

There have been many times at school where I was judged by others for going out of my way to stop by the support unit, and just say 'hi' to many of my friends with various disabilities. It was crazy how much bullying goes on just for being nice and acknowledging others. I've always been the type of person who wants to include everyone. I don't think that I'm better than anyone else; I just always try to treat people the way I want to be treated, with respect and kindness.

It's important to note, there is no need for physical violence no matter how rude a person might be. The thing I learnt from this experience was that I could stand up for myself and knock people over with my intelligence. Over the years as I have faced many people who have made fun of me because of my physical differences, this is what I've done. People have often told me I should just ignore it. Sure, sometimes it's possible to do, depending on how old the person insulting me is. My mum has even occasionally told me not to worry about it when she sees it happening and sees me getting frustrated. It's not always as simple as that though, when you deal with it as often as I have. It bothers me that I could be in a good mood, minding my own business and then someone knocks me down emotionally.

Truthfully, as hard as it might be to believe, sometimes I forget I'm different. You might wonder how that's even possible, but in all seriousness this is the only me I know. Even though I'm in pain all the time and I know I can't reach everything I want. Physically I realise I'm not your average Joe or *Jane*, but I've accepted myself.

This is me! When someone insults me as an adult, it sometimes throws me off and makes me remember; 'Oh yeah, that's right, I'm different! I feel like yelling sometimes, I've been on display since 1982, aren't you used to me yet?...

If I can offer one piece of advice; LOVE YOURSELF. Once you accept yourself for all of your differences that's when you'll truly break through!

Chapter Seventeen

Driving Towards Independence

The process of getting my driver's license was one of the most exhausting battles I had to deal with. In the state of New South Wales, Australia, which is where I live, the driving age is sixteen for obtaining your learners permit. Sometime after my sixteenth birthday I went to the RTA, (Road and Traffic Authority) to take the required computer test.

Once I had my learners permit, I went to a driving school. The school I went to did driving assessments for people with disabilities. The place was recommended to me by my rehabilitation specialist. We had discussed my desire to obtain a drivers licence at one of my appointments, so she provided me with their details.

An assessor took me out in one of their vehicles and tested various cushions to see how much height I needed to safely see above the dashboard. They also suggested additional external wide angle side mirrors, due to the limitations in my neck and inability to rotate properly. With the thought in mind that the added mirrors might aid in better visibility for me. This wasn't a necessity but simply an option if I felt like the regular side mirrors weren't providing enough visibility. I was advised to only drive an automatic vehicle due to the stress a manual car would put on my joints. After the assessment was complete, they wrote a report with their recommendations, confirming they couldn't see any issues of concern with my ability to drive. Provided I made the minor modifications to whichever car I would be driving of course.

The recommendations were as follows, an automatic vehicle with power steering, a custom-made seat cushion, and external wide angle mirrors should I deem them necessary. They even wrote that I must have my glasses on at all times. *(What did they think I was crazy and about to drive without glasses, when I can barely see without them?)*
Shakes head

Many other little people require the use of pedal extensions when they drive because of their shorter limbs. This wasn't an issue for me as my legs are fairly average in height; therefore they didn't list pedal extensions as a requirement.

The next step was finding a cushion I could use. At the time I wanted something basic because I didn't have my own car yet. I needed a cushion that I could use in any regular sedan. One day I happened to be in a store that sold many things made from foam and rubber. One of the staff members there said he would be more than happy to make me a suitable cushion for a low price; and he did. Then I had to find a local driving instructor so I could learn how to drive. I knew beforehand that I didn't want my mum teaching me because she was nervous about me driving in the first place. This made me fear that her nervous reactions would make me more anxious behind the wheel. I found an instructor who had a Toyota Corolla; this was the first car I ever drove.

When the instructor felt I was ready for the next stage, he booked me in at the RTA for the driving test so I could progress to my provisional licence. In my mind I can picture myself sitting in my instructors white Corolla. I was so nervous when the RTA assessor sat next to me as I went through the motions of completing his requests. Turn here, do a three point turn now, reverse park in this spot, etc. Yes, I was nervous, but I thought I did well.

After the driving test was complete, the assessor told me to wait for him inside the RTA. I sat in the waiting room anxiously anticipating his return. When he finally called me over, I felt all my hopes just shatter right in front of me as he said;

"Unfortunately no matter how many times you come and take the test, we will fail you. You should be assessed by a disability assessor." I couldn't believe my ears; "What, why? I've already been assessed and provided my report to the RTA."

He proceeded to say; "Well the fact that you didn't turn your neck properly to look behind you when reversing and during other instances is grounds for me to fail you every time."

Is this really happening?

"Why didn't you tell me before you let me pay for the test that this would be the outcome either way? I mentioned it to you before you got in the car that I rely more on my mirrors as I can't turn my neck as far as I should due to my fusion." I was trying to keep my cool, but inside I was crying.

"Did I actually drive unsafely? Did I do anything wrong?" He just continued to repeat himself and told me, no matter how many times I went, they would keep failing me. My disability driving school assessment report had already listed any issues, and the RTA had accepted their report as grounds for me to proceed with getting my licence. My instructor was no real help with this situation. The assessor then handed me my paper with a big fail on it and no real explanation on the form itself. Maybe he wanted to cover himself in case I reported the issue, and then there would be no written proof as to what was said.

When I got home I told my mum what happened, by then I was so upset that I couldn't hold my tears back anymore.

(Mum I'm sorry but your reaction only made it worse.)

"Maybe it's a sign Fiona, it's better for you not to drive."

I knew my mum was just worried about anything bad happening to me on the roads, but all my life she taught me to be independent. Driving was the biggest key to me truly achieving my independence, but I didn't feel her support in this. I didn't know what I could do to fight for my independence and where to go from all that; my hopes were completely shattered. At the time I needed my mum to tell me we would work it out together, instead of tell me to give up. This situation killed my spirit a little, so I threw my learners permit in a drawer and my dreams of ever driving with it.

Almost two years after I had given up on getting my licence, the decision still wasn't sitting well with me. I knew mum reacted the way she did because she feared me ending up in a car accident. I knew she loved me and thought she was protecting me. This was more about her fears. Sometimes it's not ideal to let your parents hold you back because of their fears. I reassessed my decision and thought to myself;

'No, I am not accepting no for an answer.'

By then, my learners permit had expired, so it meant I had to retake the computer test again. Unfortunately though, during the two years I wasted not continuing to fight for my independence, the RTA had changed the drivers licence process. See, originally back in 1998 the rules were, after the driving test was completed, you'd be given a red provisional licence if you passed. The provisional licence meant you could drive alone in the car but still had extra rules to comply with for a year. After the year passes, you'd then receive your full permit.

The new rules that came into play in the year 2000 meant as soon as you passed your learners test, you had to complete a logbook with a certain amount of driving hours and tasks. Once the requirements in the logbook where complete you could take the driving test to receive your provisional licence. Instead of automatically receiving your full permit after being on the red provisional licence for a year, another computer test had to be completed. But that wasn't the end of it, you also had to complete two years on a green provisional licence. Then, once those two years were complete, you'd take the final computer test and be given your full drivers licence.

When I passed my learners permit on the 1st of August 2000 and they explained the new process to me, I couldn't believe my luck. I wished I hadn't given up because then I wouldn't have had to jump through more hoops. This time I would not allow myself to be defeated. I found a new instructor again and explained my history to him. He assured me he would have my back and help me achieve the goal of getting my licence once and for all. Finally after I fulfilled the logbook, it was time to go ahead with booking the driving test. My instructor suggested we go to a different RTA. He knew I was reluctant to revisit the one that previously denied me, even if I had a different assessor.

Before booking the test, I obtained a letter from my specialist further addressing the previous concerns regarding the lack of movement in my neck. He provided the RTA with more details about my condition and championed my case. Stating as long as I complied with the road rules then I should not be penalised from receiving my licence. Along with this letter, I visited my eye specialist and requested a letter from him, confirming that my vision met the driving requirements. I was hoping this wouldn't be a repeat from my first attempt. Unfortunately, when I took the driving test this time around, I let my fears of history repeating take over me. I wasn't focussed properly, and I knew it was my fault because I made stupid mistakes I never made when I drove with my instructor. So when they told me I failed this time, I only had myself to blame. My instructor told me to wait a week or two, calm down and go again, so that's exactly what I did.

Third time's a charm, right?
Finally, I knew I completed the test with no mistakes but when I went back into the RTA office afterwards, I was still worried. I couldn't believe what came out of the assessors' mouth.

"Sorry, but no matter how many times you come we will have to fail you." No, you're not dreaming, and neither was I. It was like history repeating all over again. But this time there was one big difference; my instructor jumped to my defence and had my back. He explained how I complied by getting letters and I went through all the necessary medical assessments. So unless I made a mistake in the test then they better stop wasting my time and money. While my instructor was talking, I began to panic inside;

I thought, maybe my mum was right?
Am I fighting a losing battle?
I kept telling myself to stay calm, and that I wasn't fighting for nothing because I was a good driver. God I loved my instructor for having my back. Right after he jumped to my defence the assessor looked at me and said; "You're right, this time I can't fault your driving ability, so okay, you can have your provisional licence."

What? Am I dreaming?
Did I finally pass this ever frustrating hurdle?
I couldn't believe it, for a minute there I was starting to question whether God was trying to tell me something.

When I got home that afternoon and told my mum that I finally passed, I saw the worry in her eyes. But I also saw that she was happy for me because she knew it was important to me.

I didn't feel comfortable driving my mum's car because it had big blind spots when looking through the mirrors. Therefore, I knew I wouldn't be able to drive unless I found a car for myself that would be more suited to my needs.

I was nineteen by the time I was on my P's and I didn't have the kind of money to afford a new car outright. It felt like it would be a long road before I could even afford a car, and I didn't want a second hand one. If I were to purchase a second hand car, I feared that the possibility of it breaking down at any moment was too big of a risk for someone like me.

During this time I was only earning a small amount of disability pension from the government. See, when I was a baby my specialist had directed my mum to apply for the disability pension for me, so she did. Then when I turned sixteen she had the option to keep my disability payments until I was older or let me have it myself. It made more sense for my mum to let me manage my own disability pension and I was grateful she allowed me the choice. I appreciated that my mum put her trust in me and gave me that slice of independence. I guess that's why I was so thrown off by her initial reaction when I got knocked back by the RTA in 1998. Mum soon made up for that original difference of opinion where it seemed like she wasn't supporting my independence.

Only weeks after passing my driving test she offered to go guarantor for me to purchase my very own new car. I don't know what I would ever do without my mum, I knew she only seemed like she was holding me back because she cared. But for her to offer to be my guarantor, so I could buy my first car meant the world to me.

She made me promise I would be responsible and put away most of my pension every month so I'd keep up with the repayments. I was so excited by this prospect I didn't care if all my money for the next three years went to pay off a brand new car. My mum never made preferences she has my brother and my sister to think of too, and I wouldn't expect her to be buying each one of us a new car. Without my mum offering to be my guarantor I never would have been able to drive into my independence when I did. Thanks Mum!

Chapter Eighteen

Youth and Teenage Memories

Just like my chapter of childhood memories, I feel like now is a good time to reflect on the years of my youth in-between the last few chapters.

If I can transport you back to the time when I was undergoing the many surgeries on both my legs when I had Ilizarov done. There are quite a few significant memories that come to mind. But, before we get into some pretty intense ones, let me start by share something that was a simple, yet sweet gesture that has stuck with me.

Remember Grace? The first little person my mum met when I was a baby, and also Lynda's mum who I was flower girl for in her wedding. Grace really was one of the sweetest people, and during my major leg surgeries she always wrote me these fun quirky letters. In all her letters she would draw some of the words and put fun stickers instead of write a simple worded letter. I would then reply to her in the same way. It was clear to me that Grace wrote them to cheer me up and to give me something else to think about, but I knew she genuinely cared about me too. I always looked forward to receiving her letters I must say. To show you just how much it really meant there is no better way than for me to include a snippet from an actual letter Grace wrote me that I've held onto for all these years.

Me, Kniest & Understanding

LETTER FROM GRACE:

Dear Fiona,
Well Mate, 👁 hope that U R O.K. it wont B 2 long and u will have 2 sexy leg/s and u will B able 2 jump over the rainbow pot of gold

We R good. it is very cold here 👁'm freezing my bum off.

Kyra is good. Lynda is having a baby in January. We are pleased, it will be nice to have a little baby around and 👁 know that you will love to change the pooey bim's for Lynda.

YUK!

Lynda and David came down for the weekend but could not get home because of the snow on the road.

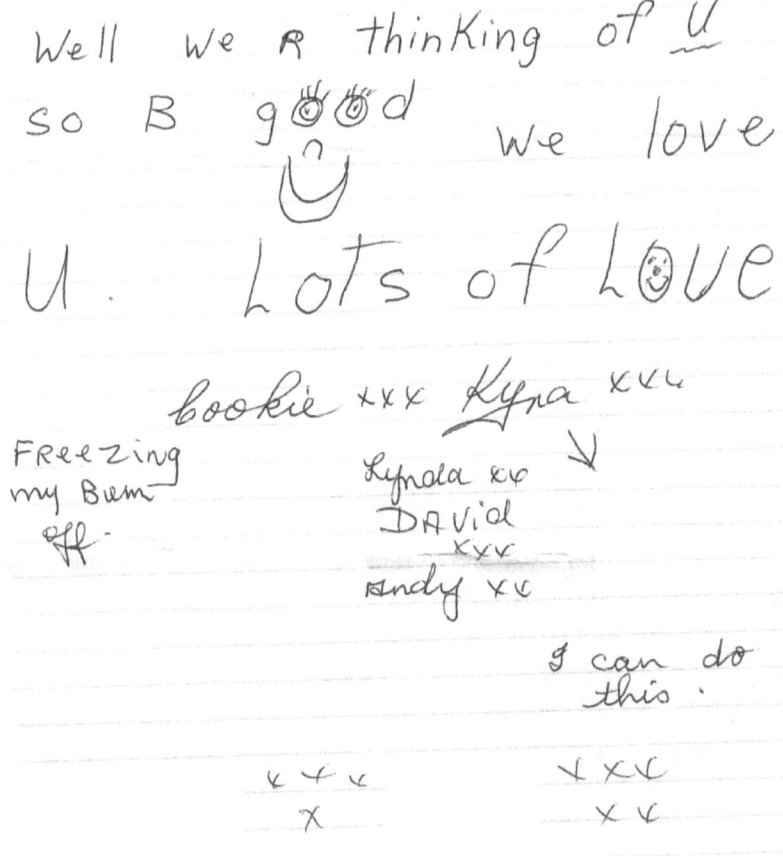

(*Unfortunately, some stickers and graphics on the letter needed to be removed due to copyright. I would have loved to share the humorous stickers Grace used to add to my letters.*)

I'll cherish these fond memories forever and I'm sure Grace would be so happy for me to be sharing them with you all. Sadly, Grace is no longer with us physically but her cheery positivity remains in my heart. I am sure she is watching over me and dancing over the rainbows in the sky.

LET'S DIVE INTO THE CHAOS

When I had the second round of Ilizarov surgery done on my right leg, and they took me to my bed in the ward, it wasn't long before chaos broke out. Whoever had stayed in that spot before me had left flowers in the cupboard next to my bed. Clearly they should have been thrown out instead of placed inside the cupboard. Also, I would have thought the nurses at least would have given it a once over before someone new came along. In case someone left anything important in the cupboard by accident. Mum hadn't brought my stuff for me from home yet because I was still pretty out of it, so the cupboard wasn't opened by us straight away either. When mum came back to visit me I was in and out of sleep because of the pain and morphine. When I was feeling more alert, I told her I was feeling itchy. Mum looked on my bed and then opened the cupboard door only to find the dead flowers and a tonne of ants. She called the nurses and had them change my bed sheets. Annoyingly, to top it off it also gave me head lice. As I was only a day or two fresh out of surgery I couldn't move much or even get up yet. This meant mum had to cut my nice long hair so she could treat it easier and get rid of the lice. I was so upset because as I have mentioned previously I love my long hair. I didn't want my mum to cut my hair but I knew at the time it was the only solution to getting rid of the lice, which was the most important thing.

(No thanks to whoever the bright spark was that couldn't carry the flowers to a bin instead of shove them inside the cupboard.)

Unfortunately for me, the chaos also went into round two of unexpected dramas. Shortly after waking up a nurse visited me to let me know she needed to take a blood sample. I wasn't in the mood to deal with a needle with all the pain I was already in. This wasn't a usual occurrence for them to request blood right after a surgery. The nurse told me that apparently a doctor had accidentally jabbed himself with a needle that was used on a patient in the operating room. He wasn't sure who the needle was used on, so they were getting blood samples from all the patients to confirm there was nothing to be concerned about. Annoyingly, the veins on the inside of my arm are always difficult to work with and doctors always struggle to draw blood from those veins. After attempting to hit my vein twice in each arm with no success I was dreading where they would stab me with the needle next. Oddly, the nurse asked me if she could take it from my groin area. I thought this was the weirdest most uncomfortable place I've ever had a blood sample taken from. Thankfully, she got her sample and left. A day or two later the nurse came back while I was sitting up in a chair next to my bed. The lab had advised her she hadn't taken a big enough sample so she needed to get more blood. OMG... Not again...

She insisted on trying both my arms again, only to receive the same result of not finding my vein. Luckily, she couldn't take it from my groin area this time because I was sitting and it would have been too difficult with the contraption on my leg. As she stood there for a moment, my annoying vein I have on my massive ankle joint was throbbing as usual. What a terrible time for her to look down and see my bulging vein on my ankle. Suddenly it was like she had won the lotto, "oh, can I take it from there?" Personally, I didn't want her to, but I didn't have much choice in the matter. That was definitely even more painful than taking blood from my groin area. I told her to please make sure she took enough because I didn't want any more needles. Mind you, I wasn't at all calm during this whole process because it was still a time when I would ball my eyes out before I even saw a needle. Fortunately, she never came back for more blood and the doctor was fine anyway, what an ordeal.

Chaos round three, yep, they say things come in threes and this was true during my Ilizarov list of unexpected dramas. Additionally after I woke up from the surgery, my eardrum was ringing loudly inside my head. I pushed the buzzer to call the nurse while I cried in pain. She told me to just ignore it and be quiet when I told her my ear was ringing. Truthfully this nurse was actually quite rude to me, and she didn't give me anything for my pain. She was acting like I was just complaining for the sake of complaining, not because there was something wrong with me. Eventually after a night of solid crying in pain, the ringing finally stopped. A few weeks later when I was at home, my grandfather in Malta called to see how I was doing.

As he was talking, I quickly realised I couldn't hear anything. Now, my grandfather is so loud when he talks it would have been impossible not to hear him, unless something was wrong. So I switched the phone over to my other ear and I could hear him speak. Straight away my mum booked me in to see a doctor. After I was examined, I told him what had happened in the hospital, but then because the ringing stopped I thought I was okay. He informed me that I had a busted eardrum, gave me antibiotics and told me to go back in a few weeks for a review. Luckily it healed as time went on without needing surgery to correct it. Now if only that nurse had taken me seriously when I told her my eardrum was ringing loudly inside my head.

As if three dramas during those surgeries weren't enough, there was one other major episode in the Ilizarov series of Fee. When the nurses were trying to show my mum how my wounds had to be cleaned, I wasn't coping very well. I was screaming throughout the hospital walls as the peroxide was stinging my open wounds. When the nurses realised it was still too fresh and they weren't able to calm me down, they took me into a special room. My mum was beside me, as the nurses gave me happy gas to try and calm me. They used happy gas because it was supposed to make me relax. Then they could continue to clean my wounds so I wouldn't get an infection. It took awhile for them to calm me down, I really struggled the first time they used peroxide on my open wounds. The nurses told my mum to continue to speak to me the whole time. They warned her not to allow me to slip into unconsciousness. As my body was so tiny, if I became unconscious it would mean they had given me too much gas; and it could have killed me.

I'm sure you can tell where this drama is about to end up. Suddenly, I closed my eyes and I stopped responding to my mum. Mum began frantically screaming and slapping me in the face, telling me to wake up. The nurses had to stop the whole procedure immediately and gave me oxygen to wake me up.

Talk about a near death experience; that would have been some warped story to tell. Young Fee tragically dies in hospital from happy gas overdose. You wouldn't read about it I tell you; no really you wouldn't because this book wouldn't even exist if that happened.

Yeah I know, sometimes my humour can be a little dark, but I can joke about it now because everything worked out just fine.

LIFE AS A SCIENCE EXPERIMENT

One of the most frustrating and embarrassing things I dealt with as a kid during medical appointments was when my specialists would bring other medical students into the room. It would be even more embarrassing when they would make me stand there in my underwear while they talked about me as if I wasn't there. Part of me felt like I was some kind of interactive science experiment in a museum. It was bad enough when I was a kid, but I felt even more violated when it continued on as I got older. Part of me figured it was because I was the only one they knew of in Australia with Kniest so they were using me as a subject of medical interest. I never once told them they were making me feel like a lab experiment because I'd hoped they would discover ways to help me throughout life. If I was expecting their help then I guess I had to co-operate too.

I recall when I went to one of my doctor appointments with Profs and he was flipping through the pages of my medical file, I suddenly felt mortified. As he was flipping the pages, I saw all these images of me throughout my file of me standing in my underwear. I felt so uncomfortable knowing they were there, that I ended up asking Profs if he could cover those photos with a piece of paper so they wouldn't be on the front of the pages. Not like doctors still couldn't look through it, if they were browsing my records, but I didn't need them jumping out at people. Plus, I knew my file was passed around so often because I was like an extinct, rare 'Fee-line' at the zoo. At least that's how they made me feel, for the most part.

Life in the Spotlight

From a young age I have appeared in multiple newspaper and magazine articles. When I was six they ran a story about me in the local paper, and then another when I was nine. I had only just got into my new primary school in grade five when the local papers were visiting. We had our own parliament at my school, almost mimicking how the real government parliament house works. This was right around the time when I became more involved and outspoken.

I was nominated by my class to be the treasurer for our school fundraising efforts. The local paper wanted to cover a story when they decided to focus their story on me. We were in a heated parliamentary debate, where I was discussing my objections to a bill on what part of the playground could be used for competitive sport practices. Treasurer Fee was already collecting her fees at a young age.

Then there were articles written about me before I left for Malta and some others afterwards. I was even in a commercial for the organisation that I went on camps with. I was speaking about my experiences, and promoting the accessibility and information about the camps they offered.

It's been an interesting adventure so far being in the spotlight without even trying. Keep an eye out, because you just never know what I'll be doing next.

Inner Soles

From a young age I had many issues with my feet, before I had all my leg surgeries my feet rolled inwards a lot. After the major Ilizarov surgeries my rehabilitation specialist was still concerned with how flat footed my feet were. She thought it would be best to have special orthopaedic boots made, to help support my feet better when walking. I had tried leg braces earlier on, but the way my hips pushed me forward, it wasn't a functional option for me, and I couldn't stand up in them.

Before we went to live in Malta, I had moulds made of my feet by a Podiatrist who designed my special boots. They were black and bulky, but around my ankle it was covered with nice soft comfy leather. So even though they weren't the most attractive looking boots, they were quite comfortable. They were about $1000 to make, which was a lot of money at the time. As unattractive as the boots were, I wore them every day because of how comfortable I felt when I walked in them. Unfortunately, I eventually grew out of them while we were living in Malta. Once I grew out of them I just tried my best to find regular shoes I could tolerate. This seemed to be an impossible task, I found joggers were the most comfortable for me, but still nowhere near as comfortable as those boots.

It wasn't until we returned to Australia and saw my specialists again that they sent me to have new orthotics made. This time they made me inner soles to fit into my joggers. I had a few different trials of various materials but eventually by the time I was seventeen the inner soles I had felt great. After going through various brands of joggers I finally found the brand that worked best for my feet with my inner soles. Sometimes I felt like I was wasting so much money trying to find shoes that didn't hurt my ankles. Occasionally, I'd wear them once or twice for a long period, and it was only then I'd realise they weren't working for me. My sister inherited many of my trial-and-error shoes that didn't work and hadn't been ruined yet by me dragging my feet. That was a bonus for her since surprisingly we wear the same size shoe as adults even though she's much taller than I am. Coincidently the joggers that work best for my feet happen to be Fila brand. Being the silly Fee that I am, I came up with my own Fila acronym:

Fiona
Is
Looking
Awesome

CLOWNING AROUND - VIVA L-KARNIVAL

In the two years I lived in Malta I was lucky enough to experience many unique opportunities. One of those opportunities happened to be taking part in a huge carnival that is celebrated in the city of Valetta, Malta. The Carnival (Karnival in Maltese) occurs during the week leading up to Ash Wednesday. It includes masked balls, fancy dress and bizarre mask competitions, lavish parties, marching bands, and a colourful parade of floats. It's a fun celebration that my school took part in. We had to learn specific dances at school for us to entertain the public in the city. I dressed up as a clown; it was the one time in my life I felt it was okay being the class clown. This was what the Carnival was all about; everyone in my class dressed up in some type of clown or unique masked outfit. It was incredibly tiring for me being in the city for as long as we were, but lucky the teachers allowed me to take refuge on a seat or a float every so often.

(Dressed for the Karnival)

LASER EYE SURGERY

On Friday the 19th of June 1998 I went back into hospital, for eye surgery. My retina was very weak and spotty in areas so my childhood eye specialist sent me to a new Ophthalmologist. He felt the best way to protect my retina from a retinal detachment would be to have laser surgery. The type of laser I had wasn't the same as the laser most people have to improve their vision. This laser treatment isn't used to improve vision but would strengthen my retina. The best way to describe this surgery; is by imagining the laser was the tool that welded my retina together to strengthen the weak spots. This is a common form of treatment when it comes to retinal degeneration.

I was placed under aesthetic while he lasered both my eyes because he felt it would be too painful for me to sit still if I was awake. This was the first surgery I had in the new children's hospital. It was better for my mum, because it was much closer than going to the one where I had my previous surgeries.

The surgery took a couple hours; when I woke up I had gooey ointment in my eyes. My eyes felt really scratchy, red and sore. Fortunately, it was only an overnight surgery, so I got to go home the next day. I had to be very careful not to get an infection in my eyes and keep up with putting the ointment on every couple hours. This was frustrating because my sleep was always interrupted by my mum waking me up to put the ointment on for me. I'm sure this wasn't any fun for her either. I was a trooper as always and went straight back to school on Monday. As soon as I was at school, I had to put the ointment on myself, so I had all weekend to practice. It's odd to say, for someone like me who didn't really enjoy going to school, I didn't like to take unnecessary days off either. The fact that I've always been a bit of a nerd and cared about having an education was the only thing keeping me there. But I couldn't wait for my school days to be over and to move onto the next important faze of my life.

IT'S ALL FUN AND GAMES UNTIL SOMEONE GETS HURT...

On one occasion I was simply playing with a Yoyo minding my own business, when a kid who was five at the time decided to jump on my back. Keep in mind he was almost the same height as me already and he was someone who knew me. I couldn't handle his weight on my back, so I was telling him to get off me, but he didn't listen. He kept yelling;

"Give me the Yoyo."

I would have happily let him borrow my Yoyo but I needed him off my back. When he wouldn't get off so I could hand it to him, I went to try to turn my body around to get him off. My back was already beginning to ache intensely, but in the process of trying to turn around my elbow nudged him off. It wasn't intentional for me to get him off in that way, but at the same time I couldn't breathe with his weight taking over my body. I knew I didn't hurt him because it was just a natural nudge from me turning, but he immediately went crying to his parents.

There I was, with tears welling up in my eyes trying to keep it together from the pain I was already feeling. At the time I was fifteen and a fairly quiet teenager. I explained exactly what happened to my mum, because she could see the pain in my eyes and asked me what was wrong. Even though she wasn't in eye shot to see the incident actually happening I couldn't hide the intense pain I was feeling.

The next day when I tried to get up in the morning I couldn't move, my back was so sore. I understand that the kid was too young to know that he shouldn't jump on my back, fair enough, he was a kid. But I spent a whole week in bed after that incident where I didn't go to school because my back was so messed up.

Many times when I'm out in public, kids tend to point and stare and say some truly horrible things. One time I was at the shopping centre walking onto the escalator, when a kid was walking behind me. He was making fun of me and trying to mimic the way I walk. This shattered me deep inside because technically this kid was familiar with me, yet he was hurting me in a way I had only known strangers to hurt me. What was even worse was instead of his parents telling him to stop being rude; they laughed.

Was this really happening?

This was even worse than the kid making fun of me; it was like his parents were encouraging him by laughing too. Instead of seeing how much something like that was so disrespectful and hurtful to me. Just because they are the adults, doesn't mean they shouldn't show respect too.

I've faced many situations like this throughout my life, where people have no filter or realise how their reactions and actions can impact and hurt me. It would be nice if everyone in the world just took a moment before being cruel to someone else and saw things from a different point of view.

Chapter Nineteen

Seeing Is Believing

We have now reached a moment in my life where my strength felt tested beyond measure. It was before Christmas in December 2002 when I faced one of the scariest medical challenges in the first twenty years of my life. As my condition dealt me what I felt to be my most devastating blow. It all began one day out of nowhere when I noticed a big blurry blob clouding my central vision. Immediately I knew I couldn't ignore the issue, this was something my specialists had warned me about throughout my whole life. I was constantly told to watch out for flashing lights, floating spots and shutter like issues affecting my vision. Realistically, no-one ever told me to watch out for blobs, but I knew this couldn't be good.

First step was instantly facing the harsh reality, even though I never liked to think about my possible loss of vision. It was always something I was well aware of due to my condition. As soon as I told my mum and tried to explain the blob she promptly rang my ophthalmologist and requested an urgent appointment. He understood the severity of my condition and how important it was to deal with it ASAP. I went into his office for him to check the back of my eye. Straight away he said that he wanted to inject me with dye so he could take pictures of the back of my eye with a special machine. The dye would aid in enhancing visibility to know exactly what was happening. He warned me that the dye would make my skin look yellow for a few days and could make me feel a bit sick. Possibly feeling sick or turning yellow was the least of my worries; I was already feeling sick with nerves internally, anyway.

It was right then that he began to explain in detail what was wrong; I had an Epiretinal membrane. An Epiretinal membrane is a serious condition that causes the vitreous jelly in the eye to form a transparent layer over the central part of the macular in the back of the eye. The transparent layer then forms like scar tissue and creates tension on the retina. This then distorts the vision of the eye, in the central macular area. I know most people reading this are thinking; what, huh? If I can put it anymore simpler, my doctor also explained it to me like this: Imagine my retina is like wet tissue paper, fragile, thinned out and weak. The membrane that formed is like super glue. Now put that together and think about the task he had to complete to try to salvage my eye. Picture trying to pull super glue off of wet tissue paper without tearing the paper, now that was the seriousness of the situation my right eye was in.

He told me that the risk of me going blind in my right eye was extremely likely, and I needed urgent surgery. It was the 18th of December 2002 when my eye specialist advised he couldn't do the surgery until January 2003 due to the Christmas holidays. This news made me very anxious, all I could do was hope and pray that my retina would remain intact until I was able to have the surgery, without causing further complications. As much as I was afraid I knew the serious reality, the sooner a situation like this is dealt with, the better my chances would be, but I had no choice but to wait it out. Sadly, when January came around my specialist advised me that he needed to push it back a few more weeks. So far my vision was still the same blob-fest I had in December; it didn't appear to be worsening. I continued to pray and hope that it would hold on until my surgery date.

Of all the surgeries I've ever had in my life, I actually would need to look up dates to confirm exactly when they were. Not in this instance though; I will never forget the 11th of February 2003. It was the day my eye surgery happened. It's the one surgery date that left an imprint on my memory forever. My specialist said I had less than 1% chance of not losing my right eye during this surgery. So I put all of my trust in his hands, and God, to help me get through the surgery with both my eyes. Before I went into the operating room I was sitting there waiting with my mum and dad. Never had I seen my dad so nervous too before I was going into have surgery. I told him I was scared, and I didn't want to be blind. He had a religious medallion with him, and said he wanted to pray with me so that I would be protected. My dad loves to joke so much that this was one of the first times I really felt he was hurting for me. Dad prayed out loud with me and gave me a hug and told me everything would be okay.

When the time came, and the medical staff wheeled me in on the bed into the operating room, I thought I was going to be sick and I couldn't stop crying. I remember the surgery bed was so uncomfortable, and there was a massive round light above my head. As they began giving me anaesthetic, I told my specialist to please do everything he could to help me. Then the last words that came out of my mouth before I passed out were;

"God, please don't let me go blind."

Before I went into surgery, the specialist had warned me if I woke up on my stomach then he wasn't able to save my eye. It would have meant I had lost my vision in my right eye, and he had to blow gas into the back of my eye. This possibility freaked me out, I was afraid to wake up. Especially knowing I had less than 1% chance of this surgery being successful. I knew it was a strong possibility I'd wake up on my stomach.

The surgery was supposed to be an hour and a half long, but ended up taking longer than expected. He was operating on my eye for a solid four hours. I'm sure my mum and dad were freaking out while they waited. Once I was out and began to wake up, I could feel a patch over my right eye. Then I began to realise I could see the blurry lights on the ceiling with my left eye. I didn't have my glasses on so everything is blurry without them. Quickly I thought to myself;

'Thank God, I'm on my back, he must have saved my eye!'

You can't even begin to understand how completely grateful I was in that moment. Even though I was still drowsy and not fully alert I just knew deep down that God was with me during my surgery to guide my specialists' hands. My faith in God is always with me every day, and especially in times of great struggle. Even though I know if that day had turned out differently God still would have been with me every step of the way to help me cope.

Thankfully I was the 1% miracle. Every surgery I had ever been through, including the ones more painful than this; I was never more scared or impacted by one of my medical challenges as I was with this one.

I had a lot of medication for the next few weeks. Every few hours I had drops that constantly had to be put in to assist the healing process. The doctor warned me to be extremely careful; to avoid getting worked up or put any strain on my eye. The first two weeks after the surgery were still a very critical time. It was important I didn't get an infection, because if I did it could have still meant the possibility of losing my eye. Once I was home from hospital, mum had to spend the first few weeks waking up every two, four and six hours to put the various drops in.

It's true what they say, when you lose one sense, your other senses are more profound. Seeing as I had a patch on my eye for the next few weeks and my eye's felt compromised, my hearing had gotten stronger. Even the sound of me whispering when I tried talking on the phone irritated me. In my head it felt like I was screaming. It totally threw off my visual perception quite a bit; I constantly misjudged how close I was walking to the wall. Each time I would knock my shoulder, I was so unbalanced and felt off centre.

Before this surgery happened, I had gone out shopping with my mum and saw this mid-sized bear with a bow tie on. I was feeling like childhood Fee because of the fear I had of losing my vision. So I picked it up and hugged it in the middle of the shop, I didn't care that I was twenty and people might have been staring at me. My mum ended up buying me that bear, she asked the hospital for an eye patch and tied it with string over his head, covering his right eye. Then she had asked a nurse to get her a hospital name tag, and attached it to his leg with the name 'Patch'. I loved it so much; my mum had indulged the inner childhood Fee, the one who always found comfort in her soft toys when things were tough. Patch is still around the house and is a constant reminder of how blessed I was to have a positive outcome that day.

All I can say is, to this day I am ever so grateful that I was the 1% exception to the rule. That even though the road to recovery was a long one, I healed from the surgery exceptionally well. I had my vision back with the correction of my glasses of course.

Things in life sometimes push us to the limit, make us question; 'Why me?' Life is hard sometimes, at times it can even feel like nothing is ever going right. When this is happening in your life it's always best to think about what is going right. Surely, there have to be positives too, like the fact that this difficult time bonded me even closer with my dad. Him being there for me with my mum and praying with me meant more to me than he will ever know. Sometimes it pays to not give up hope, because you too never know when you might be the 1% exception to the rule.

Chapter Twenty

Enemies in Low Places

I was almost a senior in high school when another little person came to my school. She was only just starting grade seven, so I was about four years ahead of her. To tell this story, I'll call her Sammy. When I first saw her walking around the school, my initial reaction was; 'Oh cool, I should introduce myself.' Even though I knew she was a few years younger than me, I thought it would be nice to have another little person to be friends with.

Although, when I first went to introduce myself to Sammy, she appeared to have a chip on her shoulder. She acted like she thought she was better than everyone. It was as if associating with another little person was a bad thing because she thought of herself as someone who wasn't different. You could say that's a good thing, that she seemed comfortable with who she was. Although on the flip side of the coin, it was like she was in denial; which you'll soon work out was closer to the truth. Even though when I first tried talking to her the reception I received was cold, I persisted because I wanted to try to become friends with her anyway.

You see, when I was about four and my mum was raising us on her own she didn't know how to drive yet. So we no longer had a way of getting to the Little People events. Then when she could drive, we were always dealing with so many medical issues or surgeries with me that I had phased out from going. Not for any other reason than life was pretty hectic in the world of Fee. The only little people I had contact with as a kid was Grace and her family. Then after we left for Malta, I never saw or hung out with any other little people, until the day Sammy came to my school.

After some time I learned more about Sammy as she finally opened up and let me into her world. It soon made sense why at first she didn't know how to react towards me. Sammy had told me she wasn't sure how to react as I was the first little person other than herself she had ever met in her life. Granted Sammy had Achondroplasia the most common form of dwarfism and I threw her off being a much rarer type. Once we got to know each other we became best friends.

Sammy came from a very strict family with good values, and as soon as her family got to know me, I felt trusted too. It was like I was a part of their family and I was her big sister. Her parents saw me as someone with good values too and placed a lot of trust in me because my dad is of the same nationality as they were. This gave them comfort in knowing I must be alright. It was good for Sammy because her parents allowed her to go out without them, as long as she was with me. I was happy to be the responsible one, and I always looked out for her. Although things got awkward when she abused the trust her parents had in me by doing things in my presence I didn't agree with.

After some time passed, she began dating a mutual school friend of ours, but the only way they could go out was if I went too. I'm fairly certain she never told her parents he was actually her boyfriend, so it put me in a tough spot. Each time they wanted to go out, I tried being the good friend and was the third wheel. I thought it was better she had someone who cared about her like I did, someone who looked out for her like family. Until on one occasion where she made me feel like I was just being used. We had all met up for a movie. They chose the movie and even though it wasn't something I was interested in, I agreed to see it too. I thought I'd be nice and let them watch what they wanted to watch. I even gave them space while they sat in the back of the cinema to watch the movie; while I sat closer to the front. It wasn't even ten minutes into the movie when I noticed they left me and didn't even let me know. This upset me more because, I soon realised I sat through an entire movie I didn't even like, all by myself and for what? I thought maybe they went to the bathroom, or they forgot to get a snack they wanted. I didn't anticipate them leaving me there.

The movie was now over and they were nowhere to be seen. I began to worry, how was I going to find her? She didn't have a phone with her so there was no way to call. Finally I found them; I was pretty hurt and angry inside.

What if her parents questioned me?

What if something bad had happened and she got herself in serious trouble? I felt responsible for her and she abused my trust, and the trust her parents had placed in me. She was my best friend, and she begged me to not say a word. I was stuck in-between a rock and a hard place. So I asked her not to put me in an awkward position like that again, and I kept my word to her. As you are reading this, I guess you might wonder why it's even relevant, but I'm getting to it I promise.

Now you understand that Sammy and I had formed a close friendship and there was nothing I wouldn't do for her. We would sleep at each other's house on weekends and spend a lot of time together during school holidays. It was when we had sleepovers I learnt that Sammy wasn't as tough, or as confident as she first made herself out to be when we first met. She was extremely insecure about her bowed legs and therefore she never wore pants. She would only wear dresses to hide her legs and not draw attention to the bowing. It wasn't until she was around me, someone she probably considered worse than her that she opened up about her insecurities.

Seeing as my legs aren't straight either ever since I had my leg surgeries. As I described in the very beginning my ankles used to roll in and therefore my knees would knock. The leg surgeries I had when I was younger made me more mobile, but as a result, they also made my legs appear less straight.

It took a lot of convincing on my part to get her to try my pants on so she could see that she wasn't as bad as she thought. Afterwards Sammy and her parents expressed that she wanted to see a specialist to correct the bowing in her legs. So I did what any good friend would do and gave her my surgeon's details. I told her to mention that she was a friend of mine and I had recommended him. Shortly after she met with him, she had Ilizarov done to her legs. Luckily for her because she had none of the hip or ankle problems I had, she healed well and her legs turned out straight, just like she had hoped. I was so happy for her and glad that I had helped give her true confidence in herself. Although this soon came back to bite me as she acted like she was better than everyone again. This upset me because occasionally she was even hurtful towards me in the comments she made. I shrugged it off as best as I could and still considered her my best friend, even though it hurt.

By this time I was finished high school, but we still saw each other regularly. A few months later, we were out shopping with her mum when we both saw two little people walking in the distance. It was a girl and a guy; they appeared to be of similar age to us. Since Sammy was now accustomed to being around me, she immediately showed interest in wanting to talk to the two people in the shop. Sammy begged me to go with her and follow them so she could say hello. It almost felt like we were chasing them down. Until we finally caught up to them and introduced ourselves. We chatted for a few minutes, and they asked us if we ever heard of the little people organisation. Of course I had, as my mum had taken me when I was young; back when it had a different name. I explained to them how I hadn't been to any events since I was a kid, and how Sammy and I met at school. They suggested we go to a meeting or a basketball social event that was coming up, so we could get involved and mingle. Sammy was suddenly very interested in going to meet with others so we went to a basketball event on the weekend just to watch and get to know people. Oddly, as much as I had no reason not to want to go to little people events, I really only went for Sammy, because she wanted to go and wouldn't go without me. By then I was nineteen when we got involved in doing things with other little people.

I still hadn't met anyone with my condition and I felt a bit out of place in the organisation. Sure I was always friendly with everyone and wanted to make friends with any person, LP or not. But I felt a sense of difference more than I felt when I hung out with Sammy or my other average height friends. The organisation was mostly all little people with Achondroplasia, with the occasional Psuedo-Achon, or person with SED. I felt like I stood out like a sore thumb; but I still made a huge effort to try and make friends with everyone.

I seemed to make better friendships at national events with people that were in different states. This was harder though because I didn't get to see those friends often. Unfortunately, because it was such a tight knit group in NSW, it felt very cliquey. Some of the members would come to me and question why I was friends with Sammy, because they thought she was odd. I didn't appreciate them trying to cause trouble behind my best friend's back. So I told them I wasn't interested in drama and I was only there for her and they should give her a chance. She was my best friend; I was loyal to her, and I barely knew those people. I didn't care about trying to fit into some clique. It bothered me as time went on and we went to a few events; I could still hear them talking badly about my friend.

This wasn't what I signed up for, not everyone was involved in all this drama but the few people who were involved were mainly from my state, so it made things difficult. I continued to go for Sammy's sake and by this time I was actually nominated to be the state treasurer of the NSW division, so I became heavily involved in meetings and events.

When 2003 rolled around and I had my serious eye surgery, Sammy's parents brought her to the hospital to come and see me. Even though I wasn't coping well emotionally with all the fear I had of possibly going blind, I noticed Sammy wasn't acting her usual self towards me. This played on my mind and was bothering me. A few days after I was home from the hospital, I called Sammy to see if everything was okay. She seemed cold towards me and I couldn't understand what I had done for her to be acting this way.

I really needed my friend during this tough time and I felt like she wasn't even there for me in an emotional capacity, which was tearing me up inside. Because it bothered me so much I asked my mum to take me to Sammy's house, I hadn't warned her I was going. I'm a very straight up person, and if something is wrong, I needed to face the issue and deal with it. Sammy was important to me, and I missed having my best friend; I hated feeling like I was losing her. When I got to her house, the look on her face was of complete shock. She didn't expect to see me and she seemed awkward. Instead of her hugging me like usual she asked me what I was doing there. I told her that I felt like we needed to talk because things didn't seem right. Her parents welcomed my mum and me into their house. Sammy had a look of complete fear on her face as she asked me if we could talk in her room. Of course I said it was fine, I just wanted to get to the bottom of all this mess. Once we were in her room, she expressed that she didn't want to let her parents know what was going on. I didn't really care about any of that, I just wanted to know what changed and why things felt as awkward as they were. Sammy explained that the people from the clique in the organisation had called her while I was in hospital and told her I was bad-mouthing her and her family. I couldn't believe my ears, I spent so much time defending Sammy to those jerks and this is how I get treated. During one of the lowest points in my life when I needed my best friend, they chose to attack our friendship, while I was defenceless. I looked Sammy directly in the eye and I said to her;

"Do you honestly think I would ever do that to you?"
"I've had your back every time they bad mouthed you and you're choosing to believe a lie, from people you know aren't really your friends." This hurt my feelings so much because Sammy and I were friends for over six years by then. Everything they told Sammy was a lie, but she didn't care, she wanted to fit into the clique so bad she disregarded our friendship in an instant. The only reason she wanted me to go in her room was because she wanted to confirm that I wouldn't go and tell her parents all the things she didn't want them to know.

This made me realise, Sammy didn't know me at all. I wasn't the kind of spiteful person to hurt her, even if she was hurting me. This situation broke my heart; I was supposed to be looking after myself and not getting upset. I still had the patch on my eye, and it was within the two weeks where I had a high risk of blindness or infection. But my friendship with Sammy meant the world to me, so much so that I put her first, before my own health. I broke down so badly and was crying so much I could barely breathe.

She said she didn't want to be friends with me anymore because now she finally felt accepted into the organisation. When I left her room; my mum kept trying to get me to stop getting worked up but I couldn't. I didn't understand how this was happening to me. Was being popular so important that she would throw our six year friendship away. We had been through so much together; I was always there for her. But when I needed her to be there for me, that was how I got treated. I never told her parents or anyone anything else after that day. This didn't stop matters from getting worse for me though, as her sister began harassing me.

See, although I still lived at my parent's house, I had my own phone line in my room. That way I wouldn't tie up my parent's phone line when I was on the internet. I couldn't understand why things continued to escalate when I kept to myself. Her sister would call my personal line and leave horrible messages on my answering machine. She would say things like;

"Why don't you go fix your ugly disabled self."

I couldn't handle any more of these messages; every time my phone rang my emotions would go into overdrive. I needed to look after my health so I let my mum and dad hear the messages on my machine. My dad got so angry that he asked me for her home number. He called, spoke to her parents, and he told them to tell their kids to stop harassing me. I felt so pathetic that my dad had to fight my battle for me, but the end of my relationship with Sammy destroyed me.

What did I do to deserve this?

After all that happened I completely pulled away from the organisation. I valued my friendship with Sammy and those few people destroyed it, and they did it when I was at one of the hardest times in my life. Granted Sammy allowed it to happen too, so obviously she didn't care about me as much as she cared about being popular. It dampened my desire to be a part of something I didn't even feel like I fit into, because I was the only one like me and I was so different. There was no way I would throw my best friend under the bus just to be around people my height, it's not like my height was ever something I focussed on, anyway. I couldn't believe it was so easy for her to choose popularity and throw me out like yesterday's garbage.

'Such is life.'

Of course, I understand that not everyone in the organisation was involved with this blow up. But because it's such a close knit group it wasn't worth it, or healthy for me to put myself there, just to be a target. It wasn't adding value to my life, if I was constantly feeling judged and out of place.

I remained friends with certain LP's that weren't involved, mostly with people who lived in other states. We stayed in contact either online or over the phone; but I stopped going to events completely. If people wanted to be my friend they could be, it'd just be outside of the organisation. The sad thing was, later on I found out, as soon as those people knew they ruined mine and Sammy's friendship, they ditched her.

Let me make something clear, I don't place any blame on the organisation itself. It boils down to those few people who tarnished my experience. An experience that could have been so positive if those few people would have welcomed us both. There was no way I would stoop to such a low level or change myself to be a puppet on a string. If people can't accept me for me and my uniqueness, then so be it. I've never been the type of person to follow trends or others. People should never make you feel like you have to change who you are to fit in.

Everyone in this world wants acceptance, no-one should ever be pushed into feeling like who they are, isn't good enough. Being cruel to others and ruining friendships to achieve acceptance doesn't sit well with me. That to me isn't genuine; I want people to like me for me, isn't that all anyone wants?

I feel as though this is where others like me or with disabilities might struggle. They desire acceptance so much so, they allow others to manipulate situations just to fit in. The older I get, the more I realised this is a constant issue for many people in life.

How a person handles these types of situations, will say a lot about their character. At the end of the day, my intentions are good towards how I approach everything in life. I could have easily taken the low road and caused trouble for Sammy, but what she clearly didn't realise was I loved her like my family. When people choose to hurt me because of their own insecurities, then I am better off without them in my life. All we can do in life is put our best foot forward, do things with the right intentions and a pure heart then let God deal with the rest.

Chapter Twenty-One

S-U-G-A-S-U-G-A

We have finally reached a time in my life where I can share the steps I took to make my greatest passion in life a reality. A time where I put myself out there, and chased my wildest dreams; by following my heart with my music. When I was in grade five and six I tried to play many instruments in our school band. This proved to be a difficult task for me, to find an instrument I could play with all the limitations in my joints. After many attempts of trial and error with a flute, clarinet, piano and guitar to name a few, I finally picked up a cornet. The cornet is a smaller version of a trumpet and I found it to be the most practical instrument for me to learn. I didn't need to stretch my fingers too far in order to hit all the notes and it was great for exercising my lungs. I played cornet with the school band for almost a year.

Then once we moved to Malta, I continued to play and learn trumpet with the band club in our village. It was a different experience, but unfortunately when the band played during the feasts I could never join in; because they walked through many streets of the village as they played. This would have been too difficult for me because I get tired walking even the shortest of distances.

By the time I was fourteen I found what I consider being my truest form of expression, as I began writing poetry. It wasn't long after, I began to turn those poems into song lyrics and heard melodies in my head. From the age of fifteen onwards while I was in high school, I took music as an elective class. This proved to be an even bigger challenge as my teacher was very insistent in me learning piano, but I struggled to play using the correct fingers. The teacher wasn't very lenient in allowing me to find my own way of adapting, so I barely scraped through music class. Whenever I needed to complete practical exams and I could use my voice as my instrument, it's exactly what I did. During that time I participated in performance evenings and singing the Australian National Anthem in assembly.

At seventeen years of age I joined a group of four other girls and we did gigs at clubs and shopping centres. Sadly, once high school was over everyone in the group went their separate ways. I finished high school at the end of 2000; although right before I left a few teachers already knew of my poetry writing. A teacher then asked me if I would be happy for one of my poems to be entered into a NSW Department of Education and Training magazine. The magazine was distributed throughout the NSW Education and Government Departments.

Obviously I was honoured my teacher thought my poem was worthy of being entered into such a magazine. The content in the magazine was filled with articles that promoted many positive stories about people with disabilities. Even though the poem that was chosen by my teacher was written by me a couple years before, when I was much younger, they still wanted to submit it to be entered. By the time it actually got published I had left school. It was published in 2001; the cool thing is it can still be found floating around to this day.

The poem that was published was called 'Feelings.' Yes, there were a few errors in the original poem that was published; I'm not sure why my teacher never allowed me to correct it first. Originally when it was written I was fairly young; actually it was my very first poem I had ever written. So why don't you continue onto the next page and you too can have a read of my poem.

S-U-G-A-S-U-G-A

FEELINGS:

As I lay on my bed and stare at the ceiling,
I find all the emotions I'm feeling.
Frightened, afraid, of what I may find,
Floating visions; in my mind.

Visions of people laughing and staring,
I can't take all this pain I'm bearing.
Why are they laughing? Is it what they see?
I guess they think they're better than me.

Guys think you're not even
good enough to get to know,
So they take one look, and
decide to go.
Girls are the same,
You're always to blame.
You're not good enough to fit in their gang,
They're always ready to blow you up with a bang.

One day I hope to be seen as a person with a name...
Like, there goes Rachael, Jackie or Sam,
WELL, MY NAME'S FIONA AND I AM WHO I AM!

It wasn't until I was nineteen that I decided to follow my dreams in the biggest way possible. I was tired of people telling me I would never achieve the dream of creating my own album. By this time I had a decent collection of poetry I'd written and ideas for how they would sound if I turned them into songs. I would no longer take no for an answer. Fortunately, I received some financial support in the beginning, from an organisation that supported people with disabilities after they finished high school. They also assisted me in finding a home studio to record in. But half way through the recording process I was advised they could no longer help with finances or my musical endeavour; so I proceeded on my own. I began recording in March 2002 and spent as much time as possible in the studio, so that I was there for every part of my production. When I wasn't in the studio, I was attending a college course on music in the business industry. Finally I completed and released my first single independently in September 2002;

'My Turn To Fly.'

I was extremely excited; straight away I began performing my own song in clubs, which created some media attention. Once my single was in my possession I went to our local radio station and met with one of the station managers. I asked him if he would consider playing my song on the air. After listening to it, he was excited not just to play my song but also to do a radio interview with me. My first radio interview was so much fun and then being in the studio when he played my song on the air was such a thrilling moment for me. He asked me if he could keep my CD to continue to play it in his regular music rotation; as if I would say no. Although part of me wasn't sure how serious he was and if he would ever really play my song again. I would listen to the station in my car all the time when I'd be going out with my mum. A few days later when I was in the car, suddenly I heard the intro to my song. It was so cool hearing myself randomly for the first time on the radio inside my car. Instantly I turned it up and just looked at my mum all excited, I was really on the air, he actually played my song.

Shortly after I was interviewed by the local newspapers, they wrote an article about me and my music, and promoted my CD.

I felt like I was becoming semi-famous at that point. It was so awesome how people were so receptive to me and my story in such a positive way.

It was then that things took a frightening turn as I was in the middle of recording my album when my eye issue took control of my happiness. My mum was being so supportive of me recording my music. Even if when I was younger she didn't seem like she wanted to encourage it, so I wouldn't get hurt. Once she knew I was serious about recording my own music, she even drove me an hour each way, every time I went into the studio. The home studio I went to was closer to the city and although I had just gotten my own car, mum didn't want me to feel overwhelmed by the intense city traffic. There were many days when she would go to a nearby shopping centre for hours while I was recording in the studio. If that's not support I don't know what is, because I guarantee that can't have been much fun for her. I'm just glad that when I had decided I would really follow my dream, my mum came along with me for the ride. Let's step into the next chapter because this is where things really get interesting.

(Studio Session Times, 2002)

Chapter Twenty-Two

My Turn to Fly

The desire to meet others with my condition continued to play on my mind and seemed like an impossible mission. I hoped to learn of others someday, and their experiences. It would have been nice to have just one other person to talk to who I could actually relate to on a deeper level. It was something I had always wished for growing up.

I pestered my specialists all the time whether they knew of anyone else in Australia that may have been diagnosed. Unfortunately, the answer would always be no. Then when I was in my late teens, I searched the internet now and then. I held onto the hope that someday I'd discover something or someone. After I had finished high school, I spent a lot of time on the internet.

It wasn't until 2001 when I finally found a website that was dedicated to Kniest. This was the most information I had found so far. They even had a guestbook forum page on the website, where people could leave questions. I read through every post on the website desperately searching for that one post where someone might say they too had Kniest. Immediately I thought to myself, I have to post something, introduce myself and hope that someone will respond. I left my email address on the post just in case; I hoped someone would answer me.

It was Tuesday the 13th of November 2001 in the United States when someone finally responded to my forum post. As soon as I checked my email and saw the subject line 'I have Kniest,' I couldn't believe my eyes, the message read:

Hey Fiona,

Well, you are in luck. I'm someone who has Kniest too. My name is Jon and I live near San Francisco in California. I'm 26 years old and didn't know I had Kniest until I was 22. Because in 1997 I joined Little People of America (LPA) and found a lot of resources on the web concerning dwarfism types. There I was able to find out on my own that I had Kniest.

I'm 55 inches tall, 4'7" (I'm not sure how tall that is in metric.) I'm the oldest of 3 brothers and one sister; I'm the only person in my family with any form of dwarfism.

In this last year I have met a few people for the first time with Kniest. A couple of people of the guestbook and I have met one little boy in our region of LPA.

So that's a good start on what's about me. Write me back and tell me more about yourself.

Take Care,

Jon

That day and that email, was the beginning of the rest of my life, I was no longer alone in the world. Finally someone I could talk to who was old enough to answer my questions. Around this time I joined many groups online for people of short stature. Suddenly I went from knowing no-one, to finding a couple more people around my age that also lived in the United States. I had made two other new friends through these groups. They were both younger than me, a guy named Aaron and girl, Amy who had Kniest. They both knew each other well before I came into the online chat scene. Amy then told me of a convention that would be happening in June 2003. Not only would there be a convention organised by the 'Little People of America' but in 2003 they would hold a special Kniest weekend straight after the regular LPA convention. This would have been a dream come true for me, I so desperately wanted to go and meet Amy, Aaron and anyone else who might attend.

As soon as I had finished my first single CD, I decided I would attempt using any sales I made towards helping me raise funds to attend the convention in the USA. By doing it this way I felt like I was at least giving something back to people, instead of just requesting a donation. As soon as I told my mum about my idea, she knew how determined I would be to try to raise enough money to go and meet others like myself. So I kept doing performances often; many of my performances were within the Maltese community in Australia.

Back in the Spotlight!

My mum then suggested that she would try to get me an interview on a local Maltese TV show. As soon as she spoke to Charlie, the presenter of the show he was intrigued by my story. He spoke to me a couple of times on the phone and asked me many questions about my condition and the convention I was trying to raise money for. This was also during the time I was still waiting for my eye surgery, it was in December 2002. He then advised me of the date, time and place where he would record his next show in front of a live audience. He told me to take my backing track so I could sing my song and asked if I felt comfortable telling my story in front of everyone. I was so nervous thinking about singing on Television but excited for the opportunity.

The day had arrived where I was being interviewed on the Maltese show. When the time came and Charlie called me to go on stage and sit on the couch I couldn't believe it was actually happening. First, he interviewed me about myself and my music I had been recording, and then he asked me to sing. He handed me the microphone, and I sang my first single; 'My Turn To Fly' on live Television. After I finished singing, everyone in the audience clapped as I sat back down. Charlie then continued to ask me all about the LPA convention in the USA and why it was so important to me that I attend. Not even a moment later he handed me an envelope and told me to read it out loud. As soon as I opened the envelope I was filled with elation and couldn't control the tears from running down my face. I got up from my seat to give Charlie a hug and thanked him from the bottom of my heart. He was sponsoring my trip to the convention. The show and some of their sponsors would cover my flights, hotels and even send me on amazing tours.

I couldn't believe I cried on national Television in front of a live audience; but come on, can you blame me? I admit I was already emotional because I was still dealing with the possibility of losing vision in my right eye. But I was crying with immense appreciation as I realised it really was 'My turn to fly.' He then encouraged the audience to buy my CD so I could use the funds to have spending money for my trip.

Charlie invited me to many of his events and allowed me to sing as often as possible. On New Year's Eve I went with my family to a Maltese ball that Charlie had organised. It was at the ball where he gave me more exciting news. A famous Maltese singer, Renato, would be coming to Australia in the beginning of 2003. Charlie said that he wanted me to learn a Maltese song and sing it with him at one of his sold out shows. I couldn't believe how my life was playing out, all these positive things were happening for me at a time where I felt I really needed God's guidance. It felt like this was his way of letting me know things would work out.

In the beginning of 2003 while I was still waiting to have my eye surgery, before it got postponed until February; I felt like I got knocked further down to the darkness of harsh reality. We received a call from our family in Malta. They told us that my mum's brother, my uncle Joe had an accident on his forklift and passed away instantly. My uncle owned his own hardware shop, next door to my grandfather's house. When we were living in Malta I used to spend a lot of time in my uncle's shop. He also had a big garage where he would cut aluminium. My uncle was always so careful, but sadly this one day something must have gone horribly wrong. I felt devastated, especially for my mum, she couldn't even go to her brother's funeral now because I was about to have my eye surgery. She couldn't leave me here in Australia to go to Malta when she knew I needed her. I couldn't help but feel responsible for her not getting the chance to be with her family. She'd already missed her mum's funeral and now because of me she was missing her only brother's. I didn't know how to deal with my emotions and sorrow from knowing my uncle Joe was gone. He was so young at forty-six; I needed to find a way to express my feelings. So I turned to the only way I knew best. I wrote a song; 'Deep within my heart.' I wrote it specifically for my uncle Joe. While I was at college I asked my teacher to help me produce my idea for the backing track; I didn't want to waste any time. As soon as I went back into the studio, I played my demo for the producer. I asked him if he could play guitar on the track and let me record my vocal there. It was important to me, so I could add it to my album; which was exactly what I did.

Only days after my surgery, was the night I performed with Renato. My eye was still healing; so I wasn't allowed to strain my face, or sing as powerfully as I'd hoped. On the night before the big show I went to the hotel where Renato was staying and met with him and his musician Joe Brown. When Joe heard one of my other songs I had recorded for my album, he said he wanted to play it on piano and sing it with me. I was honoured to be singing my song with him, it sounded so much better as a duet. Joe and I sang it together at the show, right after I sang with Renato. It was so amazing and they were both so lovely. Renato and I sang 'Xemx' together. Xemx in English means Sun, but the song is actually more about love; the lyrics are truly sweet. I was so proud of myself; it was the first time I ever learnt and sang a song in Maltese. I couldn't believe that I got to sing it with someone famous too, what a blessing. Everything that was happening in my life during this time was like a dream. It meant the world to me to have my dreams unfolding before my eyes. There were at least 800 people at Renato's show, if not more, it was the most people I had sung in front of in my life. Unfortunately all the images I have from singing with Renato are taken from far away and not the best quality for print, and I can't exactly insert my VHS tape recording here. So instead I'm including a more recent photo of us together from when he came back to Australia a couple years ago I was fortunate to spend time with him again.

(Renato and I)

As the months were nearing to my big USA trip, I was almost ready with my album. But before I finished my album, I realised many of the songs I had written from poems when I was younger, were all filled with emotional, serious lyrics. So one day while I was sitting in my car waiting somewhere, I grabbed a napkin and a pen from my glove box and began to write. This was when I came up with a fun end track for my CD.

'SugaSuga Lovin,' because nobody does it like I do...

Aha, that's right that's me...

If you can't tell it's an R 'n' B track. I felt like I needed one confident track that could just end my CD on a positive note. It was actually so hard for me to keep a straight face while recording the vocals for this track. Seeing as I wasn't an overly confident Fee, I struggled to even take my own lyrics seriously. That was actually the birth of how I got my stage name, SugaSuga. Maybe now it will make sense to you as to why I called the last chapter,

S-U-G-A-S-U-G-A.

Chapter Twenty-Three

LPA in the US of A

The time had finally arrived where I had accomplished two of my ultimate dreams in the same month. It was June 2003, and I had just completed my first album 'I Am Who I Am.' I was thrilled that I finished it before leaving for my trip to the convention in the USA. Charlie had booked everything; my mum just had to pay for her share of the trip. I couldn't believe that my mum was coming with me on the trip of a lifetime. But of course she would be, if it wasn't for her I wouldn't have even been able to go. I'm sure it couldn't have been easy for her, but there would have been no way I would have wanted to go without my mum. Charlie came to the airport the day we were leaving for our trip so he could do a follow-up story on his show. He told me to make sure I took plenty of footage with my camera so he could re-interview me on my return.

The first main stop on our trip after the layover flights was in New York City. What a long journey that was, when we finally arrived in NYC it was late at night. My mum and I both stayed at my friend Aaron's place for our first night in America. It was so surreal; Aaron got to be the very first Kniest person I ever met, physically in person. Naturally, even though we arrived fairly late at night we couldn't help but chat for hours. The next day we left for our flight to Boston to begin our amazing LPA experience. As soon as we arrived and I was walking into the hotel lobby there were already so many little people scattered throughout the hotel. I was looking for a familiar face; either someone I had gotten to know online or some of my Australian friends that I knew were going to be there. It was such an amazing week; we had also booked some of the organised tours around Boston. Such as the Salem witch tour, a city tour and even a whale watching tour. Unfortunately, on the day of the whale watching tour I was feeling so unwell and sore, I had to tell my mum to go see the whales without me so we both wouldn't miss out. I was pretty devastated because it was something I was really looking forward to. Each night during the convention there was a DJ in the big conference hall of the hotel. The nights were so overwhelming, there were so many little people everywhere, just having the best time. My mum and I would go every night to join in with the partying.

As soon as I knew I was going to LPA I even registered to sing at the conference talent show they were having. The day of the talent show I was so nervous, see right after my eye surgery I had a new issue that developed. When they had placed the breathing pipe down my throat during surgery, they used one that was too thick. This created a problem because of my neck issues and respiratory situation. My wind pipe is actually very narrow compared to most people. Upon taking out the pipe before I woke up, they scratched part of my internal lining. Every time I ate rich, saucy or acidic food or drink I always felt sick. I used to joke that it was like a fake pregnancy because it lasted nine months before it stopped being a constant daily battle. Right before I went on stage I was feeling terrible. I prayed that I could just get through my song without humiliating myself in front of hundreds of other little people.

Each time I would get on stage it was like I became a whole different, more confident Fee. Without prior planning as soon as I walked out with the microphone in hand, in front of all those little people, I said;

"Ya'll ready for some SugaSuga from Australia."

Oh, my goodness!

What was I thinking? That could have bombed and been such an embarrassing moment for me. Thankfully, it wasn't, everyone in the room actually cheered; phew!

It was one of the greatest highlights singing in front of so many little people with different forms of dwarfism. Of course, the other major highlight was being amongst other people that had Kniest like me. Who truly looked like they could pass as my brothers or sisters; as we share a lot of similar physical features.

Unexpected Dream Come True

One day during the week of the convention, I was passing through the lobby, when from the corner of my eye I noticed someone famous. I feel I should provide a bit of a back story before I tell you who I saw. When I was still in my final years of high school, a movie came out called 'Simon Birch.' The first time I ever saw the movie, I fell in love with it immediately. My best friends knew it was my favourite movie, likely because I wouldn't shut up about it. On my seventeenth birthday one of my friends, even bought me the soundtrack CD. When I first saw Simon Birch it really resonated with me because the guy who played the character of Simon had a similar genetic condition to me. I felt like even his mannerisms were so mirrored to how I walked and appeared when I was younger, before many of my leg surgeries.

I won't ruin the movie for you if you haven't seen it; but I loved it. It made me laugh, cry, and I related in such a massive way. I never imagined I'd ever have the opportunity to meet him. Throughout my life I have met some really famous people, but I'd never act like such a crazed fan. That day when I saw someone famous in the corner of my eye, it was him, Simon Birch or should I say Ian; the guy who played Simon in the movie. Instantly it was like I had a burst of energy, and I didn't care if I looked like I was totally uncool for trying to chase Ian down; while he zoomed past me in a scooter.

Eventually I caught up to him; he was only around seventeen at the time and still looked exactly how he did in the movie. "Sorry to bother you, I know I probably sound like a crazy fan, but I've seen Simon Birch, and it's my favourite movie."

"Can I please have a picture with you?"

Ian probably thought I was some crazy Australian, but he was so sweet and got up to take a picture with me. Another time during the week, I finally had a piece of paper on me; I couldn't help but ask him to sign it for me too. Meeting Ian was such a highlight, literally no word of a lie, even to this day; if someone asks me what my favourite movie is, it's still Simon Birch. I can't bring myself to change my favourite movie, and so far no other movie has gotten to me in the same way that one did. It was such an unexpected dream come true to meet him in person on this very special trip.

(Ian 'Simon Birch' and I)

MY FELLOW KNIESTIANS

After the LPA week, the time had arrived for the additional Kniest and SED extended couple of days. Aaron and Amy, who I had already been talking to online, came to attend those extended days. Naturally I had already met Aaron on my very first night in the USA. At the meetings they held, I had the opportunity to meet even more people with Kniest. For once I didn't feel like such a rarity; I met Marylou, Margaret, Abbey and young Philip who all had Kniest as well. During the meetings I even had an appointment with one of the doctors.

LPA generally organise many medical forums beforehand that take place during the week of the convention. I took my x-rays and a bit of history with me to ask a few questions. I had always wanted to know if the decisions that were made for me were the right ones. Maybe things would have been done differently if I wasn't the only one my doctors knew of in Australia. Not to say that my doctors in Australia didn't look after me, but it was only natural for me to be curious. In fact the doctor I saw during this time had actually mentioned how he knew of my doctor in Australia and he felt confident I was in good hands.

The whole experience was so eye opening and I finally felt like I had found my place where I truly fit in. The conversations I had with the other Kniestians were amazing. It's so funny because I took so much footage on that trip of me even interviewing some of my new friends. When I watch those videos back now you can see, and hear the excitement in my voice as I spoke with each of them. I was so overwhelmed by this experience it was only natural to sound the way I did. The best part was feeling comfortable and being able to talk about things I never shared with anyone before, because I finally knew people who understood me in a way no-one else could. Sure my mum can empathise and understand to a degree because she has been there for me to see most of my struggles. But it's still a different level of understanding than someone else living with the same or similar condition. Having these new friendships with other Kniestians was like I found my long lost family.

(Photos of Abbey, Margaret, Marylou and I, in top images. Then a group photo from the Kniest and SED Meeting; from left to right: Amy, Margaret, Me, Abbey, Lisa and Philip; and Aaron in the front.)

HEADED TO THE BIG APPLE

As the little people convention and Kniest events came to an end, my journey still continued. My mum and I drove back with Aaron, to Aaron's parents place in New York City to stay awhile. Amy had arranged to spend the week with us there as well, so the three of us could enjoy more time together. It was such a fantastic week, Aaron and his parents were so generous and kind to us for letting us stay at their place. We went on some awesome touristy adventures during our week in NYC. Mum and I also went on the ferry to Liberty Island. Sadly, since it was after the tragic 9/11 incident they no longer allowed people to go up into the Statue of Liberty. Aaron's mum even took us past the site where the two towers were; such a sombre feeling came over me as we drove past.

We all went to the empire state building and his mum even drove us to the Rockefeller House in Sleepy Hollow. So many amazing memories were created during this trip; especially the joy of sharing it with my mum and my friends. Aaron's mum completely spoiled us, she made the best cookies and brownies; I was in heaven. The last day I spent in New York was the day before my 21st birthday and then I was off with mum to our next destination.

CALIFORNIA DREAMING...

We left New York on the 11th of July and headed straight to Los Angeles to spend a week right near Disneyland. My 21st birthday was absolutely the coolest birthday I have ever had. Who cares that I was twenty-one and completely considered an adult in the United States now; I had the joy of living my childhood dreams. Mum and I spent the day in Universal Studios; it was better than I could have ever imagined. We went on a tour around many of the movie sets, shopped, ate amazing, unique food and went on some fun rides. The Indiana Jones ride was so intense, you had to get on the rollercoaster while it was moving. Don't even ask me how I managed to get on; thankfully I didn't end up doing the splits. At one point you think a massive boulder is going to squash you, until suddenly, the coaster takes a sharp turn and you continued through the rocky ride. We were both screaming for most of the ride, but it was hilarious and so much fun. This brings me to a story I just have to share with you all and embarrass my mum a little; love you mum. *Hehe* ☺

It's Time to Get Mummified

At Universal Studios they had a walk through ride, I'm not sure it's technically a ride but I don't know what else to call it. I asked mum if we could go through it, it was pretty dark in there and since my recent eye surgery I couldn't see well in the dark. Everything became two dimensional for me in low lighting.

I held onto my mum's arm so I wouldn't trip over and break myself. As we began walking through these people behind us were being so annoying. They had obviously been through the ride before so they kept screaming in advance and yelling "he's coming." Sometimes it even made me scream before I even knew what the bloody heck was going on.

Suddenly, a man dressed up as a mummy jumped out right in front of my mum. Never had I heard her scream so loud, she probably deafened the poor guy. Mum was screaming, I was screaming, and this poor mummy was getting beat up by my mum hitting him with her handbag and my camera bag. OMG, I was crying from laughter; it was just too good; I wish someone was actually videoing us. This walk through ride was so well done; you even felt like those creepy skin crawling bugs were running on your skin. We finally got to a point where there was a bridge. Mum looked at me in complete seriousness and said;

"Fiona you better hold on; we better run."

"The bridge is going to break."

Oh mum, this made me laugh so much. As if the bridge would break like in the movie, everyone would get injured and sue the studios. But we ran across that bridge like we were on the run from the mummy himself.

When we walked out of the ride and back onto the street, both of us had tears in our eyes from laughing and screaming. Mum said she'd had enough, no more rides for her, it was too much. Even as I'm typing this, I can picture exactly how this moment played out, it was so funny. You really had to be there; thanks mum for the memory!

❖

The rest of our week in Los Angeles was awesome; we went on a Beverly Hills and Hollywood tour. We even had a five-day pass for Disneyland to go to both sides of the theme park.

When I arrived in LA, I also had called one of my new friends Brad, who I met during the week of LPA. He actually worked in Disneyland and told me to let him know when I'd be going so we could catch up. It was so much fun; even on his rostered day off he went into work to spend the day with me in Disney. He even arranged a pass for me, so we wouldn't have to stand and queue in the lines for hours. This was awesome because I never would have been able to see and do as much as I did if I had to stand in those long exhausting lines. Brad bought me this sweet Disney autograph book. We met all the Disney characters, took photos with them and they signed my book. We went on so many fun rides; I never would have done on my own. There was one in particular; it was a car you had to drive on a track, this ride was hilarious. It was only hilarious because it was such a joint effort. I have the long legs so I was responsible for the pedals, and Brad could see over the steering while I couldn't so he had to steer. Good times, and great memories; Brad even took me out bowling with his friends and we hung out outside of Disney. Getting to spend time with my friends along my amazing journey, and not just during the week of the convention really added to how great my experience was.

While I was in LA one of my other friends Matt, called me. I knew Matt from one of the yahoo groups online, six months before we met in Boston. He expressed that he wanted to fly down to LA while I was there, so we could spend more time together before I went home. As soon as he confirmed it was okay with me and my mum, he booked his flight. So for the last two days in Los Angeles, I spent them with Matt in Disney as well. Going on rides and screaming our faces off. Who cares that I was twenty-one and an adult, I was living out my childhood that I never got to have during my actual years of childhood, because of all the surgeries I had experienced.

When my California adventure was over we all went to the airport; Matt left to go back home while mum and I went onto Vegas baby!

What Happens in Vegas, Stay's in Vegas or Does It?

Our trip was almost coming to an end, but the Maltese television show that sponsored my trip had organised some truly amazing tours and locations for us. Before we were due to fly back home, we had three days to spend in Vegas. By this time we had spent almost a month in the United States, and I was running out of spending money fast. So much so, I didn't gamble all my money away, because I didn't have much to throw away by then. It was a good thing Vegas was at the end of our trip, eh! They timed it well though; it was cool to be in Vegas just after I turned twenty-one. While we were there, Charlie from the Maltese show had even organised for us to go on a helicopter flight over Vegas at night. I'd never been on a helicopter ride before and neither had my mum. This was such a fun experience for both of us to do together. I loved it so much; it felt so different from being in a plane. All the lights were beautiful to look down on. I wish I would have taken photos while I was up there, but I did take some amazing video footage.

We even went on a day trip to the Grand Canyon; we flew there on a small twelve seater plane. It was pretty loud travelling on that type of plane; but the pilot gave us these big headphones to protect our ears from all the noise. The Grand Canyon was so extraordinary and beautiful. When we caught a bus to the visitor centre I even saw a deer just wandering on the side of the road.

The month went by so fast, I couldn't have planned a better first trip experience. We went to five different states; I met Simon Birch, and saw some of the most iconic places in America, which was awesome. But most importantly I met my fellow Kniestians and formed friendships with LP's of all different types of dwarfism.

I couldn't have asked for a better gift and will always be grateful to Charlie, as well as all of the sponsors and Maltese community who helped send me on a journey of a lifetime. When I arrived back home from my big adventure in the USA, I was re-interviewed, and they showed video highlights of my trip. One day I was watching the show after I returned and they even had a Maltese dance group dancing on Television to my song 'My turn to fly.' I thought it was so cool and unexpected.

I knew then that this trip would not be my last, but for now it's back to life as we know it.

Chapter Twenty-Four

Into the Workforce

It's about time we discuss some of the force you need, to get into the workforce. When I was in grade ten at high school, it was compulsory for all students to do at least one or two weeks of work placement. Even though my passion was always in music and wanting to sing, I was still realistic enough to know I needed a back-up plan. My back-up plan was a fairly easy decision to make, considering I also had a very nerdy interest in computers and technology. I had no idea where I wanted to do my work placement, until I approached a major Australian home loan company. First, I had to see if they would let me complete work experience there. Fortunately, they were very welcoming; at first they gave me the regular filing everyone hates to do in an office. But once they realised I was eager to prove my capabilities they gave me actual responsibilities of typing up letters and other office admin work. I enjoyed my time at my first work placement, everyone there was pleasant to work with. Once I completed my work placement they even gave me a certificate and a really high review to take back to school.

When I was in my final two years of high school I was already thinking about what my next steps should be to enter the workforce. In all honesty I couldn't wait to be done with school and move onto other things in life. I also hoped that the workplace would be a place where I'd be taken more seriously. Somewhere I didn't have to deal with immature kids bullying me for my differences. Surely, adults have to have more respect than to continue that type of behaviour in the workplace.

I sought out and initiated many possibilities to complete further work placements at various office environments. There was one in particular I completed at my local council; it was probably one of the more interesting work placements. Once the boss realised I spoke another language other than English, she asked if I'd be willing to complete a task for their library resource department. I translated a kid's book from English to Maltese and also recorded an audiotape to go along with it. This was a neat project to work on; it was great being able to do something creative.

While I was completing my final two years of high school, I also wanted to get a jump start on college. I went to TAFE (Technical and Further Education) while still attending school; I was studying Information Technology and Hospitality. The first few units of IT were so easy for me because I already knew how to use the basic windows programs. One frustrating aspect I encountered was, the teacher wanted me to complete my keyboard speed and accuracy test using the correct fingers on specific keys. This seemed ridiculous to me, obviously with my joint restrictions in my hands I wasn't able to use the supposed correct fingers. It took awhile to convince the teacher that it shouldn't matter as long as my speed and accuracy was on point. I had my own way I adapted to; typing was actually quite easy for me to do without even having to look at my keyboard. But if I had to try force my wrist or fingers into a position I couldn't achieve then of course I would fail. This almost felt like the same scenario I went through with my music teacher in high school, when it came to trying to learn piano. Only difference was computers were something I was already good at and therefore I would not allow this to prevent me from passing.

Does it really matter how you type?

Shouldn't it only matter that I can?

Thankfully, my college teacher was easier to convince than my music teacher who wouldn't budge.

Before finishing grade twelve I was provided with the option to enrol in a post school program. The program was linked to a disability organisation, the one that actually assisted me in the beginning with my musical endeavours. I went ahead with enrolling myself into the program because I thought it couldn't hurt to have support until I got my foot in the door and into the workforce.

My doctors had also organised a Neuro-developmental test to assess my abilities and limitations. They were curious to know how I might handle situations in the work place. Doing tests like that always made me feel like they too were placing judgement on my maturity and intellectual abilities. I felt like everyone was judging my every move, reaction and word that came out of my mouth.

It was especially ridiculous when doctors or organisations thought that because I would let my mum come into these appointments with me it somehow made me less independent. But when an average height person does this for moral support or because they have a good relationship with their mum, no-one blinks an eye. My mum never came with me to work placements or to college, and she wouldn't be going with me to the workplace either. These statements bothered me though because I love my mum and I didn't feel like she was there because I couldn't do it on my own. She was there because I wanted her to be and they weren't situations where it mattered to them if she was or not.

It was actually quite stupid sometimes, because they would make these statements but then instead of talk to me, they would direct their questions to my mum. She would then have to say; "why are you asking me? Fiona is right there."

In all honesty sometimes I would ask my mum to come with me, especially when I knew parking in these places was ridiculous. This allowed her to drop me off near the front door, rather than me trying to find parking *(when I did start driving)* and kill my body having to walk a terrible distance. If anything I was, and am grateful to my mum for doing things like that for me, to spare me additional pain. I didn't consider her being mindful of my needs as her not allowing me to be independent.

When I finished high school, I continued my studies at college. I went on to study and complete certification in Digital Media, as well as Music in the Business Industry, and a few other computer administrative courses. Once I had completed my computer studies and my music passion projects I was pursuing, it was time to step into the workforce.

The hunt for a job had begun; I wasn't sure exactly what type of job I wanted, I only knew I wanted to find a job that wouldn't be too physically demanding. I searched online and in local newspapers for any office jobs I felt qualified to do. When I saw a job I was interested in, I'd call and express my interest and ask if I could send them my resume. I knew getting my first job would be hard until someone would be willing to give me a chance. The one thing I always struggled with was, knowing whether I should disclose that I was a little person or a person with a disability. After discussing it with various people I decided that it shouldn't matter if I mention it, maybe then they would put me in the too hard basket. Technically, by law it's discrimination to not give someone a job because of a disability. Plus, it's not like I was applying for unrealistic work.

When I went for my first job interview, I had already sent my resume and spoken to the boss on the phone. Classic example of people judging me for my disability came from this experience. When I spoke to her on the phone, she seemed very interested in interviewing me, even mentioned how my certifications and previous work placements were a great start. She seemed positive that I would be the right fit for the job position they were hiring for. As soon as I walked into her office and introduced myself; I saw her face change right in front of me. Immediately, I could see the judgment she was placing on me, it was written all over her face. She hesitated, looked me up and down, and then told me I wasn't what they were looking for. Suddenly, she had someone else who they were going to fill the position with. I knew this was just her way of not dealing with the elephant in the room. It's funny how I'm a little person yet I can also be the elephant in the room.

(Sorry, I can't help but find humour in these situations.)
I admit though, at the time I was pretty hurt by what had happened because I knew why the door was being slammed in my face.

This didn't stop me from continuing the search, after many similar knock backs I finally got my foot in the door. I found a job in the newspaper that really interested me; it was only part time, for four hours in the afternoon, five days a week. I thought this would be perfect for my first official job; it would give me a chance to test how well I could manage. The advertisement specified that the job was linked through an employment agency. So I called and set up an interview, the person I met with at the agency was lovely. I explained to her how frustrating it was trying to get my first job and be taken seriously. The agency asked me to fill in some forms and set a time for me to complete a few computer tests. After all this was out of the way, they told me they'd get back to me if I had the job I was interested in. This seemed like a better way for me to avoid constant knock backs through multiple interviews. If the agency was to find a placement for me, I would be sent to work straight away without further interviewing processes.

After a few days had passed the agency called me back to tell me they were giving me the job I was after. They gave me the details of the company and told me what day I would be starting. Before I could begin work as a receptionist they asked me if I had a problem completing a criminal background check. Their reasoning was because the place I would be working at consisted of many kids coming through reception. This didn't bother me at all because I knew I didn't have a criminal record so I told them to go ahead with running my background check.

My very first job was great; I was earning $20 an hour which was amazing for my first official job. Being part time was a good option for me too, because it didn't put too much physical strain on my body. Everyone at the office was so nice, it was awesome; even the boss who had no idea I was a little person when the agency sent me was easy to get along with. The kids that came through every day were so polite as well, which was surprising because I feared it could be a repeat of my school days. I had no negative experiences, awkward comments or anything like that; they showed me a lot of respect.

One kid that came into my office with his mum seemed to gravitate towards me. Then one day his mum apologised in case he was bothering me and explained that he usually wasn't talkative to strangers. She continued to tell me that his auntie was a little person too and that could explain why he felt comfortable talking to me. My curiosity took over and I asked her, what his aunties name was; not that I knew many little people because back then I didn't know hardly any at all. *(No not every little person knows each other; as hard as that might be to believe.)* Although in this case it was an awesome coincidence. She told me her name, and I couldn't believe my ears. His auntie Michelle was once a friend of mine; we had met as kids in hospital when we were both undergoing different surgeries. For a while we were pen pals and even wrote to each other while I was living in Malta. Then with all my moving around and such we lost contact with each other. I handed her my number to give to Michelle so that maybe we could catch up again; what a random coincidence this was. Michelle has SED and was actually in the same age bracket as me, I was looking forward to catching up with her again.

After a few months I decided to leave my position as a receptionist because the boss wanted to hire me without using the agency. The only reason I wasn't up for doing so was because she wanted to decrease my salary by a significant amount, which I saw as a huge step backwards. I went back to the agency and asked them if they could find me another job. They offered me a temporary two week position in a company where they required people to do surveys. At first I thought to myself; 'Oh lovely, now I'm going to be an annoying person people want to hang up on.' But it was a job, and it was only for two weeks so I thought I'd give it a go. Funny enough a few days after starting, I was walking through the complex when a man called my name. I thought to myself how does someone know me here? Turns out it was the company Michelle's dad worked for. Seriously, what were the odds of me bumping into another family member of hers, it felt like a sign from the universe making sure we got back in touch with each other.

After my two weeks were up, it wasn't long before they had another short term work placement for me. Within the first week of my placement the boss was so impressed with how quick I picked up their company software; that he wanted to know if I was interested in full time employment. The only downside was they didn't have a full time job available at that particular location. There was an opening at the companies head office, which would be forty minutes away from my place.

The head office was starting a new credit check team within their company, and the position I was recommended for was to be one of their new credit check officers.

At first I thought to myself, this sounds great, but are they really going to hire me, someone with no credit checking experience?

When I went for the interview at head office, the boss was really easy to talk to; I didn't feel judged at all. The staff member who recommended me for the position had told her how well I had been doing. One thing led to another, and I was offered the position. They provided me with the training I needed for the first few weeks as they continued to hire people and put our new team together. The place I was working for was a major company that had stores Australia wide, but I was working in the main head office. The members in our team were each given regions to look after and mine covered all the store locations in Melbourne and Tasmania. I had slotted right into my role as credit check officer so well that when new people joined the team I became the go-to person who would train them. It was so awesome how much easier things were once I had my first job. All I needed was a chance to prove myself that I was capable like anyone else to do the job I was hired to do. No more agency work for me, now I was officially working full time in a good job. It was a struggle to get to that point but my determination and willingness to learn new things really helped to prove my capabilities; if only people gave me a chance.

Chapter Twenty-Five

Taking a Chance on Romance

I'm sure you are wondering right about now, where is the love? I know in my earlier chapters I had mentioned I hadn't had a boyfriend even in the beginning of high school. Funny enough when I was in Kindergarten I was popular with all the boys, I would joke with everyone and say I had four boyfriends. None of this was true though, did I think some boys were cute, of course I did; did I actually act on those thoughts, no way!

It wasn't until I was about sixteen when I had my first actual boyfriend. I was out at a Christmas party, with people from my school, some of their friends and many other people I'd never met before. During the night I was chatting a lot to one guy in particular. He knew I liked to sing, so he convinced the DJ to let me get on stage. It was around the time things were awkward with that bully at school; the one I completely lost it at when I reached my breaking point. Anyway, so I was having a deep conversation with this guy about many things when eventually he asked me if I'd want to go out with him sometime.

Truthfully I thought he was one of the sweetest guys, I actually couldn't believe he was asking me out. Not that I didn't think I was worthy of having a boyfriend, but I wasn't exactly out there or confident in that aspect of life. We dated for a while and went out with a group of my best friends regularly. Until everything came to a holt, and I was completely shattered. I found out he cheated on me with one of my best friends.

I never expected that from him or my friend. Clearly my best friend was willing to do things I wasn't comfortable with. Shattered doesn't even begin to explain how this made me feel about myself. What a terrible first relationship experience, it shut me down inside for quite some time. I never spoke to my previous best friend anymore either; right after he knew I found out, they started officially dating. It just would have been nice if he would have broken up with me first, instead of go behind my back and hurt me like that.

My second real relationship ended even worse than the first. Actually, before we got together, we were friends at school for quite some time. His best friend, who was also a great friend of mine, kept trying to encourage us to get together.

One Valentine's day at school, they were selling roses; it was then he expressed his interest in me. He gave me a rose and asked me if I would go out with him on a date. The relationship started out great, this one actually lasted about two years. We would go out over the weekend a lot with a group of our friends to the beach or the movies. He would spend time over at my parents place with me and I even went to his parents place a lot. We were still dating when we had both graduated from high school. He began work at an electronics store as a sales representative shortly after finishing school. Sometimes I would go visit him at work, until I noticed he was growing distant with me. A few of the guys he worked with began hassling him about how he was dating a little person; instead of defending me he started pulling away. Until it got to a point where I went to his house and confronted him about what was going on. He admitted he couldn't deal with the constant judgment he was copping from other people because he was dating me. I cried like an absolute idiot when I knew it was over. Sure, I didn't like people looking at us like we were a spectacle but I'd hoped he would have my back and defend me. After this relationship had ended, I completely retreated within myself.

Will anyone ever really love me for me?

Am I destined to be alone when it comes to love?

Will anyone see me for the loving person that I am and not my physical differences?

It made me feel like no-one in the average height world would ever truly accept me for who I am. I hated how insecure this made me feel about myself.

It wasn't until Sammy and I got involved with other little people that I realised how nice it was to talk to people at eye level. There were certain people I really connected with; mostly they lived in another state though. We became amazing friends, and it was then that my perception changed. Maybe it would be easier dating another little person? Maybe there was an added level of understanding that the average height guys couldn't see. Granted, I didn't grow up surrounded by little people guys at all.

A couple of LP guys expressed their interest in me; but I was never the type of person to go out with just anyone to avoid being alone. Even if I felt we connected well, sometimes I thought we were such good friends I didn't want to ruin our friendship in the way my last relationship ended.

It wasn't until I went to an Albury weekend organised by the little people organisation in Australia that I began to date a guy from Melbourne. Sometimes I would think to myself; 'Fiona what are you getting yourself into? Another state, long distance, this will be so much harder.' To top it off, part of me didn't like that I knew who his previous girlfriend was in the organisation. It's such a small community *(pun not intended)* it's hard to avoid those kinds of situations. We both visited each other but things got a little out of hand when he talked to me like I was his bitch. *(Sorry for the language but it's actually the most accurate description.)* Things ended with me having to stand up for myself in the most terrible argument I ever had in any relationship.

It really doesn't matter whether the guy is short or tall, if things are going to end badly, it will happen either way. I knew that just because I dated a little person, it didn't mean we would be perfect for each other. There were elements though, that made me feel more comfortable. Society see's an average height person with an LP and suddenly it's judgement central. But when society see's two LP's together, even if they are just friends, assumptions are always made that they are together. It's ridiculous how society put's specific people in certain boxes.

This type of judgement made me realise even though my first LP boyfriend wasn't the right fit for me, I still preferred dating LP's. Not because of what other people thought I should be doing, but because it was nice to be face to face when having a conversation. It also made me less insecure about whether they understood my limitations.

My relationship history and experiences I had could be compiled into another novel, if I was to delve into the depths of my heartaches. I feel like now is a good time to skip ahead, there may have been a few crazy relationship experiences in my past. Some not worth mentioning and others I could have definitely done without. It's time I share the most significant relationship I ever had, the one which completely changed my life in ways I never expected.

OVER LAND AND SEA

There were many friends I made through Yahoo over the years, specifically within the dwarfism groups. A female friend of mine had introduced me to a few other LP's that she knew. One guy I spoke to in particular, was always there for me, we would talk about almost anything and everything. We had been chatting online or via video chat to each other for five years as friends. We both knew we got along so well, but long distance would be hard, especially since he was from America, it seemed impossible.

Finally, we both decided we should at least meet up, we had been friends for so long, and it would be great to hang out in person. Even if nothing came of it, it seemed like the thing to do; we felt like we knew each other so well and had so much in common. He wasn't really involved in the LPA scene but because he knew how much I loved my first convention, he suggested we road trip there together.

Andy's passion for music seemed equal to mine; only I thought he was more talented than I was. He played drums, guitar, and piano. Sometimes he would play guitar or piano for me when we would video chat; I couldn't get over how talented he was. We made a plan, I took time off work and I booked a five week trip to the USA. This time I went by myself and ventured on the long journey to Pittsburgh, Pennsylvania.

It was the end of June 2006 on a cool summer's night when I landed in Pittsburgh airport. After almost twenty-four hours of travelling on a plane, I was completely exhausted. As I walked through the airport after passing customs I could see Andy walking towards me. I was so nervous; it felt like all the surrounding noise had vanished. All I could think about was; 'I wonder what's going through his mind, is he as nervous as me?' he sure looked it. When we finally came face to face, we gave each other what felt like the biggest hug. As we were talking and walking to his car, he asked me if I wanted to go check out Pittsburgh city before driving an hour to his parent's house in the mountains.

Naturally, even though I was exhausted from the flight, I was now running on adrenaline so I said; "Sure, that sounds fun." He parked the car, and we went for a walk down the city streets.

It was already dark before we left the airport, so all the lights were brightening up the streets, it was really beautiful. There was a gorgeous water fountain in the middle of where we were. It had coloured lights coming out through the ground that changed to the beat of the music that was playing. There were speakers throughout the city centre, on the light posts. It felt like a scene set from a movie, as we sat on a bench opposite the water. It was as if we were the only two people outside; we talked for what seemed like hours.

For the first time, I felt like Andy was more nervous than I was. This wasn't something I was used to, because it didn't feel like we were strangers. We already knew everything about each other before we even met in person. All I knew was, for once I wasn't troubled by the usual things that worried me. I felt like all my insecurities didn't exist around him.

After a couple days Andy and I headed off on our road trip to Milwaukee LPA convention. It was approximately a twelve hour drive; we stopped every two hours for food, to sight see or have a rest. Seeing as Andy was doing all the driving because there was no way I would drive on the wrong side of the road. The drive was amazing; we had a blast listening to my iPod through the car stereo; singing, talking and laughing.

The convention was so much fun too; I saw some of my friends I hadn't seen for three years. It was a different experience this time, firstly because my mum wasn't there; and secondly because we didn't stay in the main hotel. Andy and I stayed at a nearby hotel because at the time it seemed like a more affordable option. We were enjoying our time together so much I was dreading the day my trip would be over. While we were at the convention, my friend who actually had introduced Andy and I online was also at the convention. This was our first time hanging out in person too. She asked me if I wanted to go spend a few days with her in Buffalo after the convention, so we could spend quality time together. Andy was so nice that he offered to drive me four hours each way for me to go spend time with my friend. We had arranged that I would make the trip to see her after my birthday because Andy really wanted to spend my birthday with me.

The morning of my birthday arrived; we were already back at Andy's parents' house in Pennsylvania. At the time Andy was working night shift, so I was waiting for him to finish work. It was eight o'clock in the morning when he came into the room where I was staying. He gave me flowers, an awesome iPod pillow (in my favourite colour too) and some other cute little gifts. Never in my life had I been so spoilt by anyone, I surely didn't expect to be spoilt, but it was really sweet. Everything about Andy felt so different to anyone else I ever knew, he was caring, loving and so genuine. We connected on a level I didn't know existed, and I knew he felt it too.

Before he took me to my friend's house in Buffalo, he asked me how I would feel if he wanted to fly back to Australia with me. He told me, he just knew what we had was special and he was willing to quit his job so he could stay the maximum time a visitor's visa would allow. Of course I wanted him to come back with me, but he didn't even have a passport yet. How on earth were we going to sort everything out in time for him to fly back with me?

He filled out his passport straight away and paid extra to rush the process along. Now we just had to wait for it to arrive before we could book his flight.

In the meantime he took me to Buffalo where I spent almost a week with my friend. When he came to pick me up at the end of the week, he surprised me with flowers in a cute little vase and chocolates. I'm not usually a girly girl as I have professed a few times, not enough to expect gifts like that, but I appreciated them so much. These gestures came from his heart, he did them because he wanted to and it really made me feel special.

It felt like we were meant to be; miraculously he received his passport on time with a couple days to spare. Immediately we went online, and he got his visa approved, and he even managed to get a ticket for the same exact flight I was on.

I was so thrilled he was coming back to Australia with me; I was excited to get back home even more now. Also, because a couple days before we left my niece was born and I couldn't wait to meet her.

Things were going so well during the months Andy was in Australia. It was the first time I felt comfortable showing affection in front of my parents and not even caring how much grief they gave me about it. As the months passed it was almost time for Andy to return home. This prospect made me so sad; I had no idea what we would do once he left. I was so used to having him around, he really felt like my soul mate.

In all honesty, I didn't think relationships like ours existed until I was actually living it; let alone, I never imagined it happening to me. One day a few weeks before he had to leave, we organised a trip into the city. I wanted to take him up Centrepoint Tower in Sydney. We took my younger ten-year-old brother with us too. As we were up in the tower I noticed Andy and my brother acting a little strange. At one point Andy almost sat down next to me when I heard a loud crack.

"What was that?"

"Oh, it was nothing."

He looked so nervous about something, but I had no idea what was going on. Then as I sat on the edge of the window, in the tower; he gave my camera to my brother and asked him to take our picture. Next thing I knew Andy was down on one knee with a beautiful wooden box, and a gorgeous ring.

When he asked me to marry him right then and there; I was overwhelmed with emotions. Obviously I said;

"Yes!"

My brother was a brilliant photographer because he totally captured the moment. You could see my face was red, in shock and my eyes were filled with tears of joy. Mind you, the cracking noise was actually the ring box. *Oooops...*

My brother was in on the whole surprise, apparently so were my parents because he asked permission from them, before he asked me. Everything about the way he did things was so old school, chivalrous and sweet. I wasn't sure how we would cope being away from each other even more now.

Afterwards we began the process of applying for a fiancé visa. He had to undergo criminal record checks, medicals and so many processes. We had to prove our relationship was legitimate; it felt like the 'Never Ending Story.'

As the visa process was in the final stages, we were just waiting for his acceptance to come through. We got through it by chatting on the phone as often as we could. By the time Valentine's Day came around we were still waiting, but we knew it wouldn't be much longer. We had hoped we would be together to celebrate, but it didn't work out that way.

To my surprise Andy sent me the sweetest gift I ever received from anyone in my entire life. He sent me this beautiful bear that had a phone in his hand. As soon as you pressed the bear, the phone would ring, open up, and it sang; 'I just called to say, I love you.' If that wasn't cute enough on the inside screen of the phone there was a picture with 'I love you Fiona' written in the snow. It was winter time in America so he actually went through the effort of writing a message in the snow himself.

Seriously, how could I not feel blessed; by all the thoughtful and amazing ways he showed his love for me.

GROW OLD WITH YOU

You know, as much as I never thought I would end up married, I used to actually joke about it. See, Kniest causes all my joints to be larger than average, right. Therefore, my knuckles look extremely arthritic; the only normal looking knuckle was my ring finger. This led me to believe, maybe I was meant to get married someday. How could it be the only finger unaffected by my joint issues, it was a pretty crazy coincidence, if you asked me.

As we were leading into the months of our wedding, my parents were such a huge support to us. They fixed up our old house we lived in when I was ten-years-old and made it more accessible for us to live in once we got married. We were both so grateful for everything my parents were doing for us, without them everything would have been an even greater struggle.

A couple of weeks before the wedding we decided to move into our place early. This made it easier for when Andy's parents came down, because then they had a place to stay with us.

It was the 7th of July 2007, and it was the day every little girl probably dreams of. Although in my case, I was having a serious meltdown in the morning. I've said many times I'm not usually girly, so I really didn't own any dresses as an adult. I began to have a panic attack that my dress wasn't sitting properly or I looked terrible. Don't ask me what was wrong with me, because I knew I loved Andy more than anything in the world. It was probably a case of those wedding jitters people talk about.

We had a small intimate wedding, considering most our extended families lived overseas and couldn't make it to our special day. It was a beautiful celebration, everything turned out great. We were grateful that Andy's parents were at least able to come down to Australia for our special day.

If you didn't think Andy could get any sweeter, he could. He knew how much I loved the song from the movie; 'The Wedding Singer.' To my surprise he sang it to me, while playing guitar at our wedding reception. Andy practiced when I was at work and he had a rostered day off, so I never knew what he had planned. You know the song Adam Sandler sings to Drew Barrymore on the plane at the end of the movie. It was perfect and completely adorable.

If you don't know the song I'm talking about you should look it up, I felt it was so appropriate and sweet. I would have loved to include the lyrics with you all but I'm not best friends with Adam Sandler to get his copyright permission.

*(Princess Fiona, Proof that I am not an ogre. LOL
I know, I know, my lame jokes just keep on coming!
There had to be at least one Shrek reference somewhere.)*

Life is Not a Fairytale...

Chapter Twenty-Six

Broken and Alone

Immediately after we got married, other things in my life were changing. My specialist took me off of Fosamax because my bone density had increased by twenty percent, and by then I was on it for almost nine years. Profs was concerned that some results had come back where as much as Fosamax helped bring up bone density; it also carried risks of hip fractures. He thought it would be best to see if I could hold the bone density I had gained without continuing the medication.

Not even two weeks after I got married, we received terrible news that my grandfather in Malta had passed away. He was very sick for a long time, and he struggled greatly when his son, my uncle Joe, had passed away a few years before. This news absolutely shattered my heart, he was my only living grandparent I had in my life and now I had no-one. My poor mum, had lost her mum, her brother and now her dad. I was already sad he couldn't make it to my wedding because he was so sick. Losing my grandfather when we did, really took me out of my exciting newly married state. Of course, I still loved Andy and was happy to be married, but I felt like my heart was crushed while I mourned the loss of my only active grandparent in my life.

Almost a year into marriage life, my nephew was born. I became privileged enough to be an aunt again, and a godparent.

Three years into our marriage was when my fairytale I had been living was over, and I felt so unloved. I would drive Andy to work, say; 'I love you,' as he got out of the car, but I was left with nothing in return. This made absolutely no sense to me.

How did we go from those people we were, to this?

The majority of our marriage was amazing. Andy would leave notes in my lunch that I'd discover at work, we went on weekends away together; it was almost perfect. We never fought about anything stupid and had such a strong connection. I didn't understand where all of that went, almost in an instant. It was like I had entered into the 'Twilight Zone.'

Was this really what we had become?

Two people living as roommates in a house?

When I think back to what should have been one of the most important special days of my life, all I feel is sadness and disappointment. The song he sang for me was so special and those lyrics meant everything, but now I'm left realising they were just words. Words, I regarded as a promise of our future, to grow old together.

I couldn't take feeling the way I was, so I confronted the issue as I do with everything in life. But he didn't really want to talk about it. Suddenly, he wanted to move back home to America.

I felt like there was something he wasn't telling me.

Did I do something I wasn't aware of?

I'm not a mind reader though, so if he wasn't going to tell me, how would I ever know? For those whole three years, I asked him if he wanted to go visit his family. I would have been more than happy to go for a vacation and take time off work. Each time I asked he would say 'no;' but now all of a sudden he wanted to go back home? Right when we had actually booked flights for later in the year to go visit his parents. But then he said that wasn't enough, he didn't just want to go for a holiday. He wanted to move back there, and he didn't ask me to go with him. Basically it was over, and at the time I can honestly say I never saw it coming. I was shattered inside; he distanced himself so much from me; yet he begged me not to say anything to my family. Do you know how hard it was, going to my parents place and trying to pretend like I was okay? I felt completely dead inside myself; I wasn't great at faking my emotions so it was easier to stay away. Maybe he didn't want me to say anything to my family, because he thought they would want to know why.

For almost two months I tried so hard to keep all my hurt inside. I loved him so much, and I never wanted to be someone who got married and divorced, like it was nothing. I took our wedding vows so seriously, and I had no valid reason to help me comprehend why he wanted to throw all that away. We went through so much to be together, and I could have sworn he was my soul mate; but maybe I wasn't his.

I didn't know what to do about my flight I had booked for August; I would have never been able to get a refund. The thing that was killing me inside even more was how easy it all seemed for him. He just wanted to wait until we were meant to leave and go home then. But I couldn't keep living like that and feeling my heart rip into pieces, knowing my happily ever after was no more.

That was when I decided since I couldn't refund my ticket, I would change the destination and go to another LPA event. It had been another four years since I had been or seen any of my friends; I thought the distraction would do me good. Plus, there was no way I could face him day after day, and keep living this lie. I suggested we both change our ticket dates and he could leave after I was already gone to LPA. In my mind, I knew I didn't want to be there for that awkward, goodbye. I expressed to him that I needed to talk to my mum about it because it was driving me crazy, and he was just going to have to deal with that.

After I told my mum, I asked her to promise me she wouldn't get involved because I didn't want things to be worse.

So I left a few days before he was meant to leave and I went to the convention in Nashville Tennessee. Even though I had no reason behind why any of this was happening and I was shattered; I still made my mum promise me she would at least drop him off at the airport. I didn't have the heart to be cruel even when I felt confused and broken.

THE DECISION THAT ENDED IN DISASTER

The Decision that ended in disaster doesn't even begin to explain what I am going to share with you now. During the week I spent in Nashville, I had decent moments with old friends, but I even had moments that had me feeling more hurt and broken inside. I felt like I was already at my lowest point trying to distract myself from all the heartache I was feeling, when I ended up in a huge argument with a really good friend of mine. He had found out I was separating from my husband, and I knew he had feelings for me for the longest time, well before Andy and I had gotten together, but to me he was like family. It was then that he gave me an ultimatum that either something had to happen between us or we could no longer be friends. I was an emotional mess and if I would have allowed anything to happen between us then it would have been for all the wrong reasons. It broke me inside that he couldn't understand that it really wasn't the right time to put that kind of pressure on me. So as much as it hurt me I told him, "I guess we can't be friends then." He chose the day before my anniversary to get into the worst screaming match with me. He probably didn't pay any attention to what the date was because it wasn't as relevant to him; but I couldn't seem to clear my head. I couldn't believe this was all happening during my weakest emotional state. Right then I needed my friend more than anything, and I wished things could have been so different. Maybe then I wouldn't have gone on to make one of the worst decisions in my life.

It was the night before the convention was going to be over and I would be returning home. I was on the phone to an LP friend of mine that lived in New Jersey when I was explaining to him that I wasn't ready to go home. When I thought about returning to an empty house all by myself, knowing everywhere I'd look would be full of memories; I couldn't do it. I just wasn't ready to face my new reality. Next thing I knew I was on the phone to the airlines changing my return date and booking a flight to New Jersey for two weeks. Then I made the decision to email my boss and quit my job on the spot. I had only just started working at a new place with a boss who knew me from a previous employment but I wasn't happy where I was, so that was that.

Nothing in my life made sense anymore, I needed a fresh start. It wasn't until I made all these decisions that I contacted my mum to let her know I wouldn't be coming home as planned. At the time all this was going on, I didn't really want to talk about it with anyone, not even my mum. I didn't think she would understand that I really needed to do this for myself. Of course I knew my problems would be waiting for me, the minute I got home. But I knew I just needed more time to myself, without any real distractions. My mum seemed so angry with me on the phone; she couldn't understand why I was throwing everything in my life away. Why I didn't just let her be there for me, but obviously she couldn't stop me from making the decisions I had already made.

I went to New Jersey for two weeks, and I spent time with my friend Trevor on days he was free. Most of my time was spent in the bookstore next door to the motel I was staying in. Had I not had a massive fight with one of my best friends I probably would have asked him if I could stay with him for a while. Although having a lot of alone time was what I needed for my own sanity. Right then I couldn't deal with having to listen to everyone else's opinions on how I should be dealing with my feelings.

Well, I couldn't escape reality forever, there were only four hours left before I had to make my way to the airport. My mum had called me to make sure everything was okay, and I told her I'd message her as soon as I land at my first stop. Trevor and I were just killing some time before I had to go to the airport, so we went to a shopping centre.

After some time had passed, we were ready to leave the shops, so I could make my way to the airport. Little did I know the event that was about to unfold would change everything in my life forever. As I was turning towards the direction of the escalators to leave, in a split of a second, I felt a hard nudge against my right shoulder. The next thing I knew I was completely airborne and smashed onto the concrete floor of the shopping centre. I landed directly on my entire left side of my body. It all happened so fast I had no time to react; it was like no other fall I had ever experienced in my life.

I'd never fallen on the side of my body, I usually fall forwards and my body reacts. Usually I'm left with enough time to place my arms in front of me to break my fall. It's like an automatic Fee reaction, I may not be able to stop every fall but I generally can stop any serious damage. The next thing I knew this American woman was screaming;

"Call 911, Call 911."

I just laid there stunned for a moment on the floor, unable to believe the current state of events. As I lay motionless, I said;

"No, no, please don't call anyone, I'm fine..."

So many thoughts were running through my mind over the next few seconds. All I knew was I was in America and calling 911 meant insane medical expenses I wouldn't be able to afford. I looked over at Trevor as he stood above me; he looked like he was freaking out more than I was.

"I'm fine, accidents happen, don't worry."

Little did I know I wasn't fine at all! Quickly my thoughts turned to my mum; I had just spoken to her.

'Oh, My Gosh, mum is going to kill me; I need to get on that plane and go home.' Even though I hadn't said it out loud, I could feel it deep down; I wasn't going to be able to get on the plane. Still in a state of shock I wasn't able to judge how bad things really were. From past experience, I knew before I moved I had to allow my body a few minutes to assess if I could even get up. This was definitely a unique situation, but how serious it all was, still felt like an illusion.

When I began to realise I couldn't move, I asked Trevor to call my mum and tell her what had happened. My mum was flipping out on the other side of the phone; she couldn't understand what happened since she had just spoken to me. She was totally losing it, obviously because she was on the other side of the world and couldn't do anything to help me.

I tried so hard to get up off the floor, but I couldn't move my left leg or bend it at all. My left shoulder was also hurting like hell; I couldn't put pressure on my arm to push myself up. Even though the pain started to hit me I still hadn't cried or anything yet. Security came with a wheelchair and it felt like hours for them to safely assist me onto the chair. They wheeled me out to Trevor's car, and he insisted on taking me to emergency.

I knew at that point I wasn't going home for sure but I didn't want to accept my current circumstances. As soon as we pulled into the emergency driveway of the hospital, the paramedics came to help me out of the car. When they realised I couldn't get out, they called for a stretcher. Right when they pulled me out of the car, I yelled out in pain, it was one of the loudest screams. Still in denial, there was not a tear in my eye; even though I was in agony. They rushed me into the ER to hook me up to morphine before they could arrange for a CT scan.

The nurses asked my friend to remove my earrings and necklace, so they wouldn't get lost in all the commotion. I told Trevor to make sure he closed the clasp of my necklace because I didn't want to lose my cross. *(Most people who know me well would know that I don't like to go a day without wearing my cross. I may not come across as someone who talks a lot about faith with friends or strangers I meet, but my faith in God means a lot to me personally. I'm just not usually the type of person that likes to bring it up in actual conversation.)*

It wasn't until I came back from my CT scan when the doctor came to speak to me while I was still in the emergency department, he said; "I'm sorry to tell you, but you have a broken shoulder and two fractures in your left hip and pelvic area." It was at that very moment that all the pain and all my emotions couldn't be held in anymore. I cried the most excruciating cry; my tears wouldn't stop falling down my face. Suddenly my focus shifted and I was more concerned with what my mum would say. She was already mad at me for extending my trip, I imagined her saying;

'Now look what you've done to yourself!'
As I laid there in emergency, I felt like my whole life was flashing before my eyes. I had hit rock bottom, it felt like my life was over; when suddenly a real overwhelming sombre feeling came over me. I heard family members surrounding the guy in the bed next to me praying as he flat-lined and had passed away. It was horrible hearing the machines go crazy, the family members crying; I had a horrible eerie feeling deep inside of me.

Was I next?

Was I going to die here alone, with no family beside me?

Why didn't I just go home when I was supposed to?

I know that might sound dramatic as you're reading this but I really felt like all the walls were closing in on me and my life was over. The first few days were the hardest, I had no-one to visit me, and even Trevor hadn't stopped by to see me.

I had so many issues, I was hallucinating and my pulse was going crazy. The nurses couldn't even find my pulse on occasion, and I had episodes where I struggled for oxygen. I thought I truly was going to die there in America, all alone. The worst part was my mum had other unexplainable things she was dealing with back home, so she couldn't fly to America to be with me.

All my medical problems I was having made matters worse, I'd message her to call me; and as soon as she called I'd hang up on her. I never meant to hang up; initially I wanted to talk to her. But I would panic with anxiety and I didn't even know what I was doing. Mentally, physically and emotionally, I had no control of anything in those moments.

The stupid thing was, my friend Aaron lived in New York, but I was so messed up, I didn't even think to have someone contact him. I felt like I had isolated myself from my closest friends because I didn't want them to know all the heartache I was going through. By now you can probably tell that I still would keep my issues to myself. I was broken, alone, and my whole life felt like it was falling apart at the seams, and had crumbled to the ground with me when I fell.

Chapter Twenty-Seven

Pick up the Pieces and Start Again

The decisions we make will either make us or break us. In my case, I made a terrible decision that I have to live with for the rest of my life. As I continued to lay in the hospital bed for days by myself, I was finally stabilising. I contacted Trevor because I hadn't heard from him and I really wanted my jewellery back. When he came to the hospital to bring it to me, he was acting really weird and distant. He handed me my earrings and my necklace, only for me to discover the clasp wasn't closed and my cross was missing. This upset me more than anything because my cross was given to me by a family member and had special significance behind it. But there was nothing I could do; he claimed he knew nothing about a cross. Trevor didn't stay at the hospital long, shortly after he gave me my things he left.

The doctors continued to send me for CT scans and sent my images across the country requesting advice on how they should handle my rare condition and current situation. I was at such a loss; how was I ever going to get home?

My hospital bills were piling up, higher than I knew I would be able to afford, and because I ended up in America longer than I had planned, my travel insurance had a loophole to where I would not receive coverage. Not only was everything in my life at the worst possible point, now I would be in debt to the United States.

When I was finally in a state where I was well enough to make sense and have a conversation with my mum, she suggested I call

Andy to see if he would fly home with me. This sounded like the worst option to me, but my mum was just pulling at straws because she wanted me home and she wasn't able to get to me. I told her there was no way I was going to call him. He left me; I was still an emotional mess and I couldn't handle him seeing me at my worst. I had left for my trip before he did so I wouldn't have to have that awkward goodbye, and now she wants me to beg for his help; I just couldn't.

Although, when Trevor came with my jewellery, I asked him to post a message on social media for me. I told him to only post on my page, that there had been a slight delay in my travel plans, and I couldn't respond to my messages.

Coincidently, Andy happened to see the post, as I hadn't removed him from any of my social media, or changed my details yet. This led him to call me on my American cell phone number. When he called, part of me didn't want to answer; I wasn't sure how I would keep it together. Immediately, he asked me if I was okay or if something had happened. As soon as I told him what was going on he asked if I wanted him to come help me. Part of me wanted to say no, I wasn't his responsibility anymore; I didn't want to be a burden to anyone. But then I also heard my mum's voice in my head and I wasn't sure how else I would get home.

There he was being the sweet person I knew I married, but I had to keep telling myself to pull it together. He insisted he was coming; he didn't have a job again yet so he said he would get on the next flight and come straight to the hospital. I couldn't help but cry on the phone and thank him for helping me, even though I knew he didn't have to. He could have easily just ignored seeing the message and went on living his life. Within a matter of hours after we hung up the phone he arrived at the hospital. At that moment we both realised if we wanted the hospital to let him stay with me then we needed to say he was my husband. If they knew we were newly separated they probably wouldn't have let him stay. That was actually harder than it might sound because I knew it would mess with my emotions down the line. Thankfully, they allowed him to sleep on a recliner next to me. As awkward and hard as this was for me being in this vulnerable state, I was grateful for his kindness.

Once he was there, things were easier for me because before he came the nurses always placed my buzzer on the side of my broken arm. This created many issues when I needed to go to the bathroom since I couldn't walk. There were times I probably looked like a crazy person, especially when I was hallucinating and screaming for a nurse so that I could go to the bathroom because I couldn't get to my buzzer.

I had been in the hospital for two weeks and because they weren't sure what to do they opted to leave my bones to heal on their own. Now that Andy was there, the moment I could force myself to sit up and tolerate the hip pain they'd let me fly home. Seeing as originally Andy had a return ticket to Australia I was able to amend the date on his ticket. I assured him I would pay for a flight back to America for him as soon as I was home. This was the hardest, strangest situation to be in because obviously we still cared a lot for each other. If we didn't he wouldn't have agreed to fly home with me, but it made it hard for me to ignore my feelings and I couldn't help but hope we could fix things.

The struggle is real I tell you, the last time I saw Trevor was one other time, when he came to take Andy to a pharmacy to get my medications for the flight home. That flight was undoubtedly a terrible experience, I hope to never repeat in my life. As I passed through customs in America, even though I had my discharge forms on me they continued to give me the most painful pat-down. Andy was pushing me in the wheelchair, and I had told security I was broken so they wouldn't put too much pressure on my broken bones. It was like they still thought I was faking it or something.

Did they care that I was broken?

No!

It didn't seem like it anyway because they continued to push and rub my body checking me, as if I was some criminal. It was horrible they even forced me to take my shoes off; when it actually took the nurses at the hospital forever to get them on with how painfully sore my hip made moving my leg even the slightest bit. This truly was such a challenge not to flip out and refrain from acting like a crazy person in the airport because they were hurting me. But obviously I didn't want to give them any reason to stop me from flying home.

EMBARRASSING STORY TIME WITH FEE AGAIN...

The worst thing of all was the hospital wouldn't let me leave unless I wore an adult diaper. They knew I was in for a long journey home, and I wouldn't be able to get up during the flight. I wore it because I had no other choice; but I did have a choice if I made use of it. So my stubbornness kicked in, and even though we were travelling for twenty-eight hours; I held it in the entire trip. This was a massive challenge because every two to four hours I had to drink to swallow a bunch of painkillers and blood thinner pills.

Speaking of blood thinners, those injections they gave me in the hospital to prevent blood clots were a nightmare. Since I couldn't get up at all they wanted to ensure I wouldn't clot. Every day they would inject me in my stomach, which truly was the worst injection I ever dealt with.

I was struggling on the flight home; sitting on the plane for so long was killing my hip. If I only had a broken shoulder, things would have been much easier. There were times of turbulence that made me so nervous and were painfully adding strain to my broken bones. I sat there with a panicked look on my face when Andy grabbed my hand and told me it would be okay. Even though things weren't the same between us it was nice to know he understood how much I needed comfort at that moment.

As soon as we landed in Sydney I wanted to go to the bathroom straight away, but the wheelchair assistance person who came to help me off the plane had been instructed to take me directly to my car. When I saw my mum I told her I needed to go to the bathroom, but she insisted we go straight to hospital. My specialist was in a panic after hearing of my injury and he wanted me to check-in immediately. This was terrible; the hospital was another hour drive away from the airport. How much longer could I hold it in? The bumpiness on the road didn't help at all either. As soon as we arrived at my local hospital, I told the nurses I needed to go to the bathroom but they insisted that I had to wait until I was registered in their system.

Oh, My Gosh, seriously!

It was at least thirty hours before I got to a bathroom, I don't know how I lasted that long. Once they let me go to the bathroom, I told everyone to just leave me alone. I knew I was being incredibly stubborn, but it was bad enough I was a mess. I couldn't stand having the embarrassment of knowing I peed myself. Sure, there was a diaper involved, but gross, then I'd have to sit in it and feel crappier than I already did;

No Thank You!

Everything Has Changed

The decision that ended in disaster changed my life forever. Trevor was no longer talking to me, which upset me more considering I never got mad at him for being the one who bumped into me. In all honesty, I wasn't even sure whether it was an accident or not. It felt like the type of nudge between friends, when you are mucking around. Maybe that explains why he couldn't face me; maybe he felt guilty? I really don't know, because usually when I walk I pay more attention to where I'm going. I wasn't looking at him to know how he bumped into me. There's a part of me that wishes I had access to video footage, if there were cameras in the shopping centre, which there probably were. Even if he was mucking around or it was simply an accident, I didn't get upset with him because he clearly wouldn't have intended or expected me to end up so badly injured. Maybe he thought I was going to sue him for damages or something, isn't that what many people think is the thing to do? What upset me the most was that I had lost a friend.

Had I been the one to cause injury to someone else, I would have been there for them everyday making sure they were okay. Especially knowing I had no family to turn to, and I was all alone in another country. How could he live with the decision he made to isolate me, instead of be there for me? I could understand if I yelled at him or blamed him, and even though it was technically his fault, I never once made him feel that way.

Andy on the other hand had really stepped up to the vows of; for better or worse. He decided to stay in Australia for almost two months, until I was on crutches and could care for myself again. He knew I didn't want to move back home with my parents so he felt it was still his duty to see me through this difficult time.

It wasn't easy for me though, because I knew he was still intending to leave and he didn't want to stay. I was so vulnerable having him help me in the bathroom, with showers and everything else because I couldn't move my arm at all, or stand up.

Never in my life had I felt so disabled, so incapable of caring for myself. The fact I knew we were still separating made me feel embarrassed him seeing me in that state, and helping me with such personal issues. Before I booked his ticket for him to return home to America I had asked him if he wanted to change his mind. If maybe we could talk about why he really wanted to leave in the first place; but he didn't want to. So I had to tell myself to let go, but it wasn't easy for me to comprehend when I didn't know what the reasons were.

Even though our marriage ended, and he left for good I can't hate him, I can't be mad. Part of me will always appreciate that when I needed him the most, he was there. It took time for me to get over everything, but what doesn't kill you makes you stronger.

It's a shame we didn't have our happily ever after together, but I don't regret the time we did have. I learned a lot about myself during and after all those life experiences.

Who knows where life will take me, maybe someday I will be fortunate enough to meet my true soul mate. Someone who will help me fight my dragons, so I can be released from my castle where I turn into an ogre every night. *Wink, Wink*

REWIND AND RESTART...

Shortly after I was out of hospital, I received a call from someone I had worked with in a previous place of employment. He was calling to see if I was working, or if I wanted to go work for him. He had moved on from our old company where we both worked at, and was now the manager of a new place. I explained to him how I would have loved to work with him, but I was in a bad way. After telling him what happened, he asked me how long I needed. I couldn't believe he was actually willing to wait for me for a month or two, until I was physically capable to try and re-enter the workforce.

Even though, the new job was much further than I would have wanted to travel for work, I couldn't complain. I needed all the money I could get thanks to the insane medical expenses I paid to the hospital in America. Plus, I knew we worked well together in the past, even though he wasn't previously my boss.

If it wasn't for his patience, I would have never been able to get my head above water again. I was also extremely blessed because my local church and a Maltese organisation assisted with helping me cover part of my medical expenses I owed to the United States. When I finally went to work for him, I was still undergoing physical therapy a few times a week. He understood my current medical situation and allowed me to ease my way back into work. He was such a godsend in a time I really needed it. Thankfully, my mum even sacrificed a lot of her time in the beginning when I still couldn't drive. She would come to my house and pick me up, help me get ready and drop me off at work and then drive all the way back again in the evening. So many times in my life when I've needed support, my mum's always there.

Unfortunately all good things must come to an end, the boss who hired me had moved onto a better opportunity that was even further away. This was when things became more difficult for me, another colleague had moved into his position, but she wasn't as understanding of my physical struggles. See, after I healed from that terrible injury, my body and limitations were affected in ways I wasn't before.

I lost range of motion in my hips and sitting for long periods was uncomfortable. Even my shoulder affected my abilities; I formed a large bone callus which was too risky to be operated on and shaved down.

I was being pushed even harder at work and given more responsibilities past my agreed job position. My body was struggling to push through the pain, in the way I had in the past and I wasn't sure what else had changed; but I didn't feel like myself anymore.

To top things off, another colleague began disrespecting me in the workplace and used the 'M' word in reference to me. The first time I heard her, I asked her politely to stop using that word period; and I explained how it wasn't acceptable. She continued to disregard my feelings and harassed me more. This forced me to talk to the boss, but unfortunately they were friends so I felt like I was talking to a wall.

It got to where I was tired of my physical struggle, and the disrespect that I was dealing with in the workplace was affecting my emotional state. The right choice for me then was to quit, I had to put my health first.

NEVER BE THE SAME AGAIN

Even though I had stopped working, my body was sending me through a loop. I was barely doing anything, and I had pain radiating in places I never felt pain before. I spoke to Profs about my issue, and he started me on different medication to get my pain in a more manageable state. Unfortunately, it didn't work at all, I had moments where I was fine and then I would want to throw my body out the window. I had never struggled so much to hide my pain. When I would simply go to the shops, I'd walk a couple metres then I had to stand against the wall to try to regain my composure.

I knew something more serious was wrong; I contacted Profs again, and I asked him for a referral so I could get an MRI of my spine. As I laid there still for almost two hours in an MRI machine, I continued to sing my own song in my head over and over. I thought if I kept singing it a certain amount of times inside my head then I'd know how many minutes had passed. The sounds of the machine became the new beat of my song, within my head. Now I just had to wait for my specialist to review my MRI scans and get back to me.

It was a Sunday afternoon, and I was so worried about my scans. I needed a distraction, so I went to the movies by myself. Halfway through the movie Profs called my phone. I thought;

'This isn't going to be good.'

I walked outside of the theatre and answered my phone. He was in a panic; I had never heard him like that in my entire life of knowing him.

"Fiona, you need to come in tomorrow, first thing in the morning and make sure you bring a bag with you to prepare for emergency surgery."

Nooooo... It was worse than I could have imagined, I was crying outside the cinema. I couldn't even focus on the movie anymore so I went and sat in my car for a while before I went home. I rang my mum, who had told me Profs had called her because he thought I would need her support. I admit part of me was mad at him for calling my mum; I was an adult now it should have been my choice to tell her. Although, I know he knew I was close to my mum, and I understand he only told her because he was really concerned for me.

Things were really tough for me during the new discovery of my spine dramas. Not only did the fall in 2010 cause issues to my hip and shoulder but now I have bulged slipped discs in my spine. Sure, my spine has always been badly affected curvature wise, but the impact of me hitting the concrete had messed up my spine too. It only became more apparent once the pain of my shoulder and hip had dissipated. I wasn't sure what to do, once my specialist saw me he ran some routine checks, to see if there were other symptoms present to determine the urgency of surgery.

After much discussion he referred me to a spinal surgeon to discuss my situation further. I was fairly uneasy and uncertain about anyone touching my spine. I remembered what my neck surgeon had told me when I was younger. He explained how serious the risks were with the state and severity of my spine curvature was in; so this placed further doubt in my head.

I wanted to make the right decision for myself and I was in a constant battle with what was the right thing to do. After speaking with my friends in America who also have Kniest, Aaron suggested contacting a special clinic that dealt with skeletal dysplasias in New York. I didn't take this decision I had to make lightly, so I waited months for my spine specialist to clear me, so that I could fly to the States and be reviewed by specialists there.

I struggled so much to deal with this news that I felt myself slipping into a depression. This was so unlike me, I needed my positivity back, but how could I be positive when I found myself so confused by the biggest decision of my life. So I went to my go to outlet, and I wrote what I felt was the darkest poem I had ever written in my existence. Once I let all my feelings flow out of my pen, it allowed me to have the strength to realise how much I disliked depressed Fee. It gave me the wake-up call I needed when I read my poem back to myself.

Sometimes it's easy to lose yourself in your current situation, that you forget the positive things around you. There are times it's hard to look past a problem, and we focus too much on the negative. It's not always easy to know how to get back on track. As much as I aim to be a positive light in this world and make people around me happy, I too can fall off the tracks. I'm only human after all.

Like all good movies, or fiction novels, I'm going to have to leave you with a cliff-hanger. This part of my life is still a regular monitored situation where I don't even know the ending. I admit it has made me question if the doctors here in Australia would have braced my spine as a child, like many of my other Kniest friends overseas, if I would even be dealing with this issue to the same degree. It's upsetting but I have to just accept my current reality.

As I have allowed myself to be fully exposed on these pages, I will share my darkest poem. As sad and as depressing as the words may be, they were also the words that made me pick myself back up again.

Pick up the Pieces and Start Again

No Rhyme or Reason

If only I could tell you,
Just how I feel inside.
If only it made sense to me,
To not hide behind my pride.

I'm Feeling like a loser,
At the end of a winding road.
Losing all direction,
Everything around me is on hold.

I'm tired of the hurt,
And pain that I've gone through.
If it doesn't go away,
There's no telling what I'll do.

The old me say's you can do it,
Just hold on and be strong.
The me right now is over it,
What's the point in holding on?

There is no rhyme or reason,
For all the things we do.
Everything seems pointless,
That's probably because it's true.

Chapter Twenty-Eight

Musical Memories and Facing Fears

Music has always been a big part of my life, aside from the part's you already know of; I thought I'd share a few more fun and exciting musical memories.

Right at the time I had recorded my first single, there was a club I attended regularly, where I knew the DJ. His name was Pete and aside from doing his MC work at the club he was also a radio presenter. Each time he saw me at the club, he was always so kind to me. We would chat about what I was currently working on. As soon as he knew my first single was finished, he allowed me to sing at the club with my backing track. He even interviewed me once on his radio show, right after I released my first song. This was awesome exposure for me; one of the times he got me up to sing, there was a lady in the audience. She happened to work in centre management of a shopping centre. After I had finished singing she approached me and asked if I had a few more songs recorded. She gave me her business card and asked me to visit her at the shopping centre to discuss doing a show. She suggested I could even sing some covers, and she would help promote my CD. Naturally the prospect of doing a show in a shopping centre sounded exciting to me.

Around this time she even organised radio interviews and contacted the local newspaper. The paper ran a few featured articles about me leading up to the show.

When I performed at the centre, it was such a new, exciting experience. The local radio station was also streaming live from the centre, right next to where I was performing. I had a lot of positive feedback from the show and the audience seemed to respond well. I sang a few original tracks and covers that day; it was a unique experience I'll never forget.

DJ SugaSuga Hits the Airways

I was in the midst of doing many performances and radio interviews when I got interviewed by a local radio station. The show that interviewed me was actually a Maltese-based segment that aired a few times a week at the station. During my interview they hinted how I had the knack for radio. I joked back with them about my interest in doing my own show, of course I would have loved it, but I never thought it would happen. After we were off the air, we continued to discuss the possibility of me becoming a member of the station and doing my own show. The presenters of the Maltese show also happened to assist in the management of the station.

A week or two later I went to the station to begin training on the panel which I managed to pick up quite quickly. As soon as the managers saw how quick I picked up the panel they offered me the opportunity of having my own show. This is when DJ SugaSuga came to life and hit the airways. I had my own show two to three times a week for approximately two years. It was such a neat experience planning my playlist, interviewing people on air and being responsible for reading the weather and news updates. Right at the start of my show I always began by playing one of my own tracks, it became my signature beginning. As my confidence grew on air, I was asked to train many of the new hosts that were starting up. I became the go-to person for newcomers on how to operate the panel. The only reason I quit my radio show, was because I went into full time work. It was definitely fun and exciting while it lasted. Of course, I'll always be grateful for the time and opportunity I had to host my own show, and live the dream of being a radio presenter.

It seriously amazes me how many things in my life just snowball from being in the right place at the right time. I've really been blessed with plenty of opportunities. All I had to do was keep presenting myself in situations, and leave myself open to pursue them.

Australian Idol – Up close and Personal

It was 2003 when the first season of Australian Idol aired on TV. It wasn't long after I had finished my twelve track album 'I Am Who I Am.' Naturally with how much I love singing and music, when I saw commercials for the show I was interested straight away. I got so hooked, that when they announced a special live 'Up close and personal' show with the final top five contestants, I knew I had to go. Once I knew when tickets were going to be on sale I asked my mum if she'd be interested in going with me. Mum could tell how much I wanted to go so she said if I managed to get us both tickets, she would come. Tickets were only about fifteen dollars each so it wasn't too bad.

The night of the show was upon us, we made sure we got there early, because we wanted to find nearby parking; so I wouldn't have to walk too much. The producers of the show were amazing. As soon as they saw me, I didn't have to say anything before they told me to wait at the front of the line.

While we were waiting in line for the doors to open, the producers came and handed every single person a raffle ticket. They told everyone to keep their ticket as they would be drawing a lucky door prize. Then they issued a warning to everyone that photography and video was prohibited inside the studio. Many people were forced to hand in their cameras; they could then collect them after the show.

This is sometimes where being me has its perks. The person collecting everyone's cameras just told me not to worry; he said I could hold onto mine as long as I didn't take any flash photography. I was grateful for the pass I received in not being forced to hand in my camera, and that I avoided having to deal with collecting it at the end of the show. It was an amazing show; the producers sat me right near the front so I could see. When it was time for the lucky door prize, they drew ten ticket numbers out. As they were reading out the last number I thought; 'oh well, it's not going to be me.' But, boy was I wrong. My number was actually my lucky number twelve and my favourite colour blue. It was mine; I got to go on stage, collect my prize and meet the top five Idol contestants. I was stoked; I asked them if I could take a picture with them and they allowed me to. Thank goodness, they didn't take away my camera or I would have missed out on capturing the moment.

When the show was over before everyone was told to leave, a producer came up to me with a serious look on his face. In front of everyone he said; "I will need you to stay back, because we need to discuss the photo you took during the show." Bugger, I thought I wouldn't get in trouble for that. As soon as most people left, the producer came back over to me and my mum and said;

"Could you please follow me?"

I thought he would ask me to take the film out of my camera and hand it to him. But then I realised we went through the back stage door and he said to us;

"Oh, you're not actually in trouble, I just had to say that in front of everyone else. I thought you might like to meet the contestants properly, and have them sign something."

OMG, how awesome and generous!

I couldn't believe my luck, everyone was so nice and friendly, they all gave me hugs and signed pieces of paper for me. Honestly, I never like to use my condition as an excuse to receive special allowances but this was so awesome because I didn't even ask.

I've had similar opportunities like this throughout my life where I've had the chance to meet other bands or famous people. Some of the people I've met that come to mind were; Westlife, Delta Goodrem, Timomatic, and many of the artists that perform at the Carols in the Domain. I've even met a few actors from various TV shows and movies. It's always a wild ride and I'm forever grateful for people's generosity and kindness when they let me sit up front at a concert.

Myself Again

In 2011 I had time to truly reflect on where I was going with my life and what I really wanted to do. The one thing that kept creeping in the back of my mind was singing. It had always been such a big part of who I was before I got married. I felt like I had lost myself and who I wanted to be.

There was an opportunity to go to a music conference at the Institute of Music in Los Angeles. I had asked my boss if I could take five days off to go. He was really supportive of me having this opportunity, so he approved my time off. It was the best experience; I met so many wonderful people and I learnt so much. I had the opportunity to sing while I was there and I met some fabulous producers in the workshops. One of the producers I met was very encouraging and supportive of me making new music. So after I arrived home we began Skype sessions together.

Then in 2012 before I had the MRI for my spine and knew what was wrong, I had set out on a new adventure. I travelled to Los Angeles to work with four amazing producers: Jan, Marty, Barry and Sydney to create my EP 'Strength from Within' with four new songs. Two new tracks I had written, as well as one track which I co-wrote with Jan and Barry. The fourth track was actually written by Jan and another songwriter who allowed me to record my vocals on their song. This was the first time I had ever recorded my vocals on someone else's track, but I truly fell in love with the song and it turned out great.

This time was the most amazing, yet also the toughest, because I struggled with my pain during recording sessions. I had to take extremely strong pain killers just to get through the day.

I will never forget the awesome opportunity I had to work with four fantastic producers in the music industry. Producers who have worked with so many famous artists, like Bruce Springsteen and LeAnn Rimes to name a few. So I couldn't believe that I was lucky enough to have them work on my music with me.

(DJ SugaSuga on the airways, Me with the Top 5 Idol contestants, And Recording Session in Los Angeles)

BAND TOGETHER

In 2004 I had the opportunity to join a band as one of their lead singers. It was very different to singing solo, but I enjoyed putting myself out there and being challenged by new experiences. The band mainly sang cover songs, but they always allowed me to do my own original songs in-between our sets. We performed at various locations and even sang at a few charity events for people with disabilities. Unfortunately, like many other bands, after a while we all went our separate ways.

HOW SOMETHING BAD, CAN LEAD TO SOMETHING GOOD

As I sat in the hospital waiting room, there were two ladies sitting nearby with cameras in hand. I noticed they were talking to another patient who was seeing Profs just before me. It was during the time of my spine dilemma.

Of course I was curious what they were filming, but I also felt like they were curious about me and my condition too. We started up a conversation when they told me they were doing a documentary about Osteogenesis Imperfecta. *(Osteogenesis Imperfecta is another form of dwarfism that causes bones to be extremely brittle.)* The documentary they were working on sounded great, I was genuinely interested in seeing how their finished product would turn out. We continued to chat, and I told them about myself, my spine situation and my music. Right before it was my turn to see Profs we exchanged contact details. They were two of the loveliest people and I was glad that we had met on that particular day. This chance encounter was a positive distraction from all my issues I was dealing with at the time.

After I released my newest four track EP; 'Strength from Within,' they got back in touch with me to let me know they loved my new music. I was happy to hear from them, because you know how life is sometimes you meet people and say you will stay in touch but then you never do. This wasn't the case this time.

They asked me if I was interested in recording a music video for one of my tracks. As if I was going to say no, you should know me by now. I always want to involve myself in new and exciting ventures, even when things aren't going well for me physically. This was definitely a situation where I pushed through my pain and embraced the experiences in life that I gained.

We decided on a couple of nice scenic locations to shoot the music video at. It was such a cool and different experience, and the video turned out better than I could have ever imagined. I'm so thankful to them for working with me on such a fun creative project. I hope to continue to record more music and videos in the future.

Princess Popstar

New Years day of 2012, was spent on a cruise to New Zealand with my family. It was just my mum, dad and brother. It was a fun family vacation, New Zealand was so enchanting. During the cruise they had a karaoke competition, so I thought why not take part; it would be fun either way. There have been instances in my past where I have entered karaoke competitions, but many times I get judged before I even open my mouth. I entered the competition on the first night and met some lovely new people onboard. I got into the grand final round and it felt like a reality television show. We had camera men interviewing us for the cruise DVD that passengers could purchase.

The auditorium of the ship was filled with passengers waiting to be entertained. They were given voting cards on their tables because the audience was in charge of selecting the winner. Whoever received the most votes naturally would win. I secretly hoped I would win but there was some awesome competition and at the end of the day I was happy to be a part of a fun experience. After everyone sang, they announced that there were two singers with an equal number of votes. I was crowned Princess Popstar, and another guy who was an awesome singer was crowned Prince of pop.

I Want To Know What Love Is

In October 2012, I was at a club singing karaoke, as I like to do from time to time. When a woman came to speak to me about taking part in a musical art exhibition, she was organising at a big venue location. I was intrigued and wanted to know more so I gave her my email address so she could forward me information about the project. It was an elaborate multimedia show where participants were given the opportunity to showcase songs that reminded them of their first love. Songs that brought them joy, sorrow, or songs that reminded them of their childhood.

There were also live performances, and works of art as part of the exhibition. I was interviewed for the project, and I also took part in the live performance side of things. On opening night it was a major production, there were many of us who sang. Of course, the final song of the night the whole group sang together was;

'I want to know what love is' by Foreigner.

Musical Memories and Facing Fears

The Scars We Choose

As I approached my 30th birthday, I knew I wanted to do something a little crazy and unexpected. From a very young age I always figured by the time I'd be thirty my life would be pretty tragic. I know that might sound negative, but I knew the older I'd get the harder my life would be. I recall on my 17th birthday I told my best friend I'd likely need him to buy me a walking stick for my birthday. I joked about it many times, but I actually was worried that as I got older my body would fall apart.

I went out for lunch with my LP friend Michelle and I was telling her I wanted to do something to commemorate me turning thirty. I asked her for suggestions on what I could do when we discussed the idea of getting a tattoo. She wanted to get one herself, so she thought I'd be crazy enough to go with her. Well, this was true I am known to do outrageous things at times; but a tattoo was a big deal.

When I was younger, I always thought about what I would get if I had a tattoo. But I was so afraid of needles I never thought I'd have the guts to go through with it. At first I told Michelle I wasn't sold on the idea and I'd never want to get a generic tattoo anyone else might have. If I would get one, it had to be something meaningful to me. After lunch when I was at home I drew a tattoo design, I thought it was pretty funny because now I was really keen on the idea.

I asked a friend of mine who had a few tatts where a good reputable place would be to get my tattoo. Michelle and I called them and even went to ask a few questions before we booked ourselves in. I was actually surprised how different it felt to actual injections. After all the things I've been through; getting a tattoo was nothing, in relation to pain.

When I went back home, I called my mum to tell her I went and got a tattoo. I knew I didn't have to tell her; I was old enough to make my own decisions, plus the location of my tattoo wasn't in an obvious place. Who knows if she ever would have seen it if I didn't tell her, but man did she flip out!

Eventually when I explained myself in a way my mum could understand, she accepted my thought process and got over it. See, I see it this way; my body is filled with scars I didn't want or choose to have. Whereas, my tattoo is a scar I chose, and it looks nicer than my scars from all my surgeries.

I drew this specific design because as you are already aware music is a big part of who I am. The butterfly symbolises my very first song I ever recorded; 'My Turn To Fly.'

(My Tattoo Design)

FACING FEARS

When I was a kid, I had a terrible experience with a German Shepherd. This encounter impacted me in such a bad way, I couldn't handle being in the same room as a dog. It didn't even matter if it was a puppy. When a dog was jumpy, or barked it enhanced my feelings of anxiety. Before I would accept an invitation to a party, I would always ask them if they had any dogs. I can't even begin to explain how intense this fear was. Over the years many people tried to get me to face my fear, but a common problem was they just kept telling me to get over it. As if there was some switch I could just turn off and ignore.

My mum even tried by getting us a dog, first we had a Maltese Terrier we called Simba. Simba was such an active dog that barked a lot, and unfortunately as much as I wanted to become friends with her and leave my fears behind me I just couldn't. Simba ended up going to a new home and went to live with a family friend of ours, so we still knew how she was doing.

Eventually mum thought we would try again because my brother really wanted a dog and deep down I wanted to get past my fears. That's when mum found someone who bred Miniature Schnauzers. We all went to go see the puppies. We chose one and called him Max. Max was still only just born so we had to wait until he was about six to eight weeks old before we could take him home. I tried so hard to put my feelings of anxiety behind me, but as Max became more active no matter how much I wanted to be okay I just couldn't. It was breaking my heart inside, I loved Max so much but my fear was so intense that I thought I was going to give myself a heart attack. This meant Max had to become an outside dog and I just continued to love him from behind the glass. I hated feeling this way, in my heart of hearts I wanted to be outside playing with Max but everything I tried just kept setting me further back.

It wasn't until a boyfriend I was dating back in 2012 helped me overcome my fear. It took a couple weeks of nervous barking and leashing the dog to the coach a few metres away from where I would sit. I was struggling to control my anxiety. At one point I really thought it was useless, and I'd never get rid of my fear.

Then after an intense couple of weeks came the day my ex-boyfriend was moving out of his apartment. Someone had left the front door open, so he thought his dog might have gotten out. He was yelling her name;

"Oreo, Oreo."

When suddenly she came out from hiding in the wardrobe and actually ran and sat right behind me for protection. That was the moment my anxiety took a back seat, and I felt connected to Oreo like I never thought possible. She is such a smart dog, whenever she was around me, she would never jump or get pushy with me. If she wanted my attention, she'd sit beside my leg and slightly lean against me until I pet her, it was so sweet.

She changed my life forever from that moment on, and even though I am no longer with the guy I was seeing, we've remained friends. I'll always be grateful to him and to Oreo for changing my life in such a positive way. For helping me understand how beautiful the connection between people and their pets can be. Oreo will always be my baby girl and I'll love her forever.

(Oreo and I)

Thanks to Oreo I was able to finally have the opportunity to bond with our dog Max. When I went out to spend time with Max for the first time after I got over my fears, it was like he knew something about me was different. He seemed so excited that I went outside and was doing circles around me. I felt so silly, like I had wasted so much time being scared when I knew Max would never hurt me. Even though I lost so many years being afraid and missing out on the awesome bond I could have formed with Max from the very start, I am grateful that I finally was able to get there in the end.

The mind can really impact how we see and do things in life. I feel like for the longest time that childhood fear I formed from the incident with the German Shepherd had a hold on me that I thought I'd never get past. It may have taken me thirty years to get to the point I am at today, but I am so glad that I don't feel the need to run in the other direction every time I see a dog. Aside from the fact that I'd look so silly, and I'm too old to even try to outrun a dog.

(In Loving Memory – Max 14.11.2016)

Chapter Twenty-Nine

Out of the Blue Injuries

The older I'm getting the more my body is playing tug of war with my ability to put on a happy face, and smile through the pain. When I first wake up in the morning, my joints are particularly stiff. Until I move around a bit, it takes time for my body to adjust, and my bones to feel functional.

Almost expectantly the night after a day where I've done a seemingly simple task, I end up completely physically suffering from it. As soon as my joints try to get into relax mode, I begin to struggle to lift my feet high enough off the ground when I walk. My feet and ankle joints lock up on me and throb in the same way they used to when I was a kid. The throbbing feels like my joint is a sub woofer at a nightclub, and the music just keeps pumping. It can be such a nagging pain that it makes me have to push and force against myself to try to release and unlock them.

It's ironic really because people always say you are only as old as you feel; well if that's true, then I'm prehistoric. Any time a close family friend has asked me how I'm feeling, if ever for a moment I choose to open up and tell them old, or sore. They respond with; "Oh, come on, you're still young."

But am I really? What most people don't understand because I make every effort not to complain as much as possible; I don't know what a life without pain feels like. For me, my truth is not one day in my life has ever been pain free. Some pains I manage better than others, but the older I get I'm sure it'll only continue to get harder.

I'm not telling you this because I want pity, on the contrary, I can't stand pity. But I feel like because most people see me with a smile on my face, they think life is easy for me. If I want to truly provide better understanding I have to share the parts of me I usually like to hide. Let me tell you, sometimes there are days I am so sore, and so I don't get pity parties off of people those are days I usually spend in my room; by myself. It's not always easy to not let my pain get the best of me, but I sure as hell am going to try.

Just like my tag line on the front cover, 'Embrace the life you gain, when you push through the pain.' That is one hundred percent my life in a nutshell.

Elbow Injury

One year my aunty was visiting from Malta. While she was here, I went with her and my mum to Melbourne to visit their cousin; which makes them cousins of mine too. On the first night that we got there, it was raining. As I got out of their van at 9:00 pm, I slipped in the rain, in front of a diner. Instinctively when I fall I usually place my arms in front of me to protect my glasses from smashing into my face. As soon as mum helped me up and we went inside the diner, I knew something was off. My elbow was hurting, but I wasn't sure if it was just impact shock pains. So I held my arm still and just kept the pain to myself. Once we were at our cousin's house they gave me cream for my elbow to relieve the pain. It seemed like this only made it worse, but still I just stuck it out. By the time it was seven o'clock in the morning I had to wake my mum and cousin up for them to take me to the hospital. Only to discover I fractured my right elbow in two places.

Occasionally when I accidentally sleep on my right arm in a weird way, it tends to lock up on me. It can be quite painful having to push and force against myself to unlock it. It's crazy how I'm so used to pain, that my tolerance is so high, and until it hits an evil extreme I just bottle it up internally.

LOWER LEFT LEG SKIN FRAGILITY

Ever since my leg surgeries as a child, my lower section of my legs before my ankle joints, have become extra sensitive. My left leg of course as usual is much worse than my right. So much so that I only have to rub the bottom part of my leg, and it gets red. Sometimes even the skin feels so fragile it peels off.

There's a reason I hate public transport and the last time I ever caught a bus really reminded me why I don't use it at all. I went to grab onto the door handle to get up on the bus and I thought the door was solid in its place. But as soon as I lifted my leg and all my weight was on the handle, it moved. Right when it moved I tried to stop myself from falling and I hit the bottom part of my fragile left leg on the rim of the bus step. Instantly, my leg began to sting, and I could feel blood rushing down my leg on the inside of my jeans. I was in public, so I kept my composure but was screaming on the inside. This didn't stop me though, I went where I was going and it wasn't until I was done that I went back to my hotel. Afterwards when I went to have a shower to clean up my leg, I was yelling in agony. While I was in the shower and the water ran down my injured and bleeding leg, it continued to sting. Ever since the bus injury, that part of my leg has remained constantly red, and doesn't seem to want to heal. I guess I can just add it to my list of many scars that exist on my body. If I learnt anything that day, it was; *'Stick to your general rule of thumb Fiona. Public transport is not for you!'*

ANKLE INJURY

On the 26th of October 2014, I figured it would be just another 'Fee normal' day. I went out with my mum and brother to a Maltese show. When we arrived, and I got out of the car, I felt this weird feeling in my left ankle. As the day progressed, the pain and weirdness only got worse. It almost felt like the clip in my ankle I've had since I was six, was moving. Now I knew that probably wasn't the case, but the pain was getting harder to explain. I tried rotating my ankle so it wouldn't lock up on me when I heard a crackling sound. Umm, I've had weird pains in my life that I've grown to understand and manage, but I had no idea what was going on in that moment. I'm used to the pains that are weather induced, or due to arthritic flare-ups, or just a Fiona random attack, but this was like no other feeling.

By the time we got home I couldn't walk at all, I stood in the driveway and had mum bring my crutches. It's lucky I have them on standby from when I fractured my hip back in 2010. While I was getting ready for bed, I noticed my foot and ankle were swollen like a blimp. The next day, I got up and I still couldn't bear weight on my foot. Now I was worried, so I tried taking it easy, but I hadn't realised how bad it was yet. I'm so used to dealing with random flare-ups that sometimes I wait longer than most people might, until I assess my own body. The swelling wasn't going down, so I iced my foot and took anti-inflammatories. It got to the point that I had to see my doctor about it because it wasn't getting better. He sent me for an ultrasound, only for them to tell me I was just too arthritic and there was nothing I could do. Eventually I was able to bear weight again, without needing my crutches. Although ever since this weird situation happened my ankle constantly swells and flares up almost daily.

Hand Injury

The night before my niece's birthday one year, I was getting prepared to make her special cupcakes I had promised. When I went to my room to get something, I didn't realise how close I was to my bed post. When I turned around, I wasn't able to stop myself mid-motion. I smashed the top part of my hand into my bed post. It killed me and I had tears welling up in my eyes, but I pulled myself together and went into the kitchen anyway. I sat down at the kitchen bench, because even though I love to bake, it's always a huge physical sacrifice I make just to have a cake.

(I can't help but rhyme, even when I'm not trying.)

My hand was killing me, and began to swell up; but I persisted. It took me much longer than cupcakes should take to make, but I eventually got them done. When I hit my hand, it was around 5:00 pm. I went to bed as usual but I was struggling to sleep, I knew then the pain felt like a fracture. It was hurting too much to continue to ignore. At around 5:00 am, I woke up my mum. I felt terrible waking her up, but I knew I needed a cast or a splint for my hand. We went straight to the emergency room, but it took hours for anyone to x-ray my hand. Turned out I had a fractured hand like I suspected, so they gave me a splint. By this time I was pretty upset I missed going to see my niece early in the morning, but I made my mum take me to her school anyway. I wanted to give her the cupcakes I made for her, and apologise for not making it earlier.

As soon as I arrived at her classroom door, one of her class mates said; "Hey, your aunty Fee is here." My niece came running up to hug me and couldn't believe I still made her cupcakes with a fractured hand.

It's amazing what you can overcome when you love someone so much, that seeing them smile is worth the pain. Just like I did, when I continued to endure the pain and made those cupcakes.

Pain Clinic or Pain Provider?

During a time when I was struggling with multiple pain issues, my doctor had referred me to a special pain clinic, to see if they could help. After a full day of appointments with various medical professionals a physical therapist came in to discuss my issues. He wanted me to be the usual science experiment and was feeling up all my joints. When he said he wanted to feel the curvature of my spine, I warned him of my slipped discs and asked him not to push on my back.

He didn't listen though, it's like medical professionals don't understand, or take their patients seriously enough. As soon as I left the hospital that day, my spine became symptomatic again. I began to feel the worst pain, right where my slipped discs are.

It was a major setback I really didn't need. For over a week I couldn't do anything, I had to take the strongest pain killers and pray the symptoms disappeared.

The amount of times I have had medical appointments where the doctors are busy poking and prodding me; that they occasionally have created pain and caused issues to flare-up. It can be quite frustrating when I realise that sometimes even they don't grasp the severity of my situation, or my condition.

The opportunities I've had in life came from pushing myself every day. I'm a passionate person and allowing my physical daily pain to ruin my chance of having the life I want isn't acceptable. I want to live my dreams as much as the next person. But there's a difference; I didn't want to just say I want to live my dreams and expect them to fall in my lap. I knew if I didn't fake it till I make it, I'd get nowhere. There have been people that act like I have it easy because most people only ever see the positive parts of my life.

I never want to appear to be full of myself or arrogant because I am far from it. I'm just fighting my battles the best way I can. By having a positive outlook and personality, it helps me not to dwell on things I can't change. Yes, my health issues hold me back at times, and hinder certain possibilities. But like they say; the word impossible has 'I'm possible' in it!

Chapter Thirty

Eyes Wide Open

Every time I go into the eye specialist for a check-up I always get anxious. I have eye appointments at least once a year, sometimes even two or three times. It depends if there is something in particular my eye specialist is monitoring, or if I've recently had surgery on my eyes. Sometimes I can't count on the fact that I might not notice a difference in my vision. There have been times my specialist has noticed changes to the back of my eye that aren't visible to me. This can occasionally create enough reason for preventative surgery. As soon as I arrive for an appointment, it usually plays out like this:

My specialist's colleague calls me into an examination room. One eye at a time, I read the letter chart to confirm I still have acceptable driving vision with my glasses. When I know I've read a certain line, it's always a relief. Then she puts anaesthetic and dilating drops into my eyes, to be ready for my specialist so he can check the back of my retina on a more in-depth level. After sitting in the waiting room as I wait for the drops to take effect, I then enter my specialist's examination room. He reviews the notes in my file and then I sit in front of a machine where he places a lens on my eye to check my eye pressure. He then shines a light into my eyes while looking through the machine in every direction, as he examines every corner of my retina. This is usually when I'm nervously waiting to hear if everything is still stable, and I don't need any surgery.

Unfortunately in 2015 I was back in a position to need another eye surgery. I had just gone through a regular check-up, when my specialist advised me that he could see a few areas in my right eye that he wanted to laser. This would be a very similar surgery to the one I had when I was seventeen. Where he essentially welded my retina to strengthen the weak spots, and prevent holes from forming in my retina.

Although this time would be different yet again because he knew how dangerous putting me under anaesthetic would be; he wanted to do the surgery while I was awake. Now that I was much older he felt I could handle staying still while he lasered my eye. Sure, I didn't want to be put under anaesthetic either, but don't think the prospect of feeling him laser my eye didn't scare me. He told me to come back in a few weeks on the 14th of October so he could take his time when doing the surgery. I left his office that day feeling shattered, my right eye was the eye I nearly lost already; I was feeling all those emotions come flooding back.

When I arrived that morning, I only had a Panadeine Forte for the pain, and he put anaesthetic drops in my right eye. Then I went into a different room and sat in front of the laser machine. He told my mum she could come in if she wanted to, she just had to sit a few metres away and wear special glasses. After he turned off the lights in the room and put his own special glasses on, he told me to let him know if it got too painful, then he would put more drops in. As I sat there upright with both hands gripped to the sides of the machine, he told me not to panic if my vision goes black. He said that it would only last a few moments and then I should see again. You can't even begin to imagine the way I was feeling inside, I'm certain at one point I even murmured 'mum.' In like a seeking comfort kind of way, that everything would be okay.

Wow this was challenging, staying still, keeping my eyes wide open while he was burning my retina together. I gripped tighter to the sides of the machine, he kept telling me; "you are doing really well." It might have appeared that way to him but inside I was freaking out screaming. This was such a unique, horrible, painful experience I hoped to never repeat. But my brain spoke too soon, he told me he wanted to split it up, give it three weeks to heal. Then check the area and if need be he would do more on that day. For a minute there it was scary because my eye was pitch black like he warned me. Even though I was aware it could happen, I was still a wreck internally until my hazy vision returned. He gave me drops for my eye and covered it with a patch. I continued to put the drops in multiple times a day until I went back again on the 4th of November. Well you guessed it; it was time for round two. He still needed to cover a section of my retina. If I thought the first time was bad doing this awake, the second time was a thousand times worse. My eye was still sensitive from the first surgery so it was a lot harder to keep it open and deal with the pain. Honestly, the way I felt in that moment as I gripped the sides of the machine, was like I was a UFC fighter pinned in a terrible position and I just wanted to tap out. Boy, did I really want to tap out; I was glad when it was all over.

At this second surgery appointment my specialist discussed macular degeneration with me. I thought to myself 'just lovely, another eye condition to add to all the crap I already have.' My macular was already thin and weak, especially in my right eye because of the Epiretinal membrane I had in 2003. He wanted me to begin taking tablets for Macular degeneration on a daily basis, for the rest of my life. He explained that these tablets were more like a vitamin. They wouldn't guarantee protection of my macular; but they would hopefully slow down any recurring issues. He told me to start on them straight away, if anything it wouldn't make my situation worse; but it would hopefully make it better. On the drive home I couldn't help but let out my emotions and shed a few tears, it was hard to be strong during those two laser surgeries. I prayed to God I would heal and get a break from all these dramas. God was definitely with me in that room for me to stay as still as I did, when I was hurting as much as I was.

Almost a week after my eye surgery and I still couldn't do much yet. I had constant headaches behind my eyes, and bright devices like the TV or my phone were still too irritating for my eye. So I stayed clear from them and even wore my sun glasses inside because all the lights were bothering me.

It was storming outside, and I was just lying on my bed at around 4:30 pm. Suddenly, I must have drifted off to sleep out of sheer boredom, which is completely unlike me, especially in the middle of the afternoon. During that time, I had an awful dream that felt so real.

In my dream I was laying on my bed, exactly how I was, and when I went to open my eyes, my right eye was pitch black. I tried to scream out for my mum, but I couldn't scream for some reason either. Then it was like I forced myself to wake up, OMG what a nightmare; it scared me so much. It felt like my worst fears were coming true. I woke up in such a panic that I left my room instantly and was testing my eyes to make sure I could see. It was crazy how real it felt, I went out to the living room where my mum and dad were. Immediately I told them about my dream, and mum said; "Thank God it was just a dream."

Thank God, was right!

Chapter Thirty-One

You Are Not Alone

It was just another average Fee-day, specifically back on the 28th of September 2012, when I received a new friend request on Facebook, and a comment left on my cover photo.

The message said;

'Hi Fiona, my name is Kayla. I have Kniest too like you. Could you please accept my friend request? Since you are a singer that has Kniest, I would love to chat! I love to sing and I have sung in front of millions of people at my school, and at make a wish charity events. It's been fun, I am thirteen going on fourteen in October, okay Bye.'

As soon as I saw the message, I accepted Kayla's friend request and started a conversation with her. I couldn't believe it, even though at this point in my life I had already had the chance to meet others with Kniest from my American trips; Kayla was from Australia too. Something changed on that day; I no longer was the only one in Australia. After chatting for a while, I soon discovered Kayla was living a little over two hours away from me, in the same state. What are the chances? For thirteen years I could have gotten to know her and met her before I ever went to LPA in America. Of course I don't regret those experiences and I am so glad I've had them, but it's just mind blowing. What was even crazier was the fact we soon discovered we've had some of the same doctors.

How is it they never connected us together before?

We had to meet up of course; Kayla had an appointment coming up at the children's hospital not too far from where I live, so we arranged to meet there. Naturally my mum came with me to meet Kayla and her mum, because she wanted to meet them too. Kayla was only recently diagnosed, which explains why we didn't stumble across each other before. She has a more severe case of Kniest therefore the doctors weren't certain what condition she actually had. It took awhile for her mum to receive Kayla's genetic test results.

Since we met, Kayla and I have become really close; I am like an older sister to her. She means the world to me, and it means a lot that I get to be there for her at a younger age than anyone was for me. We are Kniestian sisters for life, and it truly warms my heart that she looks up to me. I love that Kayla came into my life before I actually finished this book. Now she has changed my story forever as I am no longer alone on this side of the globe. I look forward to many more fun memories and being a part of each other's lives forever.

(Kayla and I)

Then There Were Three...

As the saying goes, it's a small world after all. I was in the middle of my second week of recovery from my most recent eye surgery in 2015; and I had only got back into using my phone again. My eye was almost back to its normal comfort zone, and the bright glairiness was almost gone. By that point, I had gotten so bored not being able to do much since the surgery. I missed being the social Fee that I usually am and missed interacting with people.

In my need for a positive distraction from my boredom and issues, I went online. It wasn't long before I began chatting with a guy from Perth, who happened to have SED. As we were getting to know each other, he was asking me more about my condition. When he came to realise he had met someone in Perth not so long ago who he believed had Kniest. The next day as we continued to chat, he confirmed the person he thought had Kniest actually did. He gave me her name, so I could look her up on social media and connect with her if I wanted to. Surely you can guess by now, I would obviously look her up. I went from thinking I was completely alone and the only one in Australia with Kniest for the first thirty years of my life; to now having the possibility of a third person in Australia. Not to sound like a stalker; *Haha*... But, naturally I skimmed through her public pictures she had available. She definitely looked like she had Kniest, so I sent her a private message introducing myself. It wasn't too long before she replied confirming that she did in fact have Kniest. Soon after I went to bed as it was quite late in Sydney, even though Perth was three hours behind. When I woke up the next day, I was in the kitchen discussing the new person I had found out about with my mum. As I began explaining how I stumbled into meeting her online and that she was from Perth; mum asked me what her name was. The discussion continued when suddenly it was like a light bulb went off in my mum's head. "You know Fiona, when you were about seven or eight years old, I used to write to a parent in Perth."

"You, What? And you're only telling me this story now."

Mum was almost convinced it was the same person. But she said, the mum she'd wrote letters to and her had lost contact shortly after. Well we did move around a lot during that time, and my medical dramas were in full force at that age. Mum wasn't a hundred percent sure if that girl had Kniest, she said after all the dramas with me and moving around a lot it slipped her mind. Mum continued to say, she thought she had found one of the letters recently; and thought she had given it to me. This was news to me, seriously mum how could you be holding out on me like this? What a crazy turn of events.

"If you find this letter, I want to read it!"

Still, I couldn't believe the conversation we were having, I had pestered my mum, my doctors, everyone my entire childhood in search of wanting to know others like me.

How did this info slip through the cracks?

Shortly after my phone rang, it was one of my friends in the USA. We were having a catch-up session when suddenly my mum just bursts into my room, without knocking like she usually would. Letter in hand, she went on to say;

"Yup, see, it is her, I found the letter."

How bizarre, all this time it's like my mum had amnesia, then suddenly I felt like I was in the 'Twilight Zone,' again. So I really wasn't the only one in Australia all my life, I could have known someone else before? It was almost like my whole life was one confusing mess. I had been searching for someone for as long as I can remember. Surely, we could have gone to Perth before even having to go to America. Although I still don't regret those life experiences and opportunities, and maybe I wouldn't have gone at all; had I known about Lisa in Perth.

Oh, that's right, I forgot to mention earlier, her name was Lisa, and she was seven years younger than me. Making me still the oldest person I know of in Australia. It would have been cool if we would have met when we were kids. As soon as I got off the phone, I went online to message Lisa and tell her this crazy story. But she had beaten me to the punch and messaged me first, saying the exact same thing. How funny can life be sometimes, what a crazy way to end up reuniting with someone I wasn't even fully aware of. I had to meet some new guy online with SED to find out about another Kniest sister.

Four months went by of us chatting online before I finally had a chance to go visit Lisa in Perth, and meet her in person. Forming these connections are so important to me, I chased the dream of knowing others with my condition all the way to the USA; there was no way I wasn't going to make a trip to Perth.

Lisa is a hoot, we are so alike not just in our condition's characteristics but in our personalities too. I had such a great time getting to know her and her lovely family. I look forward to the chance to be in each other's presence again in the future.

All I know is that this just completes my heart, having special connections with people who really understand me. It makes me wonder;

Who else is out there?

Is there someone older than me hiding in the outback; someone I don't know about, yet? If there is, who knows how my life story will evolve from this point! It's been a wild ride so far, and as the years go on I feel less and less rare; even though I know Kniest is still quite rare around the world.

(Lisa and I)

Us Kniestians become like instant family; we are so rare that we have to stick together and be in each other's lives. It's almost like our genetic mutation, connects us genetically, even though we aren't. Does that even make sense?

❖

As the years have passed Kayla and I have continued to grow extremely close. I go along with her and her mum to Kayla's doctor appointments, and we do creative stuff together whenever we can. I love being like her older sister and close friend, and I know she appreciates knowing she is not alone navigating through the tough times. The special bonds I have with all of my Kniest friends across the globe mean everything to me. Even my other close LP friends and 'average height' friends that are in my life have impacted me in such a great way. I could go on to tell you so many more stories of those amazing friendships. They know who they are, and they know I love them for accepting me for me, which is all anyone wants from people they care about.

Chapter Thirty-Two

What Lies Ahead?

I always knew the day would come that the main doctor in my life (Profs) would retire. Even though I knew it would happen someday I secretly hoped he'd always be there.

(I know wishful thinking.)

The thought of him not being there when I'm older, when I could need his support, scared me a little. I always trusted his judgement and advice, especially considering Kniest being as rare as it is. So rare that Profs looked after both me and my new found Kniestian sister Kayla. Who will I have to turn to now when my body loses the plot on me? It was already difficult to navigate things after I became an adult because the hospital system moves you away from receiving constant care. Luckily Profs always looked out for me; he knew I needed someone who understood my condition as well as he does. Even after the age of eighteen he saw me as an out-patient. He got me through the first thirty-three years of my life, and now I would be meeting someone new.

When I met with the new specialist who was taking me on as his patient, I was thinking;

'Agh, now I have to explain my whole life story again.'

Turns out my new specialist Profs 2.0 is lovely, and so easy to talk to. I feel good knowing I have someone equally in my corner in the way Profs was. A few months after getting to know Profs 2.0, he knew I was working on this book and I had an interest in helping other people. So he asked me if I would be willing to do a speech at a medical forum. The forum focused on the topic;

'Young People, Old Joints.'

Honestly, this topic was a very relatable one as far as I was concerned. Dealing with arthritic issues, and problems with my joints since birth made this an easy speech to write. The day of the speech was on the 2nd of December 2015, and at first I was worried I would not make it. I had a follow-up appointment to check on how my right eye was healing. It was at two that same afternoon on one side of Sydney, while the speech was at five completely on the other side. It was something I really wanted to do, so I wasn't going to say no, but I knew I needed to go to my eye appointment too. So I rang my eye specialist and asked him if I could go in early. When I explained why, he was more than happy to fit me in a couple hours earlier, he told me to go in at midday instead. Thankfully, I made it on time for both. My eye appointment had gone well and the speech was a real positive experience. Everyone was listening intently to what I had to say; it made me excited about the possibilities of future talks. I took the task of speaking at this medical forum very seriously; I even put together a slideshow to sift through, during my speech.

That day, I met a couple of new doctors who showed a great deal of interest in wanting to help me in any way they could. I remained in contact with them through email and then organised an appointment a few weeks later. These new connections have been great for me. It has given me peace of mind, with different aspects of my health, for my future.

Robo-Fee...

Throughout my life, it's been a constant question of when it might be the right time for a hip replacement. You might think, but Fiona thirty-three isn't even old enough to need one of those. Unfortunately, this is a common thing for people with Kniest and other forms of dwarfism. When I was eighteen and my doctors did a full review, the orthopaedic surgeon I saw was very interested in pushing me to do further leg surgery and hip replacements. But since I was eighteen and could make my own decision, I simply said no.

Apparently, when I had Ilizarov done during my childhood the doctor had over-corrected my legs. This is why they no longer look completely straight. When I was a naive kid, I thought it had to be that way for my ankles and hips to be aligned better. The thought of further leg surgeries just to make myself more aesthetically pleasing didn't interest me. The doctor couldn't guarantee that doing further surgery wouldn't reverse my ankle and hip alignments; or that it would benefit relieving pressure off of certain joints. This just sounded like cosmetic surgery to me. Sure, I've been picked on a lot throughout my life because of my legs attracting people's attention; but I still didn't believe more painful surgeries would fix or stop that from happening in my future. Of course I would have liked my legs to look straight like they once did, but I'm not that fixated on shallow surgeries for appearance.

If people are going to concern themselves with treating me differently because of a physical difference, then they aren't worth getting to know. If the doctor had a real reason to believe my mobility would be enhanced further, then I would have thought differently. As far as my hip replacements go though; I thought eighteen was much too young. I deal with physical pain in every joint of my body, if I had to take away all my pain they'd need to turn me into RoboCop. Robo-Fee has a nice ring to it, what do you think?

(Then I can charge Fee fees for everyone who comes to see me, Hehe...) ☺
By the time I reached my thirties, I hit some really rough times with my hips, where I was ready to throw them out the window. It got to a point where I'd randomly ball my eyes out without warning from intense hip pain. This was so unlike me, because even when I'm hurting I can generally keep myself in check. That's when I knew this situation was serious, so I went to see the same doctor who told me to replace them when I was eighteen. After getting new x-rays and only spending five minutes in his office, he said he wasn't sure it was a good idea. He was concerned that my hip would shatter and the surgery wouldn't take well. I thought to myself; 'What happened to all that confident pushiness all those years ago?'

'Was I just going to be an experiment to him?'
Then he said; "Don't risk it, come back to me when you feel like you want to jump off the harbour bridge."

'Was this guy serious?'

Obviously I went when I did because it hit a level I could no longer tolerate, way to encourage negative thoughts of jumping off bridges. Well that was a waste of almost three hundred dollars to be told that. So I thought to myself, I don't know if I feel comfortable being the first person in Australia with Kniest to get a hip replacement, and trust that it's going to be okay. I wasn't up for being a lab rat again, especially not with something this important. It was a good reason to go back to an LPA convention in the USA. I knew hip replacements had been done on some of my Kniest friends over there, so I thought another LPA doctor review would be my best option.

See, LPA has impacted my life so much in a positive way. It has provided me with resources and help, especially when I feel like I'm at a loss in knowing what to do. Having all these connections makes me think more thoroughly about making the best medical choices for myself. After the review at another LPA convention I felt more confident in knowing that if I was ready to replace my hips, then I should be okay. Problem was, I couldn't afford to do the surgery in the USA and I wasn't going back to doctor doom and gloom. So I discussed my issue with other specialists I go to. After speaking with three different doctors of mine, all three of them had recommended the same doctor. I thought to myself;

'Wow, I guess I should get a referral and see what happens.'
When the time came to go to my appointment, I was curious how it was all going to pan out. As my mum and I were waiting in the waiting room there was another little person there. He seemed like he had a rare condition as well, I wasn't quite sure what he had and I am fairly familiar with most conditions. I found this to be intriguing, maybe I wouldn't be such a new, different, challenge for this doctor. Generally when I see another LP out in public, even if I don't know them, I'd say hello. But this guy seemed possibly a bit thrown by seeing me. Then I thought maybe he hasn't really been around other LP's before. I didn't want to make things awkward so I just sat there, chatting to my mum.

After we went in, I began explaining some of my history, while he checked out my x-rays. Funnily enough the doctor said;

"Did you see the other little person in the waiting room?"

I had a bit of a chuckle and told him how I was hesitant to say 'Hi' because he seemed thrown by seeing another LP. After discussing everything thoroughly we agreed he would add me to his waiting list in preparation for surgery. This way when I was ready he could get things moving along and do the surgery. Funny thing though, in the time it took me to see this new doctor, who I actually feel totally comfortable with, my intense level of hip pain had calmed down. So without giving too many more Merry-Go-Round details, we decided to hold off for now. I am still on his waiting list, in case I have a sudden episode and I go for regular reviews. This way at least he'll be ready when I really feel like I can't take it anymore.

Robo-Fee can wait,

You may meet her at a later date...

The body can be so weird at times, one minute I can be fine, well I like to call it 'Fee-normal.' Because my version of normal is a very different kind of what I'm sure others would consider normal. Then the next minute I may want to detach part of my body and want to throw it off a cliff. But then I realise I'm just paying my fee's, this too shall pass. *(Goodness me, my jokes are really bad as we near the end, sorry I just can't help myself.)*

Chapter Thirty-Three

Mission Impossible

At the age of ten, I was looking for an object in our garage, when I found something completely unrelated. Some papers had fallen out onto the floor. The moment I picked up the papers, I couldn't help but notice a page that had my name on the top of it. Curiosity got the better of me the moment I noticed my name. At the very top of the page it said something like 'Fiona's case.' It had a figure of a male and female with a short genetic description. This paper only sent me into even greater confusion as I wondered if there was more behind the story of how I got my genetic condition. Even though my mum was always open with me, when I asked her direct questions about my medical history. During my diagnosis as a baby, the process was based mostly on skeletal confirmation through x-rays and other basic tests. Unlike today, where genetic testing has advanced to a more accurate, in depth DNA blood screening.

For the majority of my life, I always wanted genetic confirmation on a more in-depth level to verify that I truly do have Kniest Dysplasia. Wouldn't it be funny as we get to the end of my book if I actually revealed I didn't have Kniest at all? As silly as it sounds, I thought about that; imagine, I publish my book and then discover I have something different. I was fairly certain this wouldn't happen, but it was still important for me to know. Would me knowing really change anything, not likely, I'd still be who I am today. But as much as doctors have treated me like a lab rat to advance their own knowledge, it was important to me to know if I was really just a random mutation.

Would my brother be at risk of carrying the gene and having a child born with Kniest if my mum was the carrier? Truthfully, it was equally possible for either parent to be carriers. If my mum wasn't a carrier then my brother wouldn't have anything to worry about. Realistically it wasn't just important for me to find out, but it could be important for my siblings too. Am I going to be upset with my parents if they were carriers? No of course not because they wouldn't have known and that would be like me saying I don't want to be who I am. The only way anyone could ever lay blame on my parents would be, if they did something knowingly creating the mutation.

There is also one other very distinct possibility, eighty percent of people born with dwarfism are born to average height parents; where it's simply just a random genetic mutation. Most people don't realise that anyone can have a child born with dwarfism, without any prior history existing.

When I was younger, I constantly remember asking Profs for my genetic test results. But it felt like I was never going to get any answers, Profs couldn't locate a biopsy or the test results he claimed were done when I was younger. I'm sure I gave him a headache constantly asking for my results.

"Is there some way I can just do the test now?"

Most people might think it's not that important and I should just take the x-ray verification from my childhood as diagnosis. Don't ask me why, inside my mind it's such a big deal. It'd be good to know, to ensure I've covered all the medical issues I encounter as accurately as possible. Secondly, my stubbornness partially stems from me putting my story out there. It wouldn't exactly make sense to name it after my condition if it turns out that's not the condition I have. From a specialist's point of view and I'm sure some other people too; they would only see this type of testing to be considered important if I was intending to have children of my own.

Seeing as I have always said I wasn't interested in having my own kids, it becomes extremely hard to convince labs to run a genetic test. It's quite a costly process, unless I want to privately pay and have the test done.

When I met with my new genetic specialist for the first time, I expressed my views and need to have that piece of my puzzle filled in. I felt like he understood my reasoning, and he offered to look into other funding options for me. At that first appointment when we discussed my genetic test, I was so honest with him about not wanting kids. I opened up about so many aspects of my life and I even joked with him, saying;

"I'd pretend I was considering having a baby if it meant they could have an excuse to run the test for me." We both laughed about it, it's actually nice that I can talk to my specialist so candidly. It's nice to not feel awkward discussing important issues, no matter the topic. But also having the ability to be myself and joke knowing he will take it the way I meant for it to be. Sometimes it's hard to find this level of comfort with a doctor. As time went on, we continued to seek an alternative medical cause for needing such a test to be done. I told him I wouldn't care if he used my results to help further their own research that's how important it is to me.

Finally, we reached the point where he sent me forms to fill and a referral to go to my local hospital and have the blood work done. My hospital would then forward it onto him so he could send it to the right place. As the waiting game continued, he had mentioned that the test could take over two months for me to receive my results.

'Will I have Kniest?'

'Is it possible a spanner will get thrown in the mix and I will have a new mutation that was never considered?'

So many thoughts were going through my mind, I was excited but nervous; I was sick of asking for twenty something years; but now I was going to finally get some answers. Mind you, it was hard not talking about it to anyone. I figured why not leave it for this book, considering my results could impact how my story ends. My mum really only knew I was on a mission to get my test done. As the weeks went by, it felt like it was dragging on forever. Over five weeks had passed; then one night I checked my email fairly late when I noticed I had a message from Profs 2.0. Suddenly, a wave of anxiety and nerves hit me. This is it! I will finally know...

The subject of the email said;

'Genetic Test Results,' instantly I felt like I needed to compose myself. Below I will provide the important section from my results:

DNA Sequencing reveals and confirms a genetic mutation in the COL2A1. To the best of my knowledge, this particular splice and change, has not been previously reported. However, the biological significance of this change is not known for certain. Analysis of additional family members may be helpful; specifically parental DNA. The patient has Kniest Dysplasia which is an autosomal dominant disorder.

Well, it's official I have Kniest, but at first when I read some of the other details, it threw me a little. I called Profs 2.0 and asked him to explain it to me in Fee terms.

He confirmed that the way my genetic mutation was spliced was actually a new variant in confirming Kniest. I should have known nothing about my life is ever black and white. It wasn't enough I struggled to get my results in the first place. This only gave me more questions I wanted answers to. Even my doctor grew interested in seeking more information about how my particular change occurred. Now I had to hope my parents would be willing to have blood tests done to get absolute accuracy. Instantly I knew my mum wouldn't hesitate to go ahead with testing. She understands how important it is for me to continue to piece my puzzle together. Mum has always known how much my research and having medical awareness means to me. After reaching this point in my book, you might realise that there will be one big problem with completing this important task. My mum didn't create me by herself and I wasn't sure how I would go about obtaining the other half of my puzzle.

The next day I told my mum the news before calling my specialist to advise him that further testing may be an issue. Mum agreed straight away to have the test done; because now her curiosity was getting the best of her too. I knew I could count on mum, she understood it wasn't ever about placing blame; it was all in the name of medical science. Even though we both knew a part of my puzzle could remain unresolved, I told her that I still wanted to try.

The one true thing I need is the one thing I can't ask just anyone for. But if I don't try and give it my best shot then I won't get the answers I so desperately seek.

In the meantime my dad came home and the first thing that came out of my mouth was; "Dad, I wish you were really my biological dad right now!" Because I knew he would do a blood test for me if I needed it. In fact I believe even though he isn't *my* biological dad, he would move mountains for all three of his children if we needed him to. It's never a question, in every other form he is my dad. But sadly, genetically speaking, this is one thing he can't do for me. I continued to explain to my dad, I had received my results and now I needed to see how I was going to find out the rest of my genetic results. My dad actually said he wished he could do the test for me.

All I know is I'm so lucky; Why, do you say?
I owe a lot of thanks to my mum and dad. Ever since my mum and my dad got together when I was five he has been my dad through and through. He showed me what having a dad was like, so any thanks I have to give belongs to both of them. When he was still only dating my mum he used to skip soccer training to take me to hydrotherapy. He even helped teach mum to drive so she could take me to all my medical appointments. My dad spent hours with me in the hospital and has been a blessing in our lives. He might not be connected to me biologically but sometimes you'd almost swear we are. I'm so blessed that I don't feel like I missed out on having two loving parents, if anything I've gained so much. I am grateful to have my immediate family that I do have. Its times like these though that I miss the closeness of my extended family back in Malta.

My need to know felt amplified to another level, part of me got a little teary when I was on my own in my room thinking about it. I knew in my heart that I'd probably never complete the puzzle. I began to try and hunt down other relatives, and I was trying to prepare myself for the important conversation. My heart was pounding inside my chest. I hadn't even seen some of my relatives in a really long time. I really don't know if I will be able to get in touch with anyone, but you are all on this journey with me as I write this part of the story; on the exact day I'm living it.

Strap in and get ready for the ride...
Immediately I hit a wall, their phone just continued to ring out; no matter what time of day I called. I wasn't even sure then if this number was still active. All I know was I wasn't giving up until I exhausted all possible avenues. When I realised this wasn't going anywhere, I got frustrated. I even tried locating them on social media, but every attempt I made just felt like mission impossible.

In the meantime my mum had her blood test weeks ago, so I was still hoping to get answers from her test. After almost two months I received an email I wasn't expecting. Last I knew my mum's blood work was sent off for testing. I could have been waiting forever thinking I was going to have half an answer when in reality nothing was happening. The lab wouldn't run the test without all the pieces of my puzzle. After a lot of discussion Profs 2.0 agreed to organise mum's test, anyway. While my mission of still hoping to piece my puzzle together continued. At this point you have to realise when I have my mind set on something I am pretty stubborn until I exhaust every option.

After almost two years of actively trying everything within my means to find the answers I desperately seek, I finally had to face defeat. I have no other choice but to accept that I'll never get the answers I truly want. To conclude; my mum's results came back confirming she doesn't carry the genetic variant, but obviously further in-depth results could not be provided without all the pieces of my puzzle. The mystery shall remain; At least I know I definitely have Kniest, and my brother is in the clear.

Chapter Thirty-Four

Point Of View

Well, if you made it this far, you can be sure you know Me, Kniest, and hopefully you have a decent understanding of both. As we near the final pages of my book, I thought I'd discuss a few topics we haven't covered that I've come across throughout my life, and I wanted to share my point of view on.

BATTLE TO BE HEARD AND UNDERSTOOD

Throughout my life, there have been many instances where the battle to be heard and understood can be a real challenge. For example, getting my first job was hard; it's difficult sometimes as an LP or a person with a disability to be taken seriously. I found that it was only after I got my first job that it was much easier to receive other employment opportunities.

By then I had already proved myself within the workforce, to be a person of determination and someone who possess a willingness to learn new things. Although, this practice of constantly feeling I had to prove myself has worked against me in the past as well. See, the moment other colleagues know you feel like you have to prove yourself, the more they abuse their power. They push you harder and give you tasks no-one else wants to do; because Fiona will do it, she has something to prove. Then you come across people in the workplace who are frustrated that you are proving yourself to be more efficient than they are, so they try to make your environment uncomfortable for you. Little do they understand or realise that the only person I've ever competed with was myself.

It's difficult enough to feel understood by the everyday public, especially when most people would never come across someone like me throughout their life. It's just as hard to have government agencies understand the nature of my condition, when I grew up being the first one in their system with Kniest. Most agencies seem to want a generalised box that everyone fits into, but the thing is, we don't all fit into the usual mould. This can be frustrating because I've always been stuck between a rock and a hard place. I don't like people to feel pity towards me, so I do my absolute best to be a positive impact with the way I try to live my life. Even when it could be just as easy to be weak and show my struggles. Trying to put your best foot forward when dealing with government agencies seems to work against you. It's as if they need to see you losing it for them to believe the struggle is real. I've dealt with these types of situations my whole life too, I've never once lied on a form, and I've never once exaggerated my situation. Why would I want to embarrass myself if I was more capable of doing things, by admitting I know I can't? The problem is too many people in society want to see what they can get away with, and the genuine ones always have to fight.

When I was healing from my massive injury in 2010, I had to deal with explaining how my situation has changed dramatically. I was still on crutches and if you've ever met me you'd know I have a clearly visible condition. The questions I was being asked made me have a complete breakdown in their office; I was so annoyed at myself for showing them weakness. But it was only then that they understood, half of what I was dealing with.

I always pride myself on showing my strength but sometimes we have to make ourselves vulnerable for people to understand. In the same way I've exposed myself on these pages. I've lived most my life trying to shield people away from seeing anything but my smile. I get up every time I've been knocked down. If my story provides some value, inspires or motivates you to see how blessed you are, then exposing my weakness to the world was worth it.

IGNORANCE IS BLISS

I especially don't like when people say 'poor thing' to me. It gives me a sinking feeling inside, like I must look so bad to be felt sorry for. It can be so much to take onboard how other people view you. When people focus on my differences more than I focus on them, it's almost as if they want to isolate me as someone who is different. Without people making those obvious acknowledgements that I'm short, or I walk different and so on; I could just go on living in ignorant bliss.

This is me, this is all I know and I love the person I am. I love that even though I have had moments of weakness I am not one of those people that let it control my whole life. I tend to look for solutions, but I also admit that sometimes other people's habits, reactions and cruelty make it difficult to do. That's when I turn to writing poetry or lyrics so that I don't let it control who I really am inside, just because of how other people might see me. Not to toot my own horn, but it takes a strong person not to dwell on every moment of every day. I've seen how easy it can be for people to slip into a rut. But I'm thankful for my stubbornness and willingness to build a bridge and move on. Do I forget the harsh reality, no, I don't have amnesia.

It's the same when I occasionally lose my temper and it does happen... I make every effort to hold a lot in and not allow things to get to me. But sometimes I turn into a kettle ready to boil. Eventually the last bubble pops before the switch on the kettle flips off, and it sends me into an over flowing mess.

Nobody will ever know anyone else's battle unless they share it with you. Even if they do, it's still only words, sympathy, and empathy. Each individual has their own journey to walk through. Each one of us can only walk in our own shoes; even with sympathy, empathy and the emotions behind trying to understand someone else's struggle. People, who live with the same or similar conditions, still have their own path to walk. With or without these similarities, the way we handle our struggles or moments in life shape us and make each experience different from anyone else's.

I Wouldn't Change A Thing

I have been asked many times if there was something I could change about myself what would I change. No matter how much I thought about this question over the years I always come back to the same answer 'NOTHING!'

Yes, sometimes other people's views or hurtful comments have really upset me. But I am who I am and if I changed even the slightest thing about myself then I wouldn't be the person you have gotten to know on these pages. I wouldn't have an appreciation for the achievements I have made. Maybe I wouldn't even be as compassionate and caring towards other people's feelings and needs. In life I do my best to treat people the way I want to be treated; with respect, without judgement of race, colour, disability, or by not being in envy of ability I may not have. Strange as it sounds I know I have things about me that are imperfect, but I think it just makes me a better person. It's hard sometimes, because I know I have the mental capacity to achieve many things in life. But my body likes to get in my way and says; 'good luck Fee, I'm not playing today.' Kniest is, and forever will be, a part of what makes me who I am, but I am a person too, first and foremost.

Here I am at the age of thirty-five... *(Actually I was thirty-two when I wrote this chapter, but this is just more proof of how long it's taken me to get to this point.)* Let me continue... Here I am at the age of thirty-five, after what feels like a lifetime of pain, heartache, travel, wonder and some truly amazing experiences.

But they all make me,
The Fee, that you see.

Chapter Thirty-Five

Spread Your Wings and Fly!

As a kid and even to this day I've always prided myself on not appearing like someone who complains a lot. I never want to be viewed as somebody who can't do things, or someone who doesn't work hard for what I want in life. Even though I've always been consciously aware throughout my entire life that there are going to be certain tasks that I simply can't do, and may never be able to do. I just never wanted to appear vulnerable, or to let others see me in that way, as much as possible.

Obviously, it's a little late now as I have just shared so many intense moments of my life, exposing myself by being vulnerable on these pages with everyone.

Sometimes when situations arose and I would be forced to say 'I can't' people would look at me in disbelief. They didn't always understand and took it as me not having enough confidence in myself. Which I feel is a very inaccurate assumption in the way I've always approached my life. There is a difference between giving up before you try, or plain stupidly in pushing past your known physical limits, possibly causing yourself irreversible damage.

From a young age I have always been an analytical thinker, especially when it comes to judging my boundaries, or listening to what my body is trying to tell me. I am one of those people who is very self aware of my capabilities and in-capabilities. Every day of my life I have tested my limits; sometimes even further than my doctors or my mum would have liked. This is how I know I can confidently be the best judge for my own wellbeing, knowing full well what consequences I could be facing based on the choices I make.

Nobody who is as headstrong to achieve things in life will ever accept defeat on something that deep down they have control over. The reality is though, for someone with my condition; I can't be too proud and go against my own better judgement by diving headfirst into a burning building with no fireproof vest on, so to speak. I'll never give up on a dream easily, within physical reasoning; you can be sure I'll give it my all, quicker than my joints can move.

I've always known, deep within my heart that God is beside me every step of the way throughout my life. When I struggled he carried me and provided me with the tools I needed to express myself; like my poetry and music. I've always felt a sense of purpose, and him telling me to just believe in myself enough to fight for what I want out of life. Maybe that's why as a teenager I was so moved by the movie 'Simon Birch,' because I saw my spirit in the character Ian played. People might think I'm crazy for believing that I am who I am for a reason. Maybe I am crazy, but I'd rather be crazy and accepting of the hand I've been dealt. Instead of waste my life full of pity, sorrow and non acceptance of who I am.

We are so conditioned into caring about how other people view us, even I have fallen victim to this situation. Not just in the average height world, but even among other little people. If you don't have a job, it's like you are looked down upon as someone who is bludging. I've never been the kind of person to judge anyone for who they are, or if they have a job or not. But it doesn't mean I don't sense others judging me when they ask me what I do and I almost instinctively hesitate. Sometimes it's easier to say I'm still a web designer or a singer songwriter. It's technically not a lie since that's who I am, but am I actively working daily, doing those things, definitely not. Ever since I quit my last official job at the end of 2011, my life has felt like a steeper slope of struggles. I like to remain positive though and don't really like to show people when I'm struggling. Of course by me publishing my honest truth, the good, bad and ugly; I'm leaving myself open to judgement.

Love me or leave me, this is who I am.

No longer can I hide behind my smile and hope that people believe I'm a strong, confident person with no worries. As much as I may not escape people feeling sorry for me; I'd like to ask that you don't. I'm grateful for the life I have, the experiences and lessons learnt. It's more than many people have experienced in their lifetime, even without my added obstacles standing in their way. Sure, I may never go on the rides at Disneyland again, because of the risks to my spine. But I am glad I was a bit more of a carefree Fee when I was in my twenties and had those fun times.

I will hold on to all my memories and achievements, even my struggles because they made me who I am. I've spent at least the first thirty years of my life fighting within a society to prove I could fit in. Whether it was in school, college, various organisations and even the workplace, especially in the workplace; I worked so hard to prove I could accomplish things most people wanted to say I couldn't, even at the expense of my own health.

Times have changed me to be a bit more cautious with my physical endeavours, only because I need to preserve the ability I have. Not send myself into constant pain for others to stop judging me. People are going to judge no matter what I do and I realise that now more than ever. I feel like I don't need to hide behind my pages, now that I've shared my life, love and different stages. Why should I care if I fit in, when I was born to stand out.

What lies ahead, in the world of Fee? Only God knows. But no matter what obstacles come my way, I will continue to;

'**EMBRACE** the life I **GAIN**, when I **PUSH** through my pain,'

Sharing my story with you has always felt like my calling. I hope to encourage others to know that anything is possible if you never give up. No matter what life throws at you, always remember it's just part of the journey. You might go through hardships in life and have 1% chance of coming out from a devastating blow. Remember you too could be the exception to the rule, like I was with my eye surgery in 2003. If things don't go the way you hoped or expected from your life, don't give up, because you have no way of knowing what's around the corner.

If I gave up every time life knocked me down, just think of all the amazing opportunities my heart would have been closed to, and missed. Life isn't easy, many times we hurt. Sure it'd be nice if we didn't have to endure the hard times. Even I sometimes wished I didn't have to go through a lot of my struggles and pain. But then I think, if I didn't, this wouldn't be my life story.

I wouldn't be me now, would I?

My hardships in life provided me with the ability to not take things for granted. If I didn't have them, then I wouldn't have built my inner strength and personality in how I appreciate life.

You've seen me go from my first breath, to that ten-year-old girl in a hospital bed with a dream to share my story; to the person I am right now achieving my childhood dream. Dreams really can come true. Thank you for taking the time and allowing me to enter into your life, by getting to know me and my story. I hope you continue along life's wonderful journey with me.

This is only the beginning...

Let's spread our wings and fly!

Acknowledgements

Once again, I thank God for instilling me with the strength to face my challenges and embrace my life to my fullest potential.

My mum, Carmen, for always being the rock I needed who taught me to stand on my own two feet. Thank you for also being a constant guide and support throughout my life.

To my dad, Ashoor, for coming into my life and being the person I am proud to call my dad. You showed me that good guys do exist because you are living proof.

Special shout out goes to my mum Carmen and brother, Brandon you both have been the key supporters in me achieving this dream of publishing my books. Thank you for your patience and for putting up with all my questions during the process. You've been my sounding boards to bounce ideas and concerns off of all the way through.

I am eternally thankful for all my family members who have been there for me throughout my life, I love you all.

My fellow Kniest brothers and sisters, thank you for being my extended family. Having you in my life has made it so much richer, I am grateful beyond words for the unique bond we have.

About the Author

Fiona Porch was born and raised in Sydney, Australia and is a budding new author who has spent her life using her trials and achievements to inspire her work. Starting with singing and song writing her first album cover title song "I Am Who I Am" was inspired from her first published work, "Feelings" a poem that was printed in the NSW Department of Education and Training Resource Magazine.

Fiona has always tried to display her emotions in such a way as to help others to leap their hurdles and pursue their goals. She now invites others to share in her experiences through her literary works, hoping that her message will become a boon for all those who want to fly.

ALSO BY: FIONA PORCH

When you need some inspiration,
With a little variation.
Why don't you have a look?
Through the pages of my book.

Happiness, sadness, loneliness and fears,
So many emotions expressed from all my years.
So why don't you get comfy and have a little stroll,
To be taken on a journey into the depths of my soul...

Available now at www.FionaPorch.com
Or leading booksellers globally.

www.ingramcontent.com/pod-product-compliance
Lightning Source LLC
Chambersburg PA
CBHW032030290426
44110CB00012B/748